Functions

Function	Purpose	Example
fclose()	Closes a disk or printer file	fclose(printer);
fgetc()	Reads a character from a file	letter = fgetc(file);
fgets()	Reads a string from a file	name = fgets(file);
fopen()	Opens a disk or printer file	fopen(FILENAME,"a");
fprintf()	Writes data to a file	fprintf(file, "%s %f", name, cost);
fputc()	Writes a character to a file	fputc(file, 'A');
fputs()	Writes a string to a file	fputs(file, "Hello");
fscanf()	Reads data from a file	fscanf(fp,"%s %f", name, &cost)
getc()	Reads a character from a file	letter = getc(file);
getchar()	Inputs a character from the keyboard	letter=getchar()
gets()	Inputs a string from the keyboard	gets(name)
putc()	Writes a character to a file	putc(file, 'A');
putchar()	Displays a character on the screen	putchar('A');
puts()	Displays a string on the screen	puts("Hello");
scanf()	Reads data from the keyboard	scanf("%s %f", name, &cost)
strcmp()	Compares two strings	cmp = strcmp(string1, string2);
strcpy()	Assigns one string to another	strcpy(new, old);
strlen()	Returns the length of a string	len = strlen(name);

◆ ◆

For every kind of computer user, there is a SYBEX book.

All computer users learn in their own way. Some need straightforward and methodical explanations. Others are just too busy for this approach. But no matter what camp you fall into, SYBEX has a book that can help you get the most out of your computer and computer software while learning at your own pace.

Beginners generally want to start at the beginning. The **ABC's** series, with its step-by-step lessons in plain language, helps you build basic skills quickly. Or you might try our **Quick & Easy** series, the friendly, full-color guide.

The **Mastering** and **Understanding** series will tell you everything you need to know about a subject. They're perfect for intermediate and advanced computer users, yet they don't make the mistake of leaving beginners behind.

If you're a busy person and are already comfortable with computers, you can choose from two SYBEX series—**Up & Running** and **Running Start**. The **Up & Running** series gets you started in just 20 lessons. Or you can get two books in one, a step-by-step tutorial and an alphabetical reference, with our **Running Start** series.

Everyone who uses computer software can also use a computer software reference. SYBEX offers the gamut—from portable **Instant References** to comprehensive **Encyclopedias**, **Desktop References**, and **Bibles**.

SYBEX even offers special titles on subjects that don't neatly fit a category—like **Tips & Tricks**, the **Shareware Treasure Chests**, and a wide range of books for Macintosh computers and software.

SYBEX books are written by authors who are expert in their subjects. In fact, many make their living as professionals, consultants or teachers in the field of computer software. And their manuscripts are thoroughly reviewed by our technical and editorial staff for accuracy and ease-of-use.

So when you want answers about computers or any popular software package, just help yourself to SYBEX.

For a complete catalog of our publications, please write:
SYBEX Inc.
2021 Challenger Drive
Alameda, CA 94501
Tel: (510) 523-8233/(800) 227-2346 Telex: 336311
Fax: (510) 523-2373

SYBEX is committed to using natural resources wisely to preserve and improve our environment. As a leader in the computer book publishing industry, we are aware that over 40% of America's solid waste is paper. This is why we have been printing the text of books like this one on recycled paper since 1982.

This year our use of recycled paper will result in the saving of more than 15,300 trees. We will lower air pollution effluents by 54,000 pounds, save 6,300,000 gallons of water, and reduce landfill by 2,700 cubic yards.

In choosing a SYBEX book you are not only making a choice for the best in skills and information, you are also choosing to enhance the quality of life for all of us.

Your First C/C++ Program

Your First C/C++ Program

Alan R. Neibauer

San Francisco • Paris • Düsseldorf • Soest

Acquisitions Editor: Dianne King
Developmental Editor: Gary Masters
Editor: James A. Compton
Technical Editor: Erik Ingenito
Book Designer: Alissa Feinberg
Production Artist: Ingrid Owen
Technical Illustrations: Cuong Le
Typesetter: Lisa Jaffe
Proofreader/Production Coordinator: Janet Boone
Indexer: Ted Laux
Cover Designer: Ingalls + Associates
Cover Photographer: David Bishop

Library of Congress Card Number: 93-87421
ISBN: 0-7821-1414-8

Manufactured in the United States of America
10 9 8 7 6 5 4 3 2 1

Warranty

SYBEX warrants the enclosed disk to be free of physical defects for a period of ninety (90) days after purchase. If you discover a defect in the disk during this warranty period, you can obtain a replacement disk at no charge by sending the defective disk, postage prepaid, with proof of purchase to:

SYBEX Inc.
Customer Service Department
2021 Challenger Drive
Alameda, CA 94501
(800)227-2346
Fax: (510) 523-2373

After the 90-day period, you can obtain a replacement disk by sending us the defective disk, proof of purchase, and a check or money order for $10, payable to SYBEX.

Disclaimer

SYBEX makes no warranty or representation, either express or implied, with respect to this software, its quality performance, merchantability, or fitness for a particular purpose. In no event will SYBEX, its distributors, or dealers be liable for direct, indirect, special, incidental, or consequential damages arising out of the use or inability to use the software even if advised of the possibility of such damage.

The exclusion of implied warranties is not permitted by some states. Therefore, the above exclusion may not apply to you. This warranty provides you with specific legal rights; there may be other rights that you may have that vary from state to state.

Shareware Distribution

The PCC compiler included on this book's diskette is a shareware program. Shareware is a distribution method, not a type of software. The chief advantage is that it gives you, the user, a chance to try a program before you buy it.

Copyright laws apply to both shareware and commercial software, and the copyright holder retains all rights. The publisher of the PCC compiler, C WARE Corporation, requires that you register your copy with them if you plan to continue using it after a 30-day trial period.

Registration, which costs $30, entitles you to use the program on any and all computers available to you, as long as you use the program on only one computer at a time. You can also copy the program for the trial use of others. As a registered user, you can obtain updates as new versions are released by calling or writing C WARE Corporation. A registration form is included in this book's Appendix.

Educational institutions wishing to use PCC for courses involving C, as well as private or commercial institutions, should contact C WARE Corporation, or refer to the file PCC.DOC.

Copy Protection

None of the programs on the disk is copy-protected. However, in all cases, reselling these programs without authorization is expressly forbidden.

Dedicated to Alice and Marty

◆ ◆

Acknowledgments

• •

A number of very talented people contributed to the production of this book.

Dianne King, acquisitions editor, and Gary Masters, developmental editor, successfully cultivated the overall project. Gary saw the merits of this book from the very beginning, and he helped organize its content and approach. Special thanks to Jim Compton, copy editor, for his keen attention to detail and his ability to smooth out even the roughest prose.

I also want to thank the fine people at C WARE Corporation, not only for their generous permission to include the PCC compiler with this book, but for producing such a complete and affordable programming tool.

My thanks also to technical editor Erik Ingenito, typesetter Lisa Jaffe, proofreader Janet Boone, indexer Ted Laux, and to Veronica Eddy and Jamie Wright for the back cover copy. The efforts of designer Alissa Feinberg and artist Ingrid Owen translated the concept of this new format to reality. Thanks also to Dr. Rudolph Langer, as well as the other people at SYBEX whose efforts contributed to this book.

Finally, my sincere thanks to Barbara Neibauer. She has grown used to reading my chapters, producing figures, and organizing my life. For this book, she learned C and C++ programming. What a wife!

Contents at a Glance

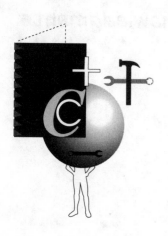

Table of Contents

• •

Two

This Is C/C++! 25

Three

Variables and Constants 39

Six

Operators 121

Seven

How Functions Function 149

Eight

Letting the Computer Decide   177

Nine

Repetition   201

Twelve

Outputting to the Disk and Printer   283

Thirteen

Putting It All Together   317

Appendix A
Using the Sample Diskette   **337**

Introduction

Forget any stories you've heard about how difficult it is to program a computer. Ignore the tales of strife and struggle. Don't worry if you are not a Ph.D. in math or science.

Learning how to write a computer program, and actually writing programs, can be fun. If you think logically, if you like solving puzzles and problems, or if you want to have control over your computer, rather than the other way around, then you're a perfect candidate for programming.

You also now have the perfect book to get you started. This book is designed for the beginner, the very beginner. In fact, it assumes that you know nothing about computer programming. (This book is also perfect if you are moving to C and C++ from other languages, such as BASIC, Pascal, and even macro languages in programs such as WordPerfect, Lotus, and Excel.)

In fact, all you need to learn programming is this book and a willing mind. The accompanying diskette even includes a powerful C compiler and an editor for writing your own programs.

Your First C/C++ Program focuses on versions of C defined by what are known as the K&R and ANSI C standards, as well as on essential aspects of C++. All of the techniques that you will learn in this book can be applied to C and C++ programs. If you are interested in C++, look for special sections, notes, and sidebars that relate specifically to this superset of the C language.

Here's What You Get

With this book, you'll learn in gradual steps how to write programs. You will find clear, easy-to-understand discussions supported by plenty of illustrations and examples. By reading the discussion, and then reviewing the figures and program listings, you will learn each aspect of programming in the proper order. Each chapter ends with useful review questions and exercises.

Although this book is designed for the beginning programmer, it is a thorough introduction. Nothing is left out. You will not only learn a programming language, you'll also discover the logic of program design and problem-solving.

You'll start by learning in Chapters 1 and 2 about the programming process, and about the structure and nature of C and C++ programs. In Chapter 3, you will learn how to communicate with a program using variables and constants.

Next, you will learn in Chapter 4 how to display information on the monitor, and in Chapter 5 how to input information from the keyboard. In Chapter 6, you will learn how to write programs using operators to perform arithmetic.

In Chapter 7, on functions, you will discover how to build your programs in sections, dividing a program into easy to manage blocks. Chapter 8 discusses decision-making, and Chapter 9 shows how to repeat instructions using loops.

As your programming skills increase, you will learn in Chapter 10 about arrays and strings, and in Chapter 11 about pointers and structures. In Chapter 12, you will learn how to read and write disk files, and how to access your printer.

To tie together your skills, Chapter 13 presents a comprehensive program example for building a database application. By reading the chapter and following the program listing, you'll learn tips for building professional applications.

The book's Appendix explains how to install and use the compiler and editor supplied on this book's diskette, and how to access the sample programs and the answers to the end-of-chapter exercises.

After reading Chapters 1 and 2, follow the instructions in the Appendix to install the programs on the diskette. You will then be ready to follow along as you read the chapters that follow. Chances are, you'll soon be striking out on your own to write programs you can use at the office, in school, or at home.

A Complete Programming Tool

If you already have a C or C++ compiler of your own, you can use it to learn C and write the programs presented here. But if you do not have a compiler, everything you need is on the enclosed disk.

The disk packaged with this book includes more than sample programs. It contains a full-featured C compiler, a linker, a comprehensive function library, and an 80-page reference manual that you can print using a word processing program or the DOS Print command.

The disk contains a text editor for writing and editing programs, and even an assembler if you later want to learn assembly language. You will also find copies of all of the programs listed in the book. You can compile and run the programs as they are, or you can open them in an editor to study or build on them.

One

What's It All About?

• •

People decide to learn computer programming for various reasons. First, of course, there is money. Most programs are written as a way to make money. Some are aimed at a specific audience or industry, others are written for mass market appeal, but the goal is the same—to create a commercial success. While you might never write that "killer" application, you can earn money by writing programs for others.

You might program just for the challenge and learning experience, the same reason others climb mountains, do crossword puzzles, or try out for the Olympic team. If you're this kind of programmer, you get personal satisfaction in completing a program. Each program is a puzzle and a mental exercise, you pitted against the computer for ultimate control.

You also might program to solve a specific problem. You need to perform a task with your computer but cannot find, or afford, a commercial program that meets your needs. The program can be as simple as recording kitchen recipes, or as complex as solving a unique business or engineering problem.

Whatever your reason is to program a computer, programming offers a sense of personal achievement and success. The gratification you get when the program works can be highly addictive. The frustration you get when it doesn't work can be shattering. But like all challenges, it's worth it.

A Computer Program

You probably have some experience running computer programs—a word processor, spreadsheet program, database, even a game or two. When you run a program, however, you only view it from the outside. You do not really see what the program is doing, just its results.

When you write a program, you see it from the inside. You know how the program works, and why it works that way. It's a much different and exciting way to look at a computer program. No matter how much experience you have running programs, no matter how computer-literate you are, writing a program presents entirely new challenges.

Have you ever given directions to someone looking for an address? Did you ever teach someone how to do something? That's what a computer program does. A computer program is nothing more than a series of instructions to your computer, telling it *exactly what to do, in exactly the correct order, in a language the computer understands.* That's it.

The computer will even tell you when it doesn't understand something, by displaying an *error message.* So you simply try again, rewriting the instruction in a way that the computer can follow. Sometimes the computer can follow your instructions even though they are wrong! Did you ever ask directions, follow them to the letter but end up in the wrong place anyway? Well, the same can happen with your program. These are the most difficult problems to solve because you may not even know that they exist.

Now let's consider our definition of a program a little further.

The Instructions Tell the Computer Exactly What to Do
The word *exactly* is the key. Each instruction must be precise. You can't leave any steps out. For example, suppose someone asks you how to get to the local post office. You tell them "Walk two blocks and turn left on Franklin Street." You just assume that they will see the post office and walk in.

C++ Notes

C++ is less procedural than C and other programming languages. Some instructions refer to "objects" and "events" rather than present a sequence of steps. However, the instructions, procedural or not, must still be explicit and complete.

With the computer you can't assume a thing. So, if you were telling the computer to find the post office, your directions would be more like this:

Walk north two blocks.

Turn left 90 degrees.

Walk straight for 50 feet.

Turn left 90 degrees.

Climb up four steps.

Open the door and walk in.

When you save a document with a word processing program, for example, the program must know exactly what steps to perform. It must know where on the disk to place the document. It must also have instructions to display some type of warning message if saving a new document would overwrite one already on your disk.

The Instructions Must Be in the Correct Order

If you tell the computer to do A, B, and then C, the computer will do them in that order. The computer can't think "Gee, this doesn't look correct, maybe I should turn up Franklin Street first instead." You can have the computer make a decision, however. Your program can decide "If her salary is over $50,000, then take out 25% in taxes, otherwise take out 15%." But you have to tell the computer when to make the decision, and what to do in each condition.

For example, let's again consider trying to save a new document with the same name as one already on your disk. It wouldn't do much good if the program saved the file, deleting the original, and then asked if that's what you wanted. It must display the message first, then decide what to do based on your input. If you give the OK, it will overwrite the one on the disk. If not, it will ask you to enter a new document name.

Programming Languages

The third requirement of a computer program is that it must be in a language that the computer can understand.

Deep inside your computer is a *microprocessor*, a single integrated circuit that controls everything that occurs within your computer. (See Figure 1.1.)

When your program tells the computer to display a message on the monitor, or print it on the printer, the microprocessor sends the appropriate electronic signals. These signals tell the computer where in memory to find the message and where to send it. Much of what the microprocessor does is invisible—you feed your program into the computer and assume that the microprocessor knows its business. But to understand how programming works, you should know a little—and just a little is necessary—about how the microprocessor works.

Technically, the microprocessor can perform only four actions. It can *move* data from one memory location to another, *change* data in a memory location, *determine* whether a memory location contains specific data, and *change* the sequence of the instructions it performs. All of these actions are performed by sending, receiving, or monitoring electronic impulses.

The computer deals with these impulses in either of two states (voltage levels); an electronic signal may be either on or off. To perform a task, we feed a series of signals—on or off states—to the microprocessor. The

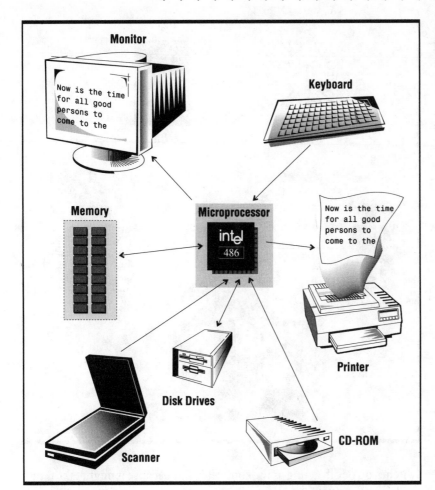

Figure 1.1
The microprocessor controls everything in your computer.

combination of ons and offs illustrated in Figure 1.2, for example, prints the character *A*.

In order to write down computer instructions at this very basic level, we use the number 0 to represent the off state and 1 to represent the on state. We call these binary digits (bits), or binary instructions, based on the binary numbering system that uses only combinations of 0 and 1 to represent all numbers.

At the birth of computers and computer programming, a program was performed by directly manipulating these on and off signals. There wasn't any microprocessor. A technician would physically turn a series of

Figure 1.2

A series of on or off
electronic impulses tell the
microprocessor what task
to perform—in this case, to
retrieve a character from
memory and send it to
the printer.

switches on or off, acting as the controller. But because it might take thousands of individual signals to perform an entire application, writing a program was a very time-consuming task.

As computers developed, it became possible to feed a program into the computer all at once, and then have the computer perform the instructions. It still required thousands of individual 0s and 1s until *assembly language* was developed.

Assembly language uses *mnemonic codes* to represent computer tasks that relate directly to the hardware. A mnemonic code is an easy-to-remember word or abbreviation that represents a complete microprocessor task. For example, the code MOV tells the computer to move some information from one memory location to another. The code JMP tells the computer

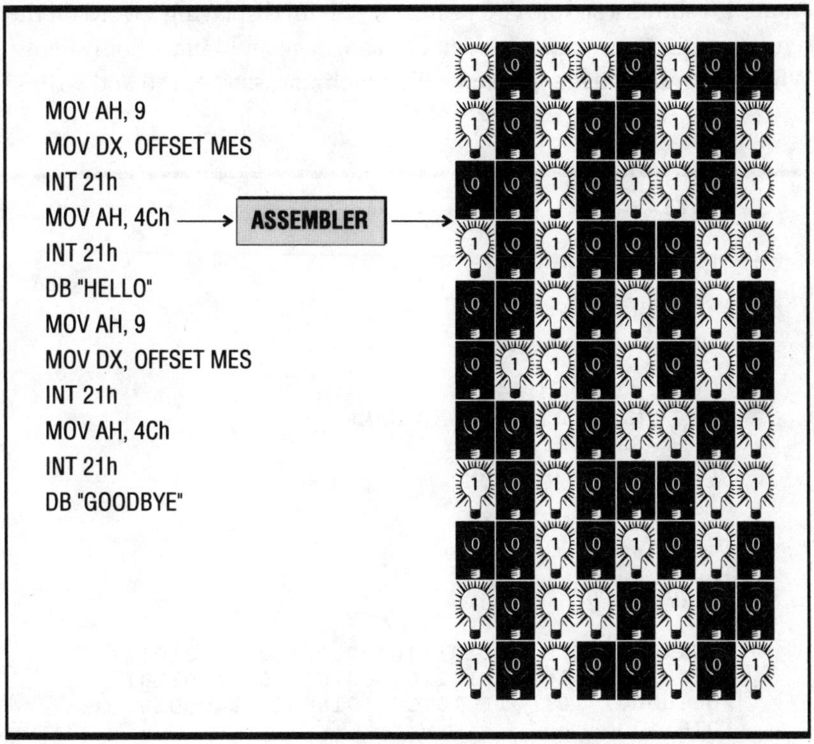

Figure 1.3

The assembler converts
assembly language instructions
to binary code.

```
MOV AH, 9
MOV DX, OFFSET MES
INT 21h
MOV AH, 4Ch   ──→  ASSEMBLER
INT 21h
DB "HELLO"
MOV AH, 9
MOV DX, OFFSET MES
INT 21h
MOV AH, 4Ch
INT 21h
DB "GOODBYE"
```

to jump to another location in memory. So instead of writing a series of 0s and 1s, the assembly language programmer can use codes such as MOV and JMP, each representing eight or more binary instructions.

As shown in Figure 1.3, a program called the assembler translates these codes into the individual electronic signals that the computer can understand. Since each code relates directly to the microprocessor's internal functions, the resulting programs run extremely fast. But assembly language is still time-consuming to use and requires a large number of codes.

Today, most programmers use a *high-level language*, whose instructions are words that people understand, not simple mnemonics or 0s and 1s. Each word represents a complete practical operation, rather than one microprocessor task. For example, the C function `puts` (for *put* a string of characters on the monitor) tells the computer to display certain information on the screen. The same function could take a number of assembly language mnemonics, and perhaps hundreds of binary electronic impulses.

Figure 1.4 shows a simple C/C++ instruction for displaying a word on the screen and its approximate Assembly Language and binary equivalents. Which programming language would you find easier to read and write?

Figure 1.4
Comparable C, assembly language, and binary instructions.

In C:

```
puts("SYBEX")
```

In Assembly Language:

```
        MOV   AH, 9
        MOV   DX, OFFSET NAME
        INT   21h
        MOV   AG, 4Ch
        INT   21h
NAME DB       "SYBEX"
```

In Binary:

```
10110100000010011011101000000000100001011
11001101001000011011010001001100110011001101
00100001010100110101100101000010010000101
01011000
```

Of course, the computer doesn't really understand what PUTS or any high-level language command means. Before the computer can actually perform a command, it must be translated into the computer's own language, binary.

This translation from human words to binary instructions is performed in either of two ways, by *compiling* or by *interpreting*.

Compilers

Compiling translates the entire program at one time, and saves it on disk so you can run the program later. To visualize how this works, let's look at a real-life situation.

Suppose you write a report in English to be presented to the French parliament. You hire a translator to convert the report into French, make as many copies as you need, and then distribute the copies. If the translator finds any grammatical errors, she will stop and report each one to you, and you'll have to correct it before she can continue translating the report. But then, if you want to use the same report a year from now, all you will do is copy and distribute the completed translation. You do not need the translator again.

As illustrated in Figure 1.5, a compiler does the same with a computer language. It is a computer program that (with the aid of another program, called the *linker*) converts all of your instructions into binary so the program can be run. The compiler makes sure that the program agrees with the rules of C or C++, then creates an *object file*, an intermediate form of the program. During the process, the compiler will tell you if it encounters an instruction it does not understand. You must correct the problem and try again. The linker then converts the object code into an executable program. This process does not run the program, it only performs the translation.

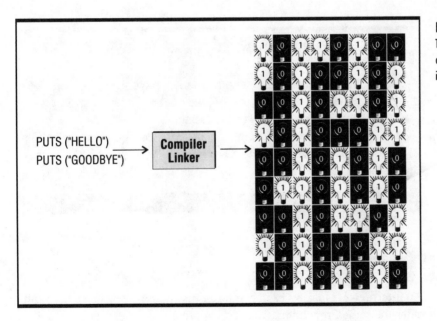

PUTS ("HELLO")
PUTS ("GOODBYE")

Compiler
Linker

Figure 1.5
The compiler and linker convert high-level language instructions to binary code.

C++ Notes

You'll soon learn that C++ is a superset of C. This means that if your program can be compiled by a C compiler, it can be compiled by a C++ compiler.

When you use a compiler, the program exists in three states. The C-language statements are stored in a text file called the *source code*. You can print and read this file, much as you can with any word processing document. You can edit this file to change the program. The compiled program is contained in an *object file* and the final results in an *executable file* that you run.

C, C++, PASCAL, COBOL, and FORTRAN are examples of compiled languages.

File-Name Extensions

With most compilers, the source code must have the extension .C, and the object code is given the extension .OBJ. The compiler provided with this book requires the .C extension for source code but the .O extension for object files. The compiler will automatically generate object files with the .O extension. Your compiler may be different.

Interpreters

An interpreter translates each computer instruction as it is run. Let's consider the same French report.

You write the report in English and hire an interpreter. As the French parliament listens, the interpreter converts the first sentence into French and reads it to the audience. Then the interpreter translates and reads the second sentence, and so on until the end of the report. Keep in mind that the report only exists in English. If you want a French Canadian to read the report a year from now, you'll have to hire an interpreter and start all over.

A computer interpreter works the same way. As shown in Figure 1.6, it translates and runs each instruction, one at a time. With an interpreter, the program never exists in anything other than its original, source-code version. The BASIC computer language supplied free with MS-DOS is an example of an interpreted language.

Why would anyone ever want to use an interpreter? When you are just learning how to program, an interpreter makes it easy to write and test your program line for line. Compiled languages require you to complete the entire program or independent, executable sections before you can test it.

So why use a compiler? Because interpreters make the mechanics of writing a program so easy, users often neglect the planning and design

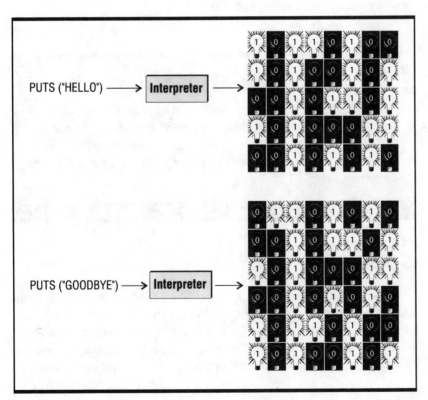

PUTS ("HELLO") ⟶ **Interpreter** ⟶

PUTS ("GOODBYE") ⟶ **Interpreter** ⟶

Figure 1.6
The interpreter translates high-level language instructions into binary code each time a program is run.

necessary to create a workable program. They jump right in, trying to write a program "on the fly," spending needless hours correcting mistakes by trial and error. If you are just learning programming, it's best to learn good habits right from the start.

Interpreted languages also run slower. You must load the interpreter into memory, then translate and run each line of the program separately. Compilers convert the program all at once. When you run a compiled program, it already exists in the form of binary instructions that can be executed directly by the computer.

Why C/C++?

C is a compiled language. It is a collection of commands and functions, in the form of familiar-looking words, that convert into binary instructions to be run by the computer. Over the past few years, C has become the language of choice over other computer languages for three very good reasons—speed, portability, and control.

C++ Notes

Remember, everything in this book applies to both the C and C++ languages. Instead of constantly referring to both languages, C/C++, we'll usually just refer to C alone. This doesn't mean that you're only learning C—you're learning both languages at the same time.

Speed

C is said to be "closer" to assembly language than other high-level languages because some C commands directly address the physical hardware of the computer. This makes compiled C programs execute quickly. In fact, they run so quickly that C can be used to write operating systems, communications and engineering applications, and even compilers.

In addition, most C compilers generate highly *optimized* code. Remember the binary instructions that the computer needs? The fewer of these the compiler must generate, the more optimized the code—and the faster the program. Some language compilers generate less optimized code, so their programs run slower.

Portability

You can also generate fast programs by writing in assembly language. However, assembly-language mnemonics vary with each family of micro-processor. If you write an assembly language program for an IBM-PC or compatible computer, and then decide to use the program on an Apple Macintosh, you'd have to rewrite the entire program.

C uses a highly standardized set of commands. For the most part, you write the program once no matter what *platform* (computer or operating system) you want to run it on. While the source-code doesn't change, you will need two compilers—one to translate the program into the binary instruction that the IBM understands, and another to translate the program into the Apple's binary instructions. But you only need to write the program itself one time.

This also means that once you learn C, you do not have to learn another language to program a different computer. You can transfer your skills from platform to platform without retraining. After all, you never know where your newly learned programming skills may lead, and it's best to be prepared.

Control

C can be an easy language to learn but it does have its requirements. In interpreted BASIC, you can just sit down at the computer and write a program off the top of your head. In C it's not quite so easy. C has a structure, a way of doing things, that forces you to think logically. You can bypass a lot of structure to write a "quick and dirty" program that doesn't do very much. But to write a serious application in C, you must do your homework first.

This structure is far from a encumbrance, however. It makes C programs much easier to design, maintain, and debug.

Function Libraries

C itself doesn't contain many commands. Unlike other languages, C does not have built-in commands for inputting and outputting information, or for handling strings. (A string is a series of characters forming a word or phrase.) The original definition of C, for example, had only 27 key-words—commands.

C's power comes from the libraries of functions provided with the compiler. A *function* is a series of instructions that perform a specific task. A *library* is a separate disk file, supplied with your compiler, that contains functions for common tasks so you do not have to write them yourself.

For instance, C does not have a command for displaying information on your monitor. This is such a common task, however, that several functions for outputting information are supplied with the C library. Instead of writing the function yourself, you just use one supplied with the compiler.

Every function has a name, such as the `puts()` function that you read about earlier. Instead of typing each of the function's instructions into your program, you just insert the function name, using the necessary punctuation and syntax. (Don't worry, you'll learn how to use the function names later.)

Some library files contain precompiled code. When the compiler encounters the name of one of these library functions in your program, it does not have to bother converting the commands into binary instruction. The conversion has already been performed. During the *linking* process (illustrated in Figure 1.7), the function's code segments—the instructions in the library for performing the function—are merged with the object file to create an executable program. Because the functions were compiled ahead of time, the compiled code is very efficient. The compiler manufacturer has refined the functions so they are fully optimized.

Some other functions are used so frequently that, depending on your compiler, their C source-code is supplied to you. These are in files called *header files*, which usually have the file extension H. Header files also contain *compiler directives*, instructions telling the compiler how certain definitions are

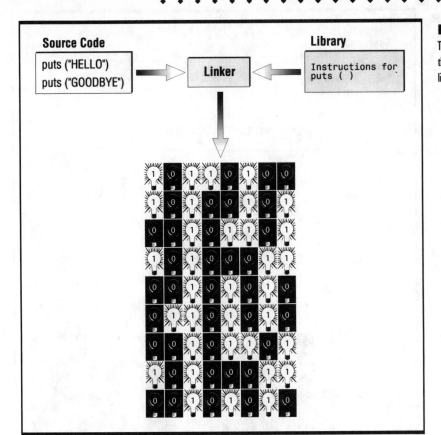

Figure 1.7

The instructions for performing the function are taken from the library during linking.

to be used. During the compiling process, the code in the header file is merged with your own program to generate the object code.

Figure 1.8 summarizes the compiler-linking process.

Header files are not compiled. Like your own C source-code files, they can be read, printed, and edited. However, you should avoid changing the header files supplied with your compiler. If you make a mistake, the compiler may no longer be able to generate object code.

In addition to the library supplied with your compiler, you can purchase specialized libraries to perform database management, high-speed graphics, communications, windowing, and other advanced functions. The more functions you have in libraries, the less work you have to do.

Figure 1.8

The compiling/linking process.

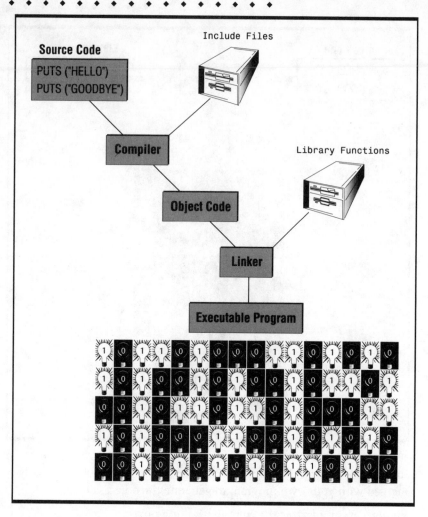

You can even create your own library of functions that you use in your programs. For example, suppose you write several programs that all perform tasks A, B, and C. You write the functions that perform these tasks and place them in your own personal library. Each time you need to use them again, they are ready and compiled.

It is the use of library files that make C portable. A compiler for an IBM-compatible computer contains library files of IBM binary instructions. A compiler for the Mac includes library files of Mac binary instructions. You simply write the C program once and then use the compilers to generate programs for both machines.

Variations on the Theme

The C programming language was developed by Dennis M. Ritchie in 1972 and defined in the book *The C Programming Language* by Ritchie and Brian W. Kernighan. An implementation of C that follows the rules described in the book is referred to as *K&R C*, for Kernighan and Ritchie. The K&R definition is considered the minimum standard implementation, so any program you write using the K&R rules of C will compile successfully on any C compiler.

Some areas of the standard, however, were not fully defined, so compiler manufacturers started to refine and extend the language on their own. To avoid confusion, the American National Standards Institute developed a new standard, called ANSI C, in 1983. ANSI C sets guidelines for extending the language and adopts standards for most C features.

The programming language known as C++ is a *superset* of C. It is not really a different language because it includes all of the commands and features of C itself, and then some. By learning C, you're learning most of C++ as well. The extensions in C++ make it easier to develop large, complex programs by defining a more "modular" approach and other enhancements. In addition, C++ focuses on Object-Oriented Programming (OOP).

What Is Object-Oriented Programming?

Honestly, there is no quick and easy way to describe object-oriented programming except to already advanced programmers. But here's a try.

Picture, if you will, a three-by-five index card file. Each card contains the name and address information of a club member:

Membership Card
> Name
> Address
> Phone Number
> Status

If a member's address changes, you have to look at the name on each card until you locate the right one. The same is true if anyone's phone number or membership status changes. If we were to write instructions for these three separate activities, they might look like this:

```
Get the cards.
Look for Smith.
Change the address to 12 West Avenue.

Get the cards.
Look for Doe.
Change the phone number to 555-1234.

Get the cards.
Look for Jones.
Change the status to inactive.
```

Notice that all of these activities involve the cards. The cards themselves are separate from the functions that you perform on them. So you have four objects to deal with—the cards and the functions of changing an address, phone number, and status.

In object-oriented programming, we combine the data we are using (the cards) with the activities we perform on them. This combination now becomes the one object we have to deal with. Visualize the object (let's call it Member_Card) looking like this:

```
Member_Card
     Name
     Address
     Phone Number
     Status
     Change_address
     Change_phone number
     Change_status
```

Because the object includes the data and the functions, we no longer have to give the compiler individual steps to make a change. The compiler will understand instructions like these:

```
Member_cards.change_address(Smith, 12 West Avenue)

Member_cards.change_phone(Doe, 555-1234)
```

```
Member_cards.change_status(Jones, inactive)
```

Don't worry if OOP seems a little abstract at this point. You don't have to learn OOP to program in C. Once you learn C, however, you'll be able to grasp OOP much easier.

What C Can and Cannot Do for You

If you are interested in writing computer programs of all types and sizes, then C is a good choice for you. There is virtually no limitation to what you can accomplish with a robust C compiler. Once you learn C, it is an easy path to move on to C++.

C's power, however, does not mean that it is the only, or even the best, way of accomplishing everything. If you need a database application, for example, you don't have to learn C. There are numerous software packages and code generators that can virtually write the application for you. You can get your database running quickly, then add features and functions to it as you work. C by itself will not help you create a database in a day. This is a limitation not just of C, but of all general-purpose programming languages. None are designed to streamline the development of a specific type of application.

Steps in Programming

Developing a program is a straightforward, logical process. If you take your time and follow the process from start to finish, you'll be a successful C programmer. Let's look at the steps in programming.

Plan the Program

Sit down, away from the computer, and think about what you want the program to accomplish. Outline the program in as much detail as possible. Most programs follow a pattern called IPO, for Input, Processing, Output.

For example, suppose you want to write a program that calculates sales tax on a purchase. What does the program need to do?

Consider the input. We need two pieces of information, the amount of the purchase and the sales tax rate. If you want to use the program for more than one purchase, you'll need to input a purchase amount each time you run the program. Chances are you'll only need one rate, that of your state, and so you can add the tax rate directly into the program code.

Next, determine the processing. In this case, we need to calculate the amount of the sales tax, multiplying the purchase price by the tax rate.

Finally, consider the output. The results of the calculation must be displayed—output—on the monitor.

The steps of this program might appear as this:

INPUT

> Tell the user to enter the amount of the purchase.
> Input the purchase amount from the keyboard.
> Tell the computer the sales tax for your state.

PROCESS

> Multiply the purchase amount by the sales tax rate.

OUTPUT

> Display the result.

Write the Program

You use an *editor* to type the program. An editor is a program like a word processor, except that it does not need the capability to format characters or paragraphs. In fact, the source code file *must* not contain any special formatting codes—the compiler wouldn't understand them and would report them as errors.

Compile the Program

After saving the source code file, use the compiler to create the intermediate object file. Instructions that the compiler cannot understand generate *compiler warnings* or *error messages*. A warning means that there is a potential problem but that the compiler can continue to generate the object code. An error message will usually stop the compiling process. If any errors appear, you need to load the source code file back into the editor and correct the problem. These are usually *syntax errors*, mistakes in the spelling, punctuation, or wording of a C command or function.

Don't be discouraged if you get errors. Even the most experienced C programmers make mistakes.

Link the Program

When no compiler errors are reported, you link the object file with your libraries to create the executable program. An error message will appear if the linker cannot find the appropriate information in the libraries. You'll have to check your source code and make sure that you are using the correct library files.

Test the Program

Now you can execute the program. If you did everything correctly, your program will run without any problems. However, two types of errors may occur.

A *run-time* error occurs when the program includes an instruction that cannot be performed. A message will appear on the screen and the program will stop. Run-time errors usually involve files or hardware devices.

For example, suppose your program includes a command to open a file called "ACCOUNT.DAT" which doesn't exist on your disk. The compiler and linker assume that the file will exist when you run the program, so they do not report any problems. However, when you run the program, the instruction cannot be performed because the file cannot be found and the program stops.

Logic errors occur when the program can follow your instructions but the instructions are wrong; that is, when they produce the wrong results. These are the most difficult problems to detect because you may not even know they exist. You must check the program's output carefully for accuracy.

Consider again the sales tax program. Suppose you made a mistake and told the program to *divide* the purchase amount by the sales tax rate, rather than *multiply* it. The compiler and linker have no way to know that you goofed, so the program appears to generate and run without any error. Unfortunately, a six-percent sales tax on $100 will be reported as $1666.66! While this mistake will be obvious, other logic errors are not as easy to detect.

If you encounter any run-time or logic errors, you must correct them, then compile and link the program again.

Learning to Program

In learning how to program a computer, you really learn two important skills.

You learn the syntax—the words, grammar, and punctuation—of the computer language itself. You learn what each command and function does, and when and how to use it.

You also learn the logic of computer programming—how to perform a task using the computer language. This is a universal skill that you can then apply to any language. Once you learn the logic of programming in one language, you can master another by just learning its syntax.

Both skills are necessary to program a computer. Luckily, you learn them both at the same time!

What You Need to Program

To program in C or C++, you need an editor, a compiler, and a linker.

You can use your everyday word processing program, instead of a special editor, to create your source code file. However, you must save the file without any formatting instructions. This is normally called ASCII or DOS TEXT output. Most word processing programs have this capability.

In the long run, however, it is usually faster to use a special editor designed for programming since the program will be saved unformatted automatically. Some editors also let you insert C programming commands by typing abbreviated keywords, or by pressing special key combinations. .

The editor provided on the disk supplied with this book will even display a sample C program to remind you of the basic structure of the language.

Your compiler will come with a linker and a set of library functions. All C libraries have the basic C functions that you'll learn about in this book, but not all libraries are the same. Many libraries include advanced functions for database management, graphics, communications, and other applications. If you are choosing your own compiler, look for one that has the functions you'll need.

In addition to these basics, there are other tools that can streamline your programming. A *debugger* helps you find run-time errors in your executable program. It displays the values of variables and the names of the functions being performed as your program runs. By watching the action, you can detect where your errors occur. A *profiler* helps you optimize your program to speed up execution time. An *assembler* allows you to add functions directly in assembly language if you want a task to run as fast as possible.

Some C compilers come packaged with an integrated development environment (IDE). With an IDE, you run one program that gives you access to the editor, compiler, linker, and other supplied tools by selecting from a menu. If you are not using an IDE, you must start the editor, type your program, then save the file. You must then exit the editor to run the compiler.

Your Future with C/C++

It appears now that there are no limits for a C programmer. It is the most popular language for system and large-scale development. While C is certainly not the only language available today, it is getting most of the attention.

New and enhanced C compilers are being developed for DOS, Windows, and all computer platforms. Extensive libraries and programming tools are available to streamline in system development. It looks like C will be around for a long time, so learning C is a sound investment.

Questions

1. What is the difference between a compiler and an interpreter?
2. Are all C compilers identical?
3. What is the difference between an Assembler and a high-level language?
4. What is a source-code file?
5. What is the difference between compiler and run-time errors?
6. What are the advantages of C? Explain.
7. What are the steps in computer programming?

Exercises

1. Outline a program that calculates regular and over-time wages based on weekly hours.
2. Outline a program that determines whether a person is eligible to retire. (The retirement age is 65.)

TWO

This Is C/C++!

• •

Figuring out what a C program does just by looking at the source code can be daunting at first. While most C commands are simply English words (like *for*), and most C functions are usually words and abbreviations (like scanf for SCAN the keyboard and Format the characters), when you combine commands and functions with C's syntax, punctuation, and spacing, you get a program that sometimes looks like anything other than English—it's no wonder they call it "code." Don't let this scare you. Once you're familiar with C, you can read a C program as easily as a good novel.

In this chapter, you'll learn about a C program's structure. You'll also learn some important programming concepts.

The Structure of a C Program

A C program contains one or more functions. Remember, a function is a series of instructions to the computer to perform a specific task. Many functions that you'll be using are already written and compiled for you in the function library supplied with your compiler. Instead of writing the individual instructions yourself, you just tell the compiler to use one of its standard functions. Only when you want to perform a task that is not in the library do you need to write your own function.

The C compiler provided with this book, for example, has a complete library of functions. It contains all of the functions specified by the K&R standard, those defined by the ANSI committee, and many additional functions. Every program you see in this book can be compiled and linked using the compiler provided.

Every C (and C++) program must begin with the function called `main()` and it looks just like this:

```
main()
```

The parentheses after `main()` are part of the function name and are necessary. Your compiler cannot generate the program if you leave them out; they tell the compiler that you are referring to a function, not the word *main*. In fact, every function must be followed by a pair of parentheses, although in most cases you'll enter something between them. From now on in this book, we'll refer to all function names by including the parentheses.

Following `main()` are your instructions. Your instructions can include C commands or the names of functions in the library or those you've written yourself. An opening brace ({) must appear before the first instruction, and a closing brace (}) must follow the last instruction. So the basic structure of a C program looks like this:

```
main()           This is the main function I want you to perform
{                and it starts here.
 ....;
 ....;           These are the instructions I want you to perform
 .....
}                and they end here.
```

The opening and closing braces ({ and }) are called *delimiters* and they mark the beginning and end of a block, or section, of code. Every function you write must start and end with braces. In addition, you may have blocks of code within a function that begin and end with their own braces.

When you start your program, the computer begins with the first instruction in the `main()` function. So here is a complete C/C++ program that writes the word OK on the screen:

```
main()
{
    puts("OK");
}
```

This program has only one instruction but it still must follow the rules of C. The quotes around OK will not be displayed—they just tell C to display the characters between them, rather than a constant or variable named OK. (You'll learn about constants and variables in Chapter 3.) Figure 2.1 shows what each part of this simple program does.

The semicolon after the instruction is called the *statement terminator*. The semicolon tells the compiler that it has reached the end of the instruction—what comes next will be another instruction or the end of the program. You must have a semicolon after every instruction:

```
main()
{
    puts("I'm OK");
    puts("You're not");
}
```

This doesn't mean that *every line* must end with a semicolon. Sometimes instructions take up more than one line on the screen. Instead of placing the semicolon at the end of the screen line, you place it at the end of the instruction.

Figure 2.1

The parts of a C/C++ program.

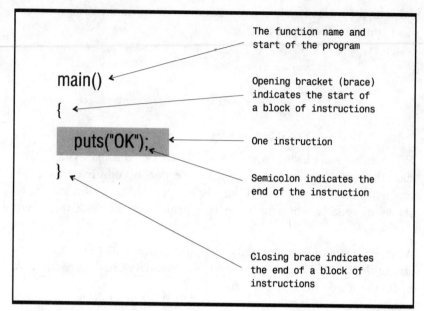

The function name and start of the program

Opening bracket (brace) indicates the start of a block of instructions

One instruction

Semicolon indicates the end of the instruction

Closing brace indicates the end of a block of instructions

Incidentally, after each `puts()` instruction, the computer moves the cursor to the start of the next line. So when you run this program with two `puts()` instructions, you will see two lines of text on the screen.

C and C++ are called free-form languages. They do not care where you put the braces or start the lines of instructions. So we could just as well write a program this way:

```
main(){ puts("OK");}
```

 **NOTE**

Some compilers do not automatically move to the next line after a `puts()` command. Refer to Chapter 4 for additional information.

The compiler will be able to perform the program either way. But to make a program more readable, we've adopted certain conventions:

- Put the `main()` function name on a line by itself.
- Put the opening and closing braces on their own lines.
- Indent the instructions. As your programs grow longer, you'll learn how indentations make program logic visible and indicate the way instructions are grouped into units.

Try to conform to these and other C conventions. They may not seem important with very small programs, but they will make longer and more complex programs much easier to handle.

While the spacing doesn't matter to the compiler, the punctuation does. If you leave out a brace, parenthesis, or semicolon, your compiler will generate an error instead of the program. These are called *syntax errors* and you must correct them before you can generate the program.

Uppercase, Lowercase

Another convention in C programs is the capitalization style. Commands and function names are always written in lowercase characters, so we use `puts()` rather than `PUTS()` or `Puts()`. You won't get an error message if you use uppercase, but the program just wouldn't look like a C program. Uppercase is reserved for things called *constants* and *symbolic names*.

The return() Function

What happens when the computer finishes performing the instructions in your program? The program stops and your computer returns to the state it was in before the program. If you ran your program from the operating system prompt, the prompt will reappear. If you ran your program from Windows, the Windows desktop will appear.

The return of control to the system or to Windows occurs automatically. Some C compilers, however, want you to be very explicit about every step, including the return to the system. For these compilers, you insert the command `return(0)` just before the `main()` function's closing brace:

```
main()
{
    puts("I'm OK");
    puts("You're not");
    return(0);
}
```

The `return()` function tells the computer to go back to the system. With most compilers, the command is optional. You won't get an error message if you don't include it. (The 0 within the parentheses may also be optional; you'll learn what it does shortly.) With the compiler provided with this book, for example, the `return()` command is optional. If you do use it, you can enter it as `return(0);` or even `return;` with no parentheses. However, if you use parentheses, you *must* include the 0 between them—you'll receive a compiler error if you use the parentheses by themselves.

If you do include the `return()` function, do not put any instructions between it and the closing brace. For example, this would be wrong:

```
main()
{
puts("I'm OK");
return(0);
puts("You're not");
}
```

The computer would return to the operating system after the first `puts()` function, and the instruction to display *You're not* would never be performed.

Using Comments

After you write and refine a C program, you'll understand it rather well. You'll know what each instruction does, and why you included it in the program.

But as your programs get more complicated, it becomes more difficult to remember the reason behind every instruction and programming nuance. It is particularly difficult if you come back to look at a program some time after you originally wrote it, or if you try to read a program written by someone else.

Adding *comments* makes your programs easier to understand. A comment is a message to anyone reading the source code. Comments can appear anywhere in a program. They are ignored by the compiler and linker. In fact, they are never added to the object code or to the executable program.

When you are first learning how to program, adding comments seems like an awful waste of time. You'd rather work on constructing the program itself. With small, simple test programs—just a few lines long—comments aren't really necessary. But down the road, you'll be thankful for comments in even the most basic program.

You begin a comment with the characters /* and end it with */, like this:

```
/*This program displays a word on the monitor*/
main()
{
    puts("OK");
    return (0);
}
```

The /* indicates the start of the comment, and */ indicates the end of the comment. C will ignore everything between the two symbols. Programmers usually place a comment at the start of each program to explain its overall purpose. Comments within a program explain a particular instruction or point of logic, and you can even add a comment after the semicolon of an instruction:

```
/*This program displays a word on the monitor*/
main()
{
    /* The word displayed is OK */
    puts("OK");
    return (0);    /*This returns to the system*/
}
```

When you include an instruction and comment on the same line, it is conventional to leave some blank space between the two. This simply makes the instruction and comment easier to read.

If you have lengthy comments, type as many lines as you want between the codes:

```
/*This program displays a word on the monitor and includes a
return() command to make it compatible with compilers that
require it.
*/
```

The closing */ code can be on its own line, or immediately after the comment.

Some programmers add an asterisk character in front of the additional lines and format the comment like this:

```
/*This program displays a word on the monitor and includes a
* return() command to make it compatible with compilers that
* require it.
*/
```

You can even get very fancy:

```
/* ***
 *      This program displays a word on the monitor      *
 *      and includes a return() command to make it       *
 *      compatible with compilers that require it.        *
 *****************************************************************
 */
```

The additional asterisks are only for appearance. They, like everything else between /* and */, are ignored.

Comments in C++

A common mistake beginning programmers make is to leave out the closing */ resulting in compiler error messages. C++ makes using comments a little easier by allowing another comment marker, the symbols //. This type of comment stops at the carriage return that ends the line, so you do not need to type an end-of-comment code:

```
// This program displays a word on the monitor
main()
{
     puts("OK");
     return (0);     //Returns to the system
}
```

If your comment runs over one line, however, each line must start with //:

```
// This program displays a word on the monitor and includes a
// return() command to make it compatible with compilers that
// require it.
```

You can still use the /* and */ comment codes in C++.

Understanding Parameters

When you use a function in a command, such as puts(), you are said to be *calling the function*. This means that you are calling on C to perform the function.

The parentheses after a function name are designed to hold zero or more parameters. A *parameter* is an item of information the function needs in order to complete its task. For example, `puts()` is a function in the library. The function contains instructions that tell the computer to put a string of characters on the screen. But what string does it display? You have to tell it by placing what you want to display in the parentheses. We call this *passing a parameter*. So in the instruction:

```
puts("HELLO");
```

the word HELLO is the parameter we are passing to the function. As illustrated in Figure 2.2, we are telling the compiler to perform the `puts()` function and to use the word HELLO when it does. The quote marks indicate that we want to display the characters H-E-L-L-O, rather than any constant or variable (again, see Chapter 3) with that name.

In this book, we've been calling an instruction like `puts("HELLO")` a function. Actually, the function itself, named `puts()`, is in the library. So

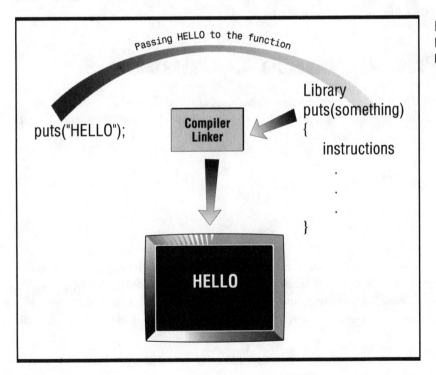

Figure 2.2

Passing a parameter to a library function.

technically, puts("HELLO") is an instruction that *calls* the puts() function and passes the word HELLO as a parameter.

The entire word HELLO is one parameter. puts() can only have one parameter—one character, word, or phrase that you want it to print. Later you'll learn about functions that can have several parameters.

Some functions do not need to be passed parameters. Many programmers, for example, perform the return(0) function by using just

```
return()
```

A parameter is not required.

You'll be learning more about parameters as you learn other C functions.

Be sure you understand the difference between how we use the function main() and any other function, such as puts(). We use main() to name the function containing our instructions to the computer. We are not calling main() but performing the commands within it. One of those commands calls the puts() function. Thus, puts() is a function called within the function main().

The #include Command

If you are writing a program that uses any disk files or prints information on a printer, you'll probably need to include the header file stdio.h with a command like this:

```
#include <stdio.h>
main()
{
    puts("OK");
    return (0);
}
```

The #include command is a directive that tells the compiler to use the information in the header file called *stdio.h*. The initials *stdio* stand for *standard input/output*, and the stdio.h file contains all the instructions the compiler needs to work with disk files and send information to the printer.

The instruction to use a header file must be given before main().

Where's the Header File?

Surrounding the name of the header file with the symbols < and > tells the compiler that the file may be located in the default *include* directory. This is a directory where the compiler's installation program will place the header files. If the file is not found in the current directory during the compilation process, the compiler will look for it in the include directory. You can also enclose the header file name in quotation marks, as in

```
#include "stdio.h"
```

In this case, however, the compiler will only look for the header file in the current directory, and it will display an error message if the file cannot be found there.

The installation program provided with this book places header files in the same directory as the compiler, C:\FIRSTC, so you can use either the symbols < and > or quotation marks. The compiler also includes a header file called MATH.H for performing complex math operations. Check the documentation file PCC.DOC that will be installed with the compiler for additional information. The documentation that comes with your compiler will explain what header file to use, and when to use it.

Some built-in C functions also need the stdio.h file to run correctly. For example, the function `getc()` inputs a single character from a source you designate, such as a file on the disk. Since so much input is obtained from the keyboard, however, C also includes the function `getchar()`. This function tells the compiler to *get* a *char*acter from the keyboard. It does so by calling `getc()` and specifying that the source is the *standard input device*. Now we know the keyboard is our standard input device, but how does the compiler know? The standard input device is defined in stdio.h. So to use the `getchar()` function in a program, you must use the `#include` command for stdio.h. The header file and library work together to complete the function.

If your compiler comes with a file called stdio.h, you may want to include it in every program just to avoid errors.

Program Design

As you learn C, you will also develop problem-solving skills—the skills you need in order to apply the language and structure of C to perform specific tasks. One such skill is the ability to divide a problem into distinct, manageable parts.

Breaking a problem into parts is a common problem-solving technique. After all, isn't a small problem easier to solve than a large one? When you are faced with a large problem that is difficult to solve, divide it into smaller, easier to handle, problems. If need be, keep dividing the problems into smaller and smaller units, until you can see a solution. When you solve each of the smaller problems, the large problem is resolved.

Do the same in designing a program. Start by dividing the overall job you want to perform into smaller jobs. If the smaller job still seems difficult to handle, subdivide it yet again. Continue to subdivide it until you can write the instructions that perform it. Once you've written all of the individual sections, and tied them together in main( ), the program is done! (In Chapter 7, you'll learn an even more efficient way of writing a program in sections.)

Dividing a program in this way also helps you find mistakes. You just ask yourself what task is not being performed correctly, then look at the section of the program that performs that task.

This process is called *troubleshooting* and it is used by professionals of all types to solve problems. For instance, when you take your car in for repair, the mechanic will ask a series of questions. When you go to a doctor, you are asked "Where does it hurt?" Your answers will help determine the particular system that may be causing the problem.

Questions

1. What is the general structure of a C program?

2. What is a statement terminator?

3. Is the `return()` function required by every C compiler?

4. What is the purpose of comments in a C program?

5. Why do you use a parameter when calling a function?

6. Does every function call require a parameter?

Exercises

1. Write a program that displays the following on the screen:

```
Welcome to my world.
Please don't rain on my parade.
```

2. Write a program that displays your name, address, and telephone number, centered on the screen.

3. Explain what is wrong with the following program:

```
main()
(
      puts("My name is Alvin);
}
```

Three

Variables and Constants

• • • • • • • • • • • • • • • • • • • •

Every program needs information of some sort. A program that calculates mortgage payments needs to know the amount, interest rate and length of the loan. A program that catalogs a stamp collection needs a description of each stamp. A program that shoots space invaders out of the sky needs to know the direction of each shot and photon torpedo.

We refer to information given to the computer as *data*. You feed data into the computer; the computer processes it following your instructions and gives you information as output. But before you input data into your program, you have to tell it what type of data it is dealing with.

For one thing, C must set aside enough memory to store each data item (without wasting any memory). Different types of data use up more or less memory space. Second, not every C function can be performed on every type of data. You'll get compiler or run-time errors if you try to give the program a word when it needs a number.

When you write your program, you have to tell it the type of each piece of data it will be using, both as input and as output. You can't leave anything out, and you can't change your mind when the program is running.

We classify a data item by the type of value it holds. (Note that *value* doesn't necessarily mean a numeric value, since data can be letters, words, and phrases as well as numbers.)

C++ Notes

C++ has the same data types as C. Some C and C++ compilers, however, have additional data types not defined in the original K&R specification of the language.

Character Data

Values of the character data type—abbreviated char—can be single letters, numerals, or other keyboard characters. For each piece of type char data, the computer reserves just enough space to store a single character. So if you're using five different pieces of char data, your computer will set aside five character spaces, as illustrated in Figure 3.1.

Figure 3.1
Each char-type data item occupies one memory location.

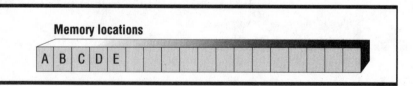

Memory locations

| A | B | C | D | E | | | | | | | | | | | | | |

Characters include the 26 uppercase letters:

A B C D E F G H I J K L M N O P Q R S T U V W X Y Z

the 26 lowercase letters:

a b c d e f g h i j k l m n o p q r s t u v w x y z

the ten numeric digits:

1 2 3 4 5 6 7 8 9 0

and the symbols you can enter from the keyboard:

! @ # $ % ^ & * ( ) _ + ¦ \ } {] [" ' : ; ? / > . < , ~ '

If you were writing a multiple-choice test, for example, you could input your answer—A, B, C, or D—as a piece of char data.

As you'll see later in this chapter, a char can also be a special control code that C stores in the same space as a single character.

Note that a char data item can also be a single numeric digit, such as 1, 2, or 3. But C makes a distinction between the character "1" and the number 1. As a *character*, "1" cannot be used in a mathematical operation because it does not have a numeric value. As a *number*, 1 can be used in math. But, as you'll soon learn, C can store the character "1" in half the space it uses to store the number 1.

Strings

A *string* is a group of characters, such as a word, phrase, or sentence. C does not have a separate string data type, as some other languages do. Instead, you work with a string as a series of char-type values, using something called an *array*.

A string can include any combination of letters, numbers, punctuation marks, and special codes that can be used individually as char data items. C distinguishes between a string of all numeric digits and a number. The string "123" does not have the value one hundred and twenty-three, it is just the combination of the characters "1", "2", and "3".

In this book, you'll work with strings starting in this chapter, although you will not learn about arrays in detail until Chapter 10. That's because strings are so useful in every sort of program, and because you can start using them without knowing all of their technical basis.

 NOTE

Some C and C++ compilers provide special string data types and a library of string functions. The compiler that comes with this book includes string-handling functions, but no special string types. For other compilers, check your documentation to see what features are available and how to access them.

Integers

If you'll be performing math with a piece of data, you must use a numeric data type. C has several numeric types, each differing in the range of values it can be assigned and how much memory it occupies.

An integer number—abbreviated `int`—is a number with no decimal places. It can be a positive or negative number, as well as zero, but it cannot have any decimal places.

A common C axiom is "Use an `int` for counting." Use an `int` to count the number of times something occurred, or when counting anything that only comes in whole units.

As shown in Figure 3.2, each piece of `int` data requires the storage space of two characters, whether it is the number 2 or 2000. But in order to use only two spaces for each number, C must limit the value of `int` data to between −32,768 and 32,767. Numbers outside that range require more than two storage spaces.

Figure 3.2

`int` type data occupy two memory locations.

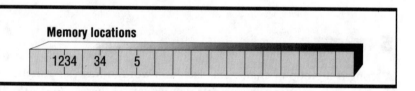

To handle all sorts of numbers, most C compilers define several types of integer numbers. The values you can assign to these types vary between compilers.

`short int`	A positive integer number between 0 and 255
`int`	An integer number between −32,768 and 32,767
`long int`	An integer number between −2,147,483,648 and 2,147,483,647
`unsigned long`	A positive integer number between 0 and 4,294,967,295

Long and `unsigned long` integers require four spaces in memory. Most compilers, including the one supplied with this book, do not recognize a separate `short int` type—you can use it in a program but it acts the same as an `int` type. This book's compiler recognizes an `unsigned int` with a range from 0 to 65535.

Decimal Numbers

Numbers that may contain a decimal place are called *floating-point* values, so C has a `float` data type for working with decimal numbers. Since floating-point numbers can be extremely small or large, their ranges of values are often expressed in exponential numbers. For example, a `float` value can be a number as large as 3.4E+38. This notation says, "Move the decimal point to the right 38 places, adding as many zeroes as needed."

There are additional data types for handling even wider ranges of numbers:

`float`	number between 3.4E–38 and 3.4E+38
`double`	number between 1.7E–308 and 1.7E+308
`long double`	number between 3.4E–4932 and 1.1E+4932

Floating-point types have limits in precision, which vary among compilers. For example, the number 6.12345678912345 is within the valid *range* of a `float` type but may be stored in your system as only 6.12345. This `float` type is said to be *single precision*, which means it is limited to 5 or 6 decimal places. A `double` type is called *double precision* and is accurate to 14 or 15 decimal places. The compiler supplied with this book has a `float` type with seven digits of precision, and a `double` with 13 digits of precision. It does not support the `long double` type.

`Float` types occupy four memory spaces; `doubles` use eight spaces, and `long doubles` take up ten spaces.

Figure 3.3 summarizes the memory requirements of common C types.

Figure 3.3
Summary of memory
requirements.

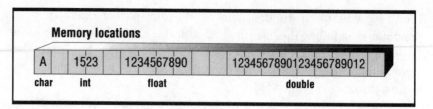

Memory locations

A	1523	1234567890	1234567890123456789012
char	int	float	double

Why Integers?

In the world outside of computer programming, we normally do not worry about the distinction between integers and decimal numbers. If you are using a calculator to perform math, you just press the keys. If a number has decimal places, you enter them. If a number doesn't have decimal places, you don't worry about it. So why does C bother with the distinction? Why are there so many different types of numbers? Isn't a number just a number?

Part of the answer to these questions involves computer storage. Memory costs money, and when your computer runs out of it your program just stops working. A good programmer tries to conserve memory, using as little as possible. Using integers instead of `float` values, and `chars` instead of strings, saves memory.

In addition, operations performed with integers run faster than those with decimal numbers. If your program does a great deal of math, using integers where possible is a wise decision. You may not notice the difference with small programs on a fast computer. But the speed difference is dramatic in engineering and graphics applications.

As you learn how to program, always select the data type that best suits your immediate needs. Develop the habit of using integers when possible—whenever you know a number won't need a decimal place.

Constants and Variables

Once you know the type of each piece of data you need, you must decide how you are going to input it into the computer. While there are many commands that input data, you must first classify each piece of data as either a constant or a variable.

A *constant* will remain the same throughout the entire program. In fact, you give a constant a value when you write the program, not when you run it, and its value cannot change unless you change the program. If you know the value of a piece of data ahead of time, and it will not change, use a constant.

For example, suppose you live in a state with a 5 percent sales tax. When you compute the charge for a taxable item, the rate will always be computed at 5 percent. So the value 0.05, a `float` type of value, can be stored as a constant.

The value of a *variable*, on the other hand, may change each time you run the program. You assign its value as the program is running. In an order entry system, for instance, the sales tax rate may not change, but the amount of the order probably will. Not every purchase is for the same amount. So you would input the amount of the order as a variable.

Most programs use both constants and variables. When you write your program, you have to know how each piece of information will be used— as a constant or a variable. That's just one of the decisions you have to make in planning your program.

Naming Constants and Variables

You have to give a name to each constant and variable that you use in your program. The maximum length of variable names depends on your compiler. Some compilers limit you to eight characters, others allow names up to 32 characters or more. In some cases, variable names can contain more characters than are significant. For example, you may be able to use 32-character names, but the first eight must be unique. To the computer, the variables `accountspayable` and `accountsreceivable` are the same because their first eight characters are the same. The compiler included with this book allows for variable names of up to 31 significant characters.

Variable and constant names may include uppercase and lowercase letters, and the underline character (_). Use any combination of letters and numbers, but start all names with a letter. Programmers use the underline to separate words, making names easier to read and more meaningful, as in `city_tax` rather than `citytax`.

Try to select names that describe how you are using the data. The name `city_tax` means more than `ctax`, and `amt_due` tells you more than `due`. Avoid names such as A and B unless you're writing a very simple program.

You cannot use a C command (or *keyword*) for a variable or constant name. If you use a keyword as a variable or constant name, the compiler will generate an error message and stop compiling your program. The following lists show all the C and C++ keywords, including those in the original K&R definition of C, those added in ANSI C, and those added in C++. Your compiler may have additional commands that are also keywords, so check your documentation. If you get an error message when compiling, and you are certain the instruction is correct, make sure you have not used a keyword for a constant or variable name.

Here are the K&R C Keywords:

auto	goto
break	if
case	int
char	long
continue	register
default	return
do	short
double	sizeof
else	static
entry	struct
extern	switch
float	typedef
for	union

ANSI C adds these keywords:

const
enum
signed
void
volatile

Chapter 3: Variables and Constants

C++ adds these keywords:

catch	inline
cin	new
class	operator
cout	private
delete	pro-·
friend	tected

Names are case-sensitive. If you name a variable TAX, you cannot later re-fer to it as Tax or tax. In fact, you could have three separate variables named TAX, Tax, and tax, each holding a different value and of a different type. (Of course, actually doing that would make your program very dif-ficult to follow and debug.) Some beginning programmers make the mis-take of changing the spelling or capitalization of a variable or constant in different parts of the program. This results in compiler or run-time errors that are often difficult to track down and correct.

The C convention (illustrated in Figure 3.4) is to use all lowercase letters for variable names, and all uppercase characters for constant names. While you will not get an error message if you violate the convention,

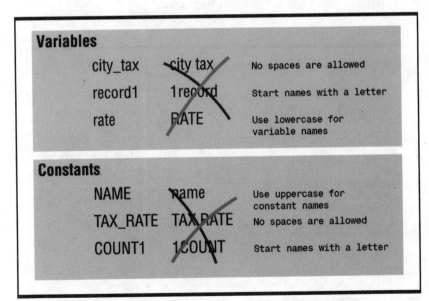

Figure 3.4
C conventions for naming variables and constants.

there is a good reason to obey the rule. Using different cases makes it easy to clearly distinguish variables from constants within a program. This makes it easier to read your program and to track what's going on.

You have to tell your C program the name and type of every variable and constant.

Declaring a Constant

Declaring a constant means telling the C compiler the constant's name and value. You do this before the main() function using the #define compiler directive, which has this general syntax:

```
#define NAME VALUE
```

There is no semicolon after the directive, and you must put at least one space between the directive, the constant name, and the assigned value. The exact syntax is based on the type of data you are defining—numeric, char, or string. (Refer to Figure 3.5.)

Before the compiler begins to create the object code, it substitutes each occurrence of the constant name with the value (like an automatic search-and-replace in a word processing program). In essence, the constant name itself is never converted into object code.

Figure 3.5
Syntax for declaring constants.

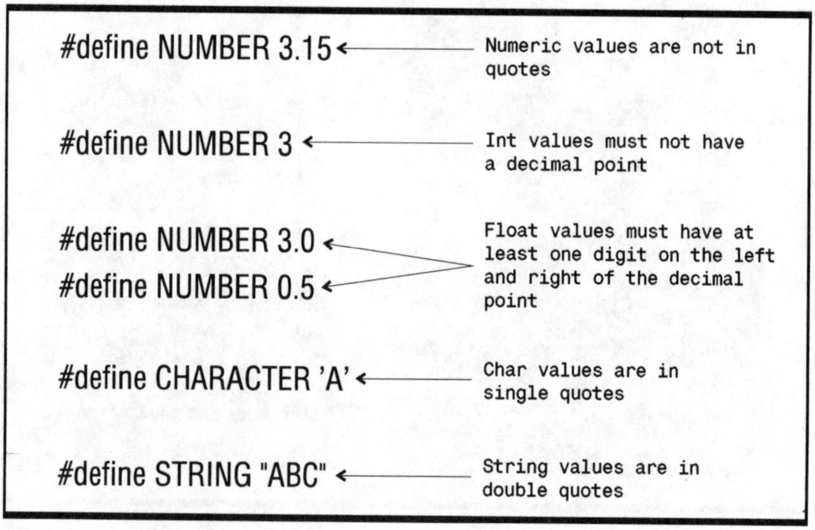

#define NUMBER 3.15 ←	Numeric values are not in quotes
#define NUMBER 3 ←	Int values must not have a decimal point
#define NUMBER 3.0 ← #define NUMBER 0.5 ←	Float values must have at least one digit on the left and right of the decimal point
#define CHARACTER 'A' ←	Char values are in single quotes
#define STRING "ABC" ←	String values are in double quotes

You declare a numeric constant by specifying the constant's name and value. For example, this directive:

```
#define PI 3.14
```

creates a constant called PI and gives it the value 3.14 (see Figure 3.6).

Whenever the compiler sees PI in the source code (for example, in a formula), it substitutes the value 3.14 (see Figure 3.7).

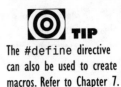

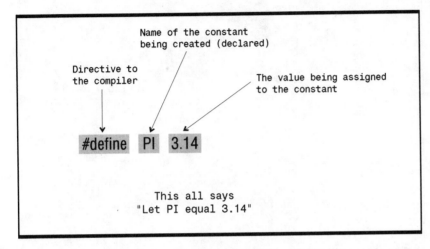

Figure 3.6
Declaring a constant.

You do not have to state the data type explicitly when you define a constant. Instead, C assigns the constant a data type based on the value given in the #define directive. In the example above, the constant PI is assigned the float data type because its value, 3.14, is a decimal number. In the directive

```
#define COUNT 5
```

the constant COUNT is assigned the int data type because 5 is an integer number.

To declare a float type, make sure the value has at least one digit to the left and right of the decimal point. If the value does not have any decimal places, add a decimal point and several trailing zeroes anyway, as in

```
#define RATE 5.00
```

Without the decimal placed, C would assume the constant was an int type rather than a float. To declare values less than one, add a leading

Figure 3.7

The compiler substitutes the
value for the name.

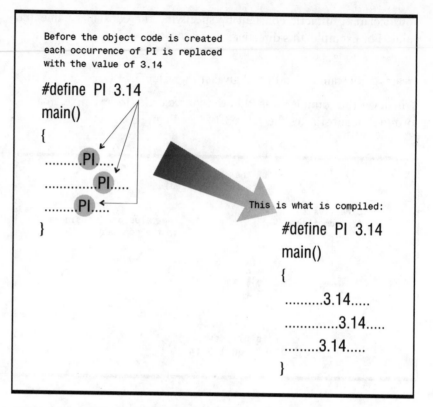

zero before the decimal numbers, as in

```
#define RATE 0.56
```

C would generate a compiler error if you declared

```
#define RATE .56
```

With char data, the *value* assigned must be in single quotes:

```
#define INIT 'A'
```

Similarly, to declare a string, enclose the value in quotes:

```
#define FRIEND "George"
main()
{
puts(FRIEND);
}
```

Just remember that the quotes do not become part of the value.

When you use a constant *name* as a parameter, in this case with `puts()`, you do not enclose it in quotes. This tells the compiler to use the value assigned to the constant, not the characters that make up its name—in this case, the value assigned to FRIEND, not the characters F-R-I-E-N-D. If you wanted to display the word FRIEND, your command would be

```
puts("FRIEND");
```

After the `#define FRIEND "George"` directive, whenever the compiler sees FRIEND in the program, it substitutes "George". So the instruction

```
puts(FRIEND);
```

actually calls the `puts()` function as

```
puts("George");
```

and displays the name George on the screen. If your program began with this line:

```
#define FRIEND "Hazel"
```

the name Hazel would appear on the screen. Why? Because the directive defined the name FRIEND as having the value Hazel.

Constants in C++

C++ and some C compilers provide an additional way to declare a constant. Using the `const` modifier, you declare a constant, specify its type, and assign it a value. You use the `const` modifier within a function, however, not as a directive before `main()`, as in this program segment:

```
main()
{
      const int CHILDREN = 8;
      const char INIT = 'C';
```

These commands declare an `int` constant with the value 8 and a `char` constant with the value C. They perform the same function as

```
#define CHILDREN 8
#define INIT 'C'
```

 NOTE

The const command is useful because it allows the programmer to create constants that are local to specific functions. However, to insure compatibility with all C and C++ compilers, most programmers continue to use the `#define` directive to declare constants.

Why Constants?

If a value is not going to change in a program, why bother using a constant? Why not just use the value directly in a program instruction? For example, if you start a program with

```
#define PHONE "555-1234"
```

you can display the phone number in a command like this:

```
puts(PHONE);
```

But since the value of the phone number will not change in the program, you could just as well display it directly:

```
puts("555-1234");
```

After all, the results will be exactly the same, and it saves you the trouble of writing a #define directive and naming a constant.

However, using constants makes a program easier to change. Suppose, for example, that a program displays your phone number 20 times. If you change your phone number and did not use a constant, you would have to edit all 20 puts() commands. You could also mistakenly change only 19 puts() commands, causing the incorrect phone number to appear in one instance. If you used a constant, however, you would only have to make one change—inserting the new phone number in the #define directive. As shown in Figure 3.8, every puts() command would be updated automatically.

The same applies to numeric constants. Instead of using the directive

```
#define TAX 0.06
```

and performing calculations using the constant TAX, you could use the value 0.06 in your formulas. But suppose your state increases its tax rate to 6.5 percent. If you did not use a constant, you'd have to change the value each time it was used, rather than change the #define directive just once.

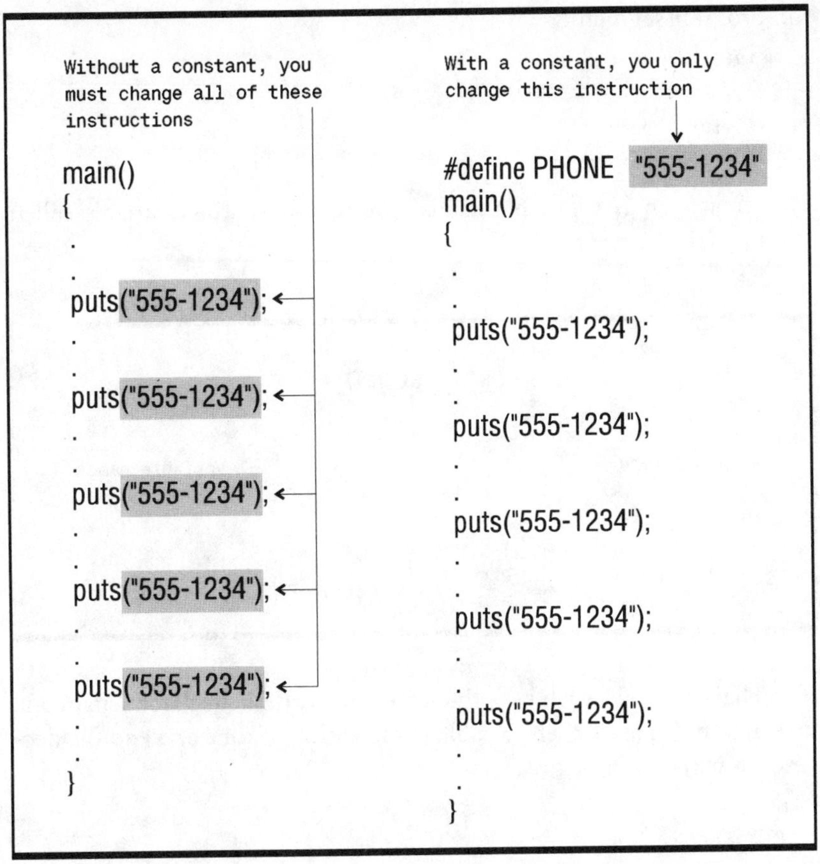

Figure 3.8
Use constants to make it
easier to change your program.

Without a constant, you
must change all of these
instructions

```
main()
{
    .
    .
    puts("555-1234");  ←
    .
    .
    puts("555-1234");  ←
    .
    .
    puts("555-1234");  ←
    .
    .
    puts("555-1234");  ←
    .
    .
    puts("555-1234");  ←
    .
    .
}
```

With a constant, you only
change this instruction

```
#define PHONE "555-1234"
main()
{
    .
    .
    puts("555-1234");
    .
    .
    puts("555-1234");
    .
    .
    puts("555-1234");
    .
    .
    puts("555-1234");
    .
    .
    puts("555-1234");
    .
    .
}
```

Declaring a Variable

Declaring a variable means providing the C compiler with the variable's
name and type, and you must explicitly state the data type of the variable's value. The general syntax for declaring a variable is this:

```
type name;
```

The number of spaces between the type and name are up to you, as
long as you have at least one. A typical variable declaration looks like

this program segment:

```
main()
{
    int  count;
    float tax_rate;
```

This creates an `int` variable named count, and a `float` variable called tax_rate (see Figure 3.9).

Figure 3.9

Declaring variables.

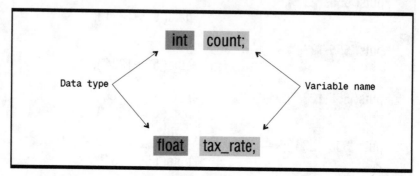

If you have several variables of the same type, you can declare them in one instruction. Separate each variable name with a comma and end the declaration with a semicolon, as in

```
main()
{
    int count, children, year;
    float tax_rate, discount;
}
```

This creates five variables—three `int` values and two `float` values. Declare variables in a group within the `main()` function, after its opening brace and before any other instructions. You can also declare single variables before `main()`, like this:

```
int count;
main()
{
}
```

In a simple program, you can declare variables in either location. (When you use multiple functions, more complex rules of C will determine where you declare variables. These are discussed in Chapter 7.)

Assigning Values

Some variables have an *initial* value—the value you want the variable to have when you start the program. Unlike a constant, this value can change as the program runs. You assign an initial value either in the declaration or as a separate instruction.

With numeric and `char` data (we'll discuss strings in a moment), you can assign the value as part of the declaration:

```
main()
{
     int count=5;
     char initial='A';
     float rate=0.55;
```

This instruction declares a variable named count and assigns it the initial value of 5. It also declares a `char` variable named initial and assigns it the letter A, and a `float` variable with the value 0.55. The value of the `char` variable must be in single quotes, and `float` values must have at least one digit to the left and to the right of the decimal point.

Once you declare a variable, you can also assign it a value in a separate instruction using the = symbol, like this:

```
count=5;
initial='A';
rate=0.55;
```

The assigned value is only the initial value. As variables, the initial values can be changed as the program runs.

If you will not know a variable's initial value until the program is run, you can assign a value by accepting it from the keyboard, from a disk file, or through a calculation. You'll learn these methods later.

Declaring String Variables

Remember, C does not contain a string type and it does not have any built-in string functions. Fortunately, C does allow us to work with string-type data through the use of arrays. We've previously defined a string as a series of characters. That's exactly what a string is—a series of `char` variables collected into something called an array. The characters of the string are stored together, in consecutive memory storage locations. A variable that has the value "Hello" would look something like Figure 3.10. Each character is stored in a separate memory location, just like a single `char` variable, but you can display the entire string as a unit in one `puts()` command. The symbol `\0` is a special code C inserts after a string. It marks the end of the string so that functions such as `puts()` know where to stop retrieving characters to display.

Figure 3.10
String data in memory.

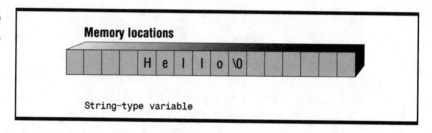

You already know how to declare a string constant—by using a `#define` directive and surrounding the characters in quotes, as in

```
#define CLIENT "Joe Public"
```

NOTE
The `\0` symbol is called a null terminator and is considered a single character.

To declare a string variable, you use the `char` variable type and specify the maximum number of characters that the variable can hold. The syntax is this:

```
char VARNAME[N];
```

VARNAME is the name of the variable, and N is the maximum number of characters. The number is always in square brackets, [and].

The number in the brackets should actually be one more than the maximum number of characters you want to use. C needs the extra character to store the `\0` code. For example, a variable to store abbreviated state names might be declared like this

```
char state[3];
```

As illustrated in Figure 3.11, this creates a string variable named state that can store two characters in addition to the null terminator (`\0`).

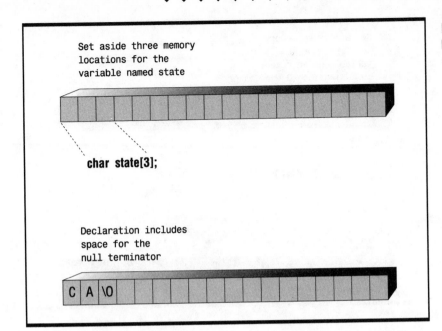

Figure 3.11
Declaring a string variable.

Set aside three memory
locations for the
variable named state

char state[3];

Declaration includes
space for the
null terminator

C A \0

You cannot assign more characters to the variable than you declare. That's because C sets aside just enough space to store the maximum number of characters. So think carefully before declaring the variable.

For example, suppose you need a variable to store a client's name. You declare it this way:

```
char client[10];
```

Your program might run flawlessly until you obtain an order from Mr. Flugglehoffen. When you try to assign this client's name, your program will stop with a run-time error, as in Figure 3.12.

You could declare the variable with some large number, such as

```
char client[80];
```

But if you have several variables like this, you'll be wasting quite a bit of your computer's resources.

Once you declare a string variable, you can assign the variable a value. As with all variables, you can assign an initial value or accept the value from the keyboard or from a disk file. (You'll learn how to accept a string from the keyboard in the next chapter.) In K&R C, you cannot directly assign

Figure 3.12

You cannot assign a string more characters than have been reserved.

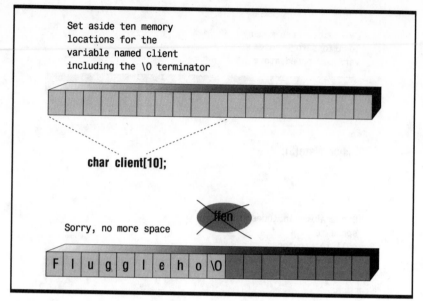

a value to a string in a statement, as this program tries to do:

```
main()
{
    char client[15];
    client="Joe";
    puts(client);
}
```

The statement

```
client="Joe";
```

is not allowed. But if you want to assign an initial value to a string variable, you do so when you declare the variables using one of two methods. You can assign the value by declaring the variable before main(), like this:

```
char client[]="Flugglehoffen";
main()
{
    puts(client);
}
```

Notice that there is no maximum number of characters in the square brackets. The maximum number allowed will depend on your compiler, but it is usually limited to the number of characters in the initial value (see Figure 3.13). Also notice that you only use the variable name in the `puts()` function—you do not have to use any square brackets.

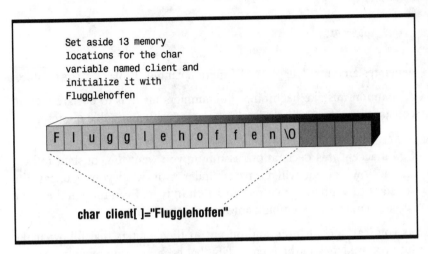

Set aside 13 memory locations for the char variable named client and initialize it with Flugglehoffen

char client[ ]="Flugglehoffen"

Figure 3.13

Declaring an initial value for a string.

Another way to assign an initial value, within the `main()` function, is a little more complex:

```
main()
{
    static char greet[] = "Hello";
    puts(greet);
}
```

The declaration is performed within the `main()` function but begins with the word `static`. A `static` variable can be used only in the function where it was declared. If you want to assign an initial value to a string variable in main(), it must be declared as a `static` variable. You'll learn more about this in Chapter 7.

Data Types and Functions

The type you assign to a constant or variable determines which functions can use it. Most functions must be passed a specific type of data as a parameter. For example, `puts()` requires a string of characters, so the program

```
#define PI 3.14
main()
{
    puts(PI);
}
```

generates an error. The `puts()` function cannot display a `float` value.

A common mistake beginning programmers make is to declare a `char` constant by surrounding a single character value in double quotes:

```
#define initial "A"
```

C will accept this declaration, assuming you want the constant to be a string. However, you will receive compiler errors when you try to pass the constant to a function that requires a `char` type. Even though the value is one character, the double quotes mark it as a string.

As you learn about input and output in the chapters that follow, make sure you understand the type of data that each function requires.

Literals

A *literal* is any piece of data that you type directly into a C instruction. For example, any number, character, or string that you type as an initial value is a literal. In the instruction

```
count=5;
```

the number 5 is a literal value. This means that you want that exact number assigned to the variable. In the instructions

```
#define INIT 'C'
rate=0.55;
client="Joe";
puts("555-1234");
```

the character C, the number 0.55, the word Joe, and the phone number 555-1234 are literals.

Planning Your Program

Data is critical to every C and C++ program. If you don't plan your use of data ahead of time, your chances of encountering compiler and run-time errors grow significantly.

Throughout this chapter, we've been discussing variables and constants in terms of the data you must feed into the program. You must also consider the data that you want to get out of the program as information. Chances are, you'll have to declare variables to store this information as well.

In fact, many programmers plan their programs starting with the output. By deciding what information they want to get out of the program, they can determine what information must be input and how it must be processed.

As an example, let's consider a program that calculates the sales tax on an order. Here are the steps in developing the necessary constants and variables:

1. Decide what pieces of information your program needs:

- The output will be the total of the sale plus the state sales tax.

- In order to determine that output, you'll need to input the amount of the order and the sales tax rate. The amount of the order is a dollar amount, so you'll need a float variable. You can call it sale. The sales tax rate is fixed by your state, so you'll need a float constant. Call it TAX_RATE.

- The program must multiply the order amount by the sales tax rate. For example, if the order is $25.00, and the sales tax rate is 0.05, the tax is $1.25. You will need a float variable to store the amount of the tax. Call it sales_tax.

- The program must add the tax to the order for a total. The total in our example is $26.25. To display the output, you'll need a float variable that will store the total order. Call it total.

2. Write the `#define` directives for any constants:

```
#define TAX_RATE 0.05
```

3. Write the variable declarations:

```
float sale, sales_tax, total
```

Once you've planned for your data, you are ready to write the program.

Questions

1. What is a char data type?

2. How does the character "3" differ from the number 3?

3. What data type would you use for a variable storing a dollar amount?

4. Why would a program need to use the long int data type?

5. Why would you use a double float type?

6. What is the difference between a constant and a variable?

7. How do you declare a constant?

8. Does C have a string data type?

9. Can a variable have the same value throughout the entire program?

10. How do you change the value of a constant?

Exercises

1. Decide what types of data you need, and write their declarations, for a program that computes the total weekly salary of an individual who gets double-time for every hour over 40 per week.

2. Decide what types of data you need, and write their declarations, for a program that computes the sum and average of four numbers.

3. Explain what is wrong in the following program segment:

```
char client[3]="Ajax";
main()
float   tax_due;
char   name(10);
int     count(5);
tax_due="$1,635.00";
```

```
int age;
age = 12;
printf("I am %d years old", age);
```

Four

Output in C/C++

. . . .

O

utput sends a copy of data in the computer's memory to another location—displaying it on the monitor, printing it on a printer, or saving it in a disk file. More exotic types of output save data on a tape, transmit it through a modem, or fax it through the telephone line.

Outputting data does not erase it from the computer's memory, nor does it change the way data is stored. It simply makes a copy of the data and sends it elsewhere.

TIP

All of the output commands
in C are also supported by
C++ compilers.

In this chapter, you will learn how to output data to the screen.

The command you use to output depends on the type of the data being output and how you want it to appear. The most straightforward forms of output work with strings and `char` data.

The puts() Function

You should already be quite familiar with the `puts()` function, which displays a string on the monitor. The parameter (the information in parentheses, which you want to display) must be one of the following types:

- A string literal:

```
puts("Hello there");
```

- A string constant:

```
#define MESSAGE "Hello there"
main()
{
    puts(MESSAGE);
}
```

 NOTE

Remember, a *literal* is an exact value that you type in a C or C++ instruction, instead of a variable or constant name.

- A string variable:

```
char greeting[]="Hello there"
main()
{
    puts(greeting);
}
```

Any other type of constant, variable, or literal value will generate a compiler error. A string literal, but not a constant or variable name, must be enclosed in double quotes.

Most compilers perform a new-line command after the `puts()` function. This means that after the data is displayed, the cursor will move to the start of the next line.

 NOTE

Because the PCC compiler does not add the new-line command automatically, we use the \n code in `puts()` instructions shown in this book. If you are using a compiler that does perform the new-line command, you can leave the \n codes out of your `puts()` instructions.

However, some compilers, including the PCC shareware compiler provided on this book's accompanying diskette, do not perform the new line automatically. With these compilers, you have to generate a new line with the \n control code. (See the discussion of control codes later in this chapter.) While this may seem like a drawback, it can actually be quite useful. By not including a new-line command after a `puts()` function, you can use several `puts()` instructions to display information on one line on the screen. You only use the `\n` code when you want the cursor to move to the next screen line.

The putchar() Function

The `putchar()` function displays a single `char` value on the monitor. The parameter must be one of these:

- A `char` literal:

```
putchar('H');
```

- A `char` constant:

```
#define INITIAL 'H'
main()
{
        putchar(INITIAL);
}
```

- A `char` variable:

```
main()
{
        char letter;
        letter = 'G';
        putchar(letter);
}
```

Only one character is allowed. The instruction

```
putchar('Hi');
```

would generate a compiler error.

If you are displaying a `char` literal or a control code, it must be in single quotes.

Most C compilers do not add a new-line command after a `putchar()` instruction. The cursor will remain immediately after the displayed character, without going to the next line. To move to the next line, you must use the `\n` control code, discussed later in this chapter.

 TIP

Your compiler may include the function `putch()`, which has the same effect as `putchar()`.

A Dual Personality

On some systems, you need to include the stdio header file to use the putchar() function. With these systems, the putchar() function is derived from another function, putc(). The putc() function, as you'll learn in Chapter 11, sends output to a specified device, such as a disk or printer. The stdio header file contains information that uses putc() to perform the putchar() function.

Because putc() can output to a disk file, certain special rules apply to it, and thus to putchar(). Some codes that must be written to a disk file may not fit in the single memory space reserved for a char item. To accommodate these codes, the putc() and putchar() functions were originally designed to use an int type. The compiler internally converts the int to a character. So with compilers that support the K&R specification, you could write a program this way:

```
main()
{
    int letter;
    letter = 'G';
    putchar(letter);
}
```

Even though the variable named letter is declared as an int type, a character is assigned to it as an initial value. The program will still compile and run without a problem.

Some programmers remain true to the K&R standard and always use putchar() with an int type. The choice is yours.

Control Codes

You can control the way the cursor moves on your monitor, and some other computer functions, by outputting special codes, called *escape sequences*. Each sequence begins with the backslash character (\), which identifies the character that follows it as an *escape character*. The backslash is followed by a keystroke representing the function you want to perform. When the compiler encounters the backslash, it does not display the next character but performs the function indicated by it.

Use the escape sequence in quotes within a `puts()` function, or in single quotes within a `putchar()` function. Even though the sequence is two typed characters, C treats the sequence as one character in a `putchar()` instruction.

The New-line Code

The sequence \n performs a new-line command, moving the cursor to the start of the next line. Use the command to move to the next line after `putchar()` displays a character. If your instructions are:

```
putchar('A');
putchar('\n');
```

the screen displays the letter A and the cursor moves to the start of the next line. Notice that the \n code, like any other literal in the `putchar()` parameter, is enclosed in single quotes. Because the letter *n* follows a backslash, the compiler performs the new-line function instead of displaying the character *n* on the screen.

In a `puts()` command, you can combine the code with a literal within the same set of quotes. The instruction

```
puts("William Watson\n");
```

displays the name William Watson on the screen and places the cursor on the next line. The new-line code must be within the parameter's quotes. If your compiler automatically inserts a new-line command after a `puts()` function, the cursor will appear **two** lines down. Here's how it works:

1. The name William Watson is displayed.
2. The \n code performs a new-line command, moving the cursor to the start of the line under the name.
3. The `puts()` function ends. If your compiler adds a new-line automatically, the cursor will move down another line.

While the \n code is most commonly used at the end of an instruction, it can appear anywhere inside the parameter's quotes. This command

```
puts("A\nB\nC");
```

displays three lines of text:

```
A
B
C
```

The compiler displays the letter A, performs a new-line command, displays the letter B, performs a new-line command, and displays the letter C. If your compiler adds a new-line command automatically, the cursor will be on the line below the letter C.

The Tab Code

The \t tab command moves the cursor to the next preset tab stop on the screen. To see how the tab code works, use this program:

```
main()
{
        puts("12345678901234567892123456789312345678941 2345"\n);
        puts("0\t1\t2\t3\t4\t5\n");
}
```

The program displays a line of numbers for you to use to count character positions. It then displays the number 0 at the far left of the screen, and the numbers 1 to 5 at the next five tab stops:

```
12345678901234567892123456789312345678941 2345;
0       1       2       3       4       5
```

You can use the code to create evenly spaced columns of text or numbers:

```
main()
{
 puts("Friends, their debts, and how long they have owed
me:\n");
 puts("Alan\t\tJeff\t\tNancy\t\tTom\n");
 puts("$1.50\t\t$2.45\t\t$6.24\t\t$3.56\n");
 puts("10 days\t\t5 days\t\t15 days\t\t1 day\n");
}
```

The output of this program is shown in Figure 4.1. Notice that two tab codes were used between each column to space them out across the screen. Also note that there are no extra spaces between the tab code and the text that follows. Any extra spaces would be displayed on the screen, and the columns would not align correctly.

```
Friends, their debts, and how long they have owed me:

Alan            Jeff            Nancy           Tom
$1.50           $2.45           $6.24           $3.56
10 days         5 days          15 days         1 day
```

Figure 4.1
Output using tab stops.

The Return Code

The \r code performs a carriage return, moving the cursor to the start of the same line, without moving down to the next line. If you display something, move the cursor back to the start of the line, and then display something else, the first text will be overtyped.

Figure 4.2 illustrates the difference between a carriage return and a new-line command. When you are typing on your keyboard, pressing the Enter or Return key performs what C calls a new-line command. Some programmers call this a combination carriage return and line feed, abbreviated CR/LF. The /r return code in C does *not* move down to the next line.

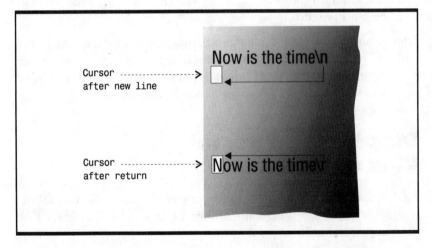

Figure 4.2
The difference between a carriage return and new-line command.

The effect of using the \r code can be seen in this instruction:

```
puts("Left\rRight");
```

The screen displays only the word Right. Here's why: After displaying the word *Left*, the \r code moves the cursor back to the start of the line. The word *Right* is displayed, replacing the characters of the word *Left*.

The \r code by itself is nondestructive; it does not erase the characters on the line as it moves back. Only displaying other characters before moving the cursor again will erase existing text.

The Backspace Code

Unlike the \r code, which backs the cursor to the start of the line, the \b code moves the cursor just one position to the left. It, too, is nondestructive in that it does not erase a character it encounters.

If you use the return or backspace codes to move the cursor, and then issue a new-line command, the cursor moves to the next line without affecting the text. The new-line command does *not* insert a blank line (as pressing the Enter key does in a word processing program).

The Formfeed Code

When you are sending output to the printer (as you'll learn how to do later), the formfeed code (\f) ejects the current page. This code is recognized by most printers.

After printing a report, for example, most programmers output the formfeed code to insure that the last report page is ejected. If you display the code on screen with `puts()` or `putchar()`, a small graphic character will appear but it will not otherwise affect the display.

Displaying Special Characters

You can use control codes to output a variety of special characters. Programmers frequently use escape sequences to display characters that aren't available otherwise:

Code	Function
\'	displays a single quote
\"	displays a double quote
\\	displays a backslash

For example, suppose you want to display the text

```
We call her "Sam"
```

including the quotes around the name Sam. If you entered the `puts()` command like this

```
puts("We call her "Sam"");
```

your compiler would generate an error message. Remember, the `puts()` parameter must begin and end with quotes, so that C will know when the string starts and ends. In this incorrect statement, your compiler would interpret the parameter as "We call her" followed by the additional characters SAM"" outside the closing quote but before the closing parentheses. To the compiler, there is just too much information on the line.

To print the text correctly, use this instruction:

```
puts("We call her \"Sam\"");
```

Figure 4.3 shows how the compiler interprets this line.

In addition to printing quotes and the backslash, you can use control codes to display a variety of graphic characters. IBM/PC and compatible

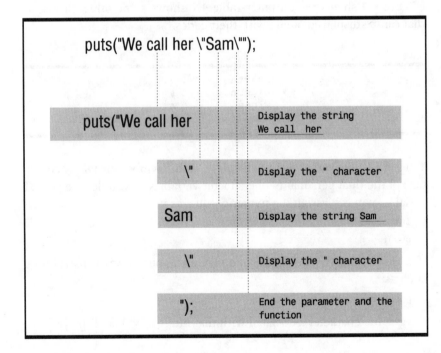

Figure 4.3
Outputting quote characters.

computers can display a set of characters known as the PC character set (or the Extended ASCII set), which includes all of the letters, numbers, and punctuation marks you can type on the keyboard, as well as some graphic symbols and Greek letters. Each character in the set is identified by a unique number. For example, the number 3 represents a heart symbol. To display a character, you place the number that represents it after the backslash, in three digits, like this:

```
putchar('\003');
```

That instruction displays the heart character. To display all of the card suits, use this program:

```
main()
{
    puts("Hearts \003\n");
    puts("Diamonds \004\n");
    puts("Clubs \005"\n);
    puts("Spades \006\n");
}
```

The `puts()` instructions display the name of the suite and its character. (Figure 4.4 shows the output.) Table 4.1 shows some other characters that can be displayed, along with their codes.

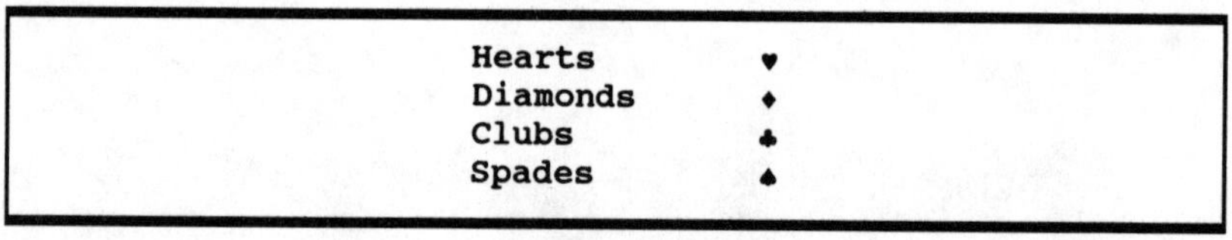

Figure 4.4

Output of graphic characters.

```
              Hearts        ♥
              Diamonds      ♦
              Clubs         ♣
              Spades        ♠
```

You can also use `putchar()` to display graphic symbols by taking advantage of the dual personality of character variables. If you declare an `int` variable, you can assign it a numeric value, as in

```
int count;
count = 5;
```

If you then use the variable as a `char` in the `putchar()` instruction, such as

```
putchar(count);
```

the graphic character associated with that number will be displayed.

Table 4.1
Some Useful Character Codes

Octal Code	Character	Octal Code	Character
001	☺	352	Ω
002	☻	353	δ
003	♥	354	∞
004	◆	355	ø
005	♣	356	∈
006	♠	357	∩
256	~(	360	≡
257	»	361	±
260	▒	362	≥
261	█	363	≤
262	█	364	⌠
340	α	365	⌡
341	β	366	÷
342	Γ	367	≈
343	π	370	°
344	Σ	371	•
345	σ	372	·
346	μ	373	√
347	τ	374	ⁿ
350	Φ	375	²
351	θ		

One number in the IBM/PC character set doesn't display a character but rings a bell! The escape sequence \007 sounds your computer's internal bell. This program, for example, rings the bell twice to attract the viewer's attention:

```
#define BELL '\007'  /*BELL is easier to remember*/
main()      /* than \007*/
{
     putchar(BELL);  /* Sound the bell */
     putchar(BELL);  /* Sound the bell */
     puts("Attention Shoppers!\n");
     puts("There is now a sale in sporting goods"\n);
}
```

The `#define` directive declares a constant called BELL with the value \007. Even though the value consists of four keystrokes, the compiler accepts it as a single `char` constant. Your bell sounds when you output the constant BELL in a `putchar()` instruction.

The Versatile printf() Function

The `puts()` and `putchar()` functions are quite useful but they have several limitations. Neither can output numeric data, and each can only display one *argument*, or parameter. Both `puts()` and `putchar()` can only display one thing.

C and C++ have a more versatile function called `printf()`. `Printf()` can display data of all types and can work with multiple arguments in one parameter. In addition, `printf()` can format how the data appears.

At the simplest level, you can use `printf()` in place of `puts()` to output a string:

```
#define MESSAGE "Hello!"
main()
{
    printf(MESSAGE);
    printf(" Welcome to my world, now get out!");
}
```

Like `puts()`, `printf()` will display string literals in quotes, and the values of string constants and variables.

TIP

C++ has an additional all-purpose output command, cout. See Output in C++ later in this chapter.

Displaying Numbers

In order to output numeric data, and to format all data types, you must divide the `printf()` parameter into the two parts shown in Figure 4.5.

The first part is called the *control string* or *format string*. The control string, in quotes, shows the compiler where you want the data to appear on the displayed line. It includes any literal text you want to display, along with placeholders, called *format specifiers*, indicating the type and position of data.

Each specifier starts with the percent symbol (%) followed by a letter indicating the data type:

%d	displays an integer number
%u	displays an unsigned integer
%f	displays a decimal number, `float` or `double`
%e	displays a number in scientific notation
%g	displays a decimal number in the shortest of decimal or scientific notation
%c	displays a `char`
%s	displays a string

So the first part of a `printf()` instruction can look like this:

```
printf("%d"
```

The % symbol tells the compiler that a format specifier will follow. (To display the % symbol itself, use two in a row, as in `printf("%%");`.) The next character, d, tells the compiler to display an int value, formatted as a decimal (base 10) number (see Figure 4.6).

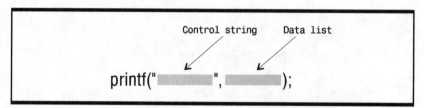

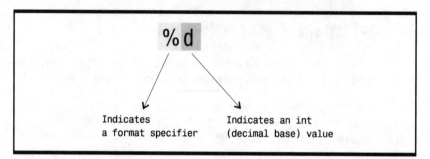

The second part of the parameter is the *data list*, containing the values, constants, or variables that you want to display. We separate the data list from the control string with a comma, placing a comma between each piece of data. When the compiler creates the object code, it substitutes the data in the list for the placeholders.

A complete, but very simple, `printf()` instruction looks like this:

```
printf("%d", 12);
```

When these instructions are performed, the value 12 will be inserted at the position of the placeholder, the %d format specifier (see Figure 4.7). In this example, the `printf()` command is actually passing two parameters to the library function—the control string and one literal value, the number 12.

The control string can also include literal text along with the format specifiers for displaying data. As an example, look at this line:

```
printf("I am %d years old", 12);
```

The control string here is

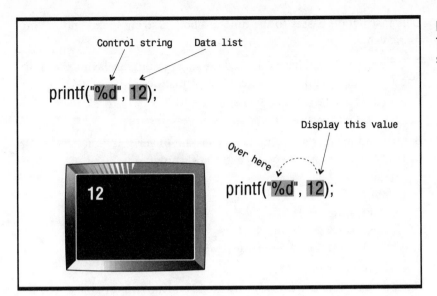

Figure 4.7
The value replaces the format specifier.

```
"I am %d years old"
```

The format specifier, %d, shows that you want to display a number between the words *I am* and *years old*. (See Figure 4.8.) The compiler substitutes the number 12 for the format specifier to output:

```
I am 12 years old
```

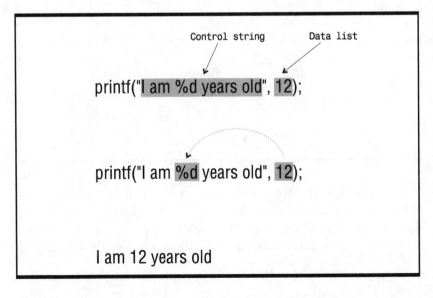

Figure 4.8
Using a format specifier within literal text.

This instruction passes to the function both a string literal and the numeric value.

Of course, you could have achieved the same result, displaying the entire line as a string literal, with either of these instructions:

```
printf("I am 12 years old");
puts("I am 12 years old");
```

But to combine text with a numeric constant or variable, you have to use `printf()` and a format specifier, as in this program:

```
main()
{
    int age;
    age = 12;
    printf("I am %d years old", age);
}
```

Here, the program displays a string literal and an `int` variable in one instruction (as shown in Figure 4.9).

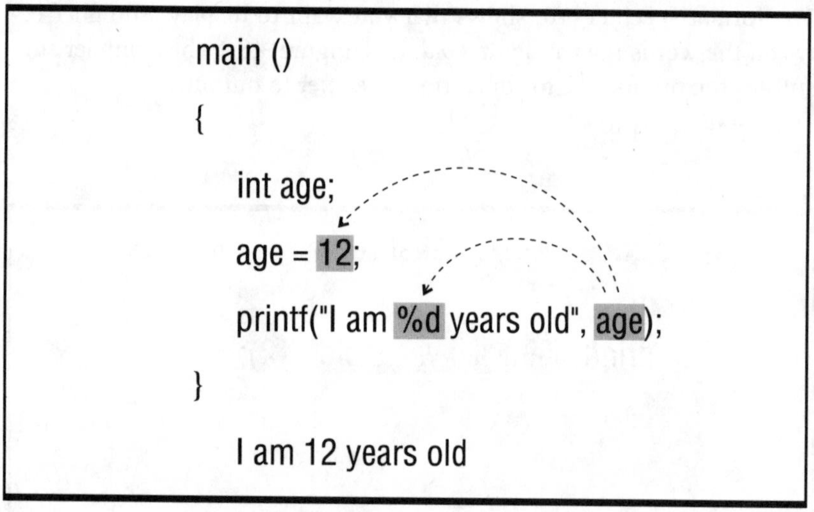

Figure 4.9
The value of a variable replaces the format specifier.

```
main ()

{

    int age;

    age = 12;

    printf("I am %d years old", age);

}

I am 12 years old
```

You can pass any number of parameters to display multiple arguments, but you must include a format specifier for each argument. The values in the data list must appear in the same order as their specifiers. The first item in the list is substituted for the first format specifier, the second item for the second specifier, and so on. Look at this program:

```
main()
{
    int lucky_1, lucky_2;
    lucky_1 = 12;
    lucky_2 = 21;
    printf("My lucky numbers are %d and %d", lucky_1, lucky_2);
}
```

The program declares two int variables, lucky_1 and lucky_2, and then assigns them initial values. The data list in the printf() instruction contains two variables (arguments) that must be displayed, so the control string must have two format specifiers. Since both variables are int type, both format specifiers must be %d, as shown in Figure 4.10.

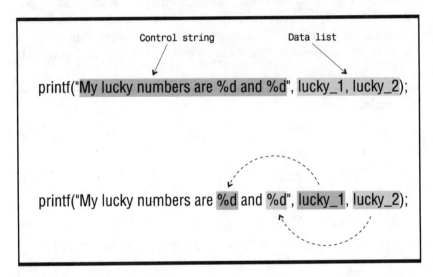

Figure 4.10
Using two format specifiers.

The compiler substitutes the values of the variables for the format specifiers to display:

```
My lucky numbers are 12 and 21
```

The value of lucky_1, the first item in the data list, is displayed in the position of the first specifier. The value of lucky_2, the second data item, is displayed in the position of the second specifier. If the items had been reversed:

```
printf("My lucky numbers are %d and %d", lucky_2, lucky_1);
```

the values would have been displayed in this order:

```
My lucky numbers are 21 and 12
```

The data type should match the type indicated by the format specifier. For example, this program displays a float variable and an int variable with one printf() function:

```
main()
{
    int   count;
    float amount;
    count = 5;
    amount = 45.58;
    printf("The cost is %f for %d items", amount, count);
}
```

The value of the first item in the data list, a float, is inserted at the position of the first specifier, %f. The value of the second item, an int, is inserted at the position of the second specifier, %d. The program compiles and runs without error because the types match. As shown in Figure 4.11,

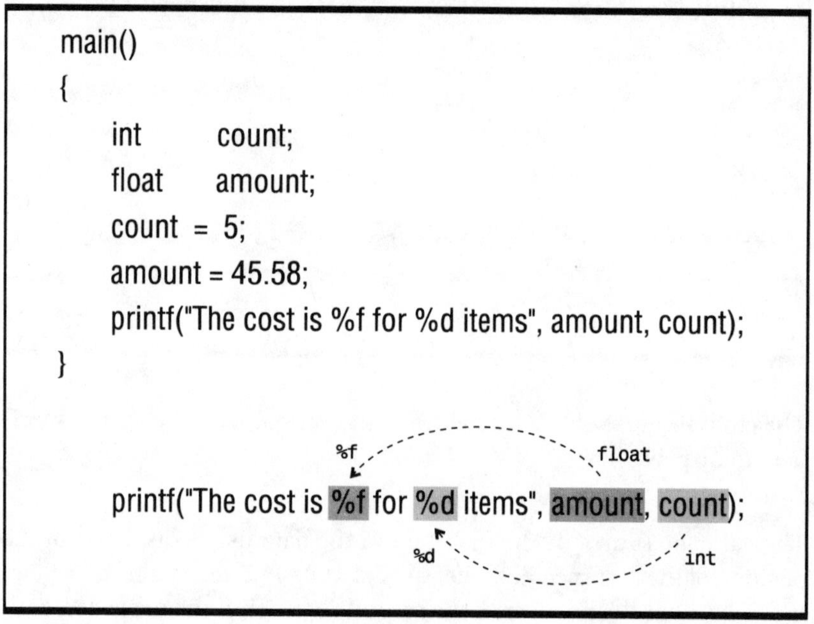

Figure 4.11
The data type must match the format specifier.

```
main()
{
    int       count;
    float     amount;
    count = 5;
    amount = 45.58;
    printf("The cost is %f for %d items", amount, count);
}



                               %f ............................ float

    printf("The cost is %f for %d items", amount, count);

                               %d ............................ int
```

a `float` value is substituted for the `%f` specifier and an `int` for the `%d` specifier. The output is

```
The cost is 45.580000 for 5 items
```

(The number of zeros that appear will depend on your compiler. You'll learn why they appear shortly.) However, if the `printf()` instruction had been written like this:

```
printf("The cost is %f for %d items", count, amount);
```

the compiler may not detect an error but the output might appear meaningless, as in

```
The cost is -2.002149E37 for 16454 items
```

The numeric types do not match the format specifiers. You can display multiple arguments, of different types, all in the same parameter, only as long as the data types match the specifier types.

Line Feed

The `printf()` function does not automatically add a new-line command after displaying data. After the parameter is displayed, the cursor remains on the same line following the last character.

If you want the cursor to go to the next line, you must include the `\n` control code within the format string, like this:

```
printf("The cost is %f for %d items\n", amount, count);
```

Place the `\n` code where you want the new line to start (not necessarily at the end). The instruction

```
printf("The cost is %f\nfor %d items\n", amount, count);
```

displays two lines:

```
The cost is 45.580000
for 5 items
```

You can use any of the other control codes to control the spacing of the line, sound the bell, or display special characters.

Converting Data Types

There are two additional format specifiers that convert an `int` number to its octal or hexadecimal equivalent:

`%o`	Converts a value to octal—use the lowercase letter o, not the number 0.
`%x`	Converts a value to hexadecimal.

To convert a decimal number to another format, use the `%o` or `%x` specifier in the control string and the decimal number in the data list. This program, for example, prints the hexadecimal and octal equivalent of the decimal number 17:

```
main()
{
    printf("%d is %x in hex and %o in octal/n", 17,17,17);
}
```

The output will be

```
17 is 11 in hex and 21 in octal
```

Remember that you needed the octal number to print graphic characters and symbols. If you know the decimal number of the character you want to print, use a program like the one shown to convert the number to octal.

Dual-Personality Characters

As you learned earlier in the section on `putchar()`, `char` variables can also be declared as `int` types. So you can assign a letter to an `int` and display it with `putchar()` or `printf()`, as in:

```
main()
{
    int a;
    a='A';
    putchar(a);
    putchar('\n');
    printf("%c",a);
}
```

When you run this program, the letter *A* will appear twice. It is displayed as a character using `putchar()`, and as a character using the `%c` specifier in `printf()`. But whether you declare a character's type as `char` or `int`, you can use the %d specifier to convert the character into its ASCII number:

```
main()
{
    char a;
    a='A';
    printf("The ASCII code of %c is %d\n",a,a);
}
```

Here, the same variable is displayed using the %c and %d specifiers. The output is:

```
The ASCII code of A is 65
```

It displays the character A using the %c specifier and the number 65—the ASCII code of the letter A—using the %d specifier.

The program would run just as well, and display exactly the same output, if the variable a was declared as an int type.

Formatting Output

You can also use the printf() function to format the displayed appearance of data. You control the spacing and number of characters displayed by using *field-width specifiers*.

Without a width specifier, for example, float numbers will be displayed with six decimal places. That is why the instruction

```
printf("The cost is %f for %d items", amount, count);
```

will display

```
The cost is 45.580000 for 5 items
```

Depending on your system, and how the value was calculated, it might also appear something like this:

```
The cost is 45.579998 for 5 items
```

You use a field-width specifier to customize the way numbers and text are displayed.

To specify the number of decimal places, use the format

```
%.nf
```

where *n* is the number of places desired (see Figure 4.12). For example,

```
printf("The cost is %.2f", amount);
```

Figure 4.12

Specifying decimal places.

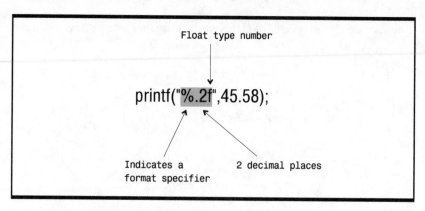

will display the **float** amount with only two decimal places:

```
The cost is 45.58
```

Similarly, the instruction

```
printf("The cost is %.3f", amount);
```

will display the amount with three decimal places:

```
The cost is 45.580
```

Figure 4.13 summarizes how to control the number of decimal places.

You can also control the total width of the field—the number of spaces the entire value will occupy—using this format:

```
%N.nf
```

where N is the total width of the field. For example,

```
printf("The cost is %8.2f", amount);
```

will display

```
The cost is    45.58
```

with three extra spaces before the number. To understand this, visualize the field-width specifier telling the compiler to print the value in a box eight spaces wide, as in Figure 4.14. The number itself, 45.58, uses five of those spaces—the decimal point counts as a character. The unused spaces appear as blanks in front of the number.

If you specify a field width smaller than the number itself, C will display the entire number anyway. Rather than delete characters from the number, it ignores the field width specified. The command:

```
printf("The cost is %2.2f", amount);
```

printf("%f",45.58);

45.580000

printf("%.2f",45.58);

45.58

printf("%.3f",45.58);

45.580

printf("%.0f",45.58);

45

Figure 4.13
Controlling decimal places.

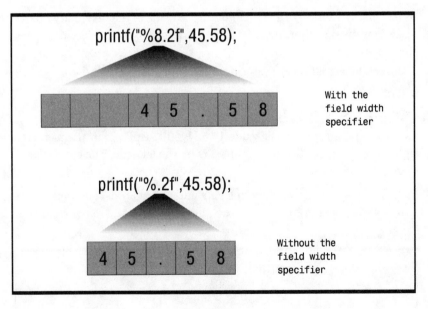

printf("%8.2f",45.58);

| | | | 4 | 5 | . | 5 | 8 |

With the field width specifier

printf("%.2f",45.58);

| 4 | 5 | . | 5 | 8 |

Without the field width specifier

Figure 4.14
A field-width specifier controls the spacing on screen.

will display

```
The cost is 45.58
```

You can also add the extra spaces but fill them with 0s rather than blanks, as in Figure 4.15. Just put a 0 before the width number:

```
printf("The cost is %08.2f", amount);
```

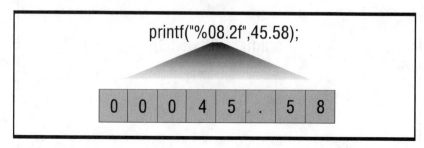

Figure 4.15

Displaying leading zeroes.

The instruction will display

```
The cost is 00045.58
```

To left-justify values—place them on the left side of the imaginary box—place a minus sign after the %, as in **%-8.2f**. The extra spaces will appear after the value:

```
printf("The cost is %-8.2f in US currency", amount);
```

will display

```
The cost is 45.58    in US currency
```

As shown in Figure 4.16, the value 45.58 is still displayed in an imaginary eight-space box, but this time is appears on the left side. The extra spaces follow the value.

Field-width specifiers work with string and character data as well. Extra spaces will appear in front of the text, moving the string to the right side

Figure 4.16

Left-justifying characters on the screen.

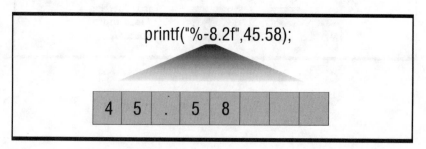

of the imaginary box. For example, if the string variable named `message` has the value "Hello", the command:

```
printf("I just called to say %7s there", message);
```

will display

```
I just called to say   Hello there
```

As illustrated in Figure 4.17, two extra spaces are inserted before the string value.

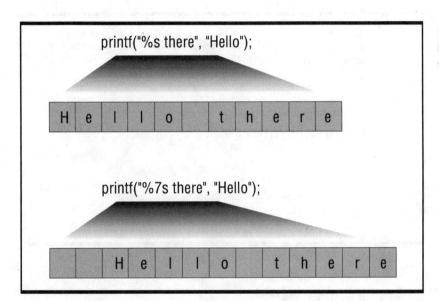

Figure 4.17
Using a field width specifier with a string.

Choosing the Right Output Command

When you are planning your output, consider which output command or function best suits your purpose.

To display just text or characters, use `puts()` or `putchar()`. Because they do not perform any formatting, these functions execute faster and their code takes up less disk space than code generated by `printf()`. With `puts()`, first determine whether your compiler automatically inserts the new-line command. If your compiler does not add the command, and you forget to, you'll only need to spend time editing your program. Forgetting to use \n with printf() is a very common oversight.

The printf() function is slower and uses more disk space. But it is ideal when you want to output numeric values, format a string, or combine text and numbers on the same line. Just carefully enter the line, matching format specifiers with literals, constants, and variables in the data list. Figure 4.18 illustrates the most important rules for printf() instructions.

Figure 4.18
Rules for using printf().

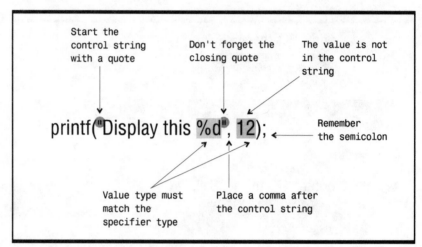

Output in C++

All of the output techniques discussed so far can be used whether you are working in C or C++. However, C++ has an additional way to output data of all types.

The C++ instruction cout displays data on the monitor. Combined with the characters <<, called the *insertion* operator, cout can display literals and the values of constants and variables without the need for format specifiers.

If you have a C++ compiler, check your documentation. You may need to use a special header file to take advantage of the cout command, and the cin command that you'll learn about in the next chapter. In some compilers, for example, the file called iostream.h must be specified in an

`#include` command at the start of your program. See Chapter 2 for additional information on the `#include` command and the use of header files.

The basic structure of `cout` is shown in Figure 4.19. Following the command `cout` are two < characters. These tell `cout` to display the information that follows. The information can be a literal in quotes, or the name of a variable or constant.

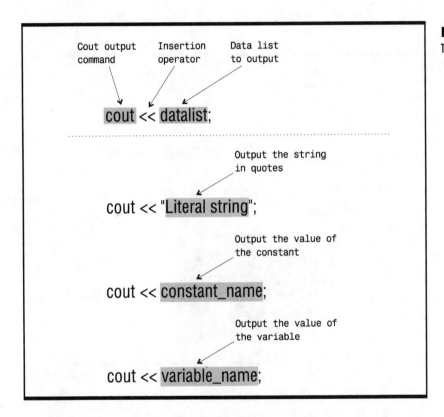

Figure 4.19
The `cout` command in C++.

For example, the instruction

```
cout << "Hi, my name is Sam. Gee, you look familiar";
```

displays the string literal in quotes. The instructions

```
int count;
count = 4509;
cout << count;
```

display the number 4509, the value of the variable named `count`.

To display multiple arguments, separate each with an insertion operator, as in Figure 4.20. For example, the instructions

```
int age;
age = 43;
cout << "You are " << age << " years old.";
```

display the text

```
You are 43 years old.
```

Figure 4.20

Multiple arguments using cout.

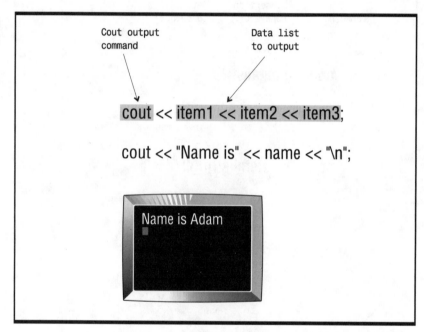

The `cout` command displays each item as it is directed by the insertion operators, in the order they appear in the instruction.

Line `printf()`, `cout` does not automatically add a new-line command after displaying data. To move to the next line, add the `\n` code where you want the line to begin, as illustrated in Figure 4.20.

Format specifiers are not required with `cout`, but they are optional. A *form* function is available for controlling the width, spacing, and number of decimal values using format specifiers. Using the form function in C++

is beyond the scope of this book. If you have a C++ compiler, check with your documentation to learn more about it. Also, check your documentation to see if you need to include a special header file to use `cout`.

Program Design

Output—anything you send to the screen, printer, etc.—is a critical part of any program, so take the time to plan each output carefully.

Start your program using output instructions that explain its purpose:

```
puts("   Welcome to the Mortgage Calculator\n");
puts("This program calculates mortgage payments.\n");
puts("You will enter the amount of the mortgage loan,\n");
puts("the interest rate, and the number of years of the load.\n");
```

In the next chapter, you'll learn about input—getting information into the program from the keyboard. But before asking for information, make sure you tell the user, even if it is yourself, exactly what to enter. Use an output line for each input item:

```
puts("Please enter the amount of the mortgage loan:");
```

When you are ready to display results, make the display easy to read and meaningful:

```
printf("Monthly principle payment: %7.2f\n", princ);
printf("Interest payment:          %7.2f\n", interest);
printf("Total monthly payment:     %7.2f\n", total);
```

The extra spaces between the colons and the format specifiers, the alignment of the specifiers, and the specifiers themselves, combine to align the numeric values like this:

```
Monthly principle payment: 256.25
Interest payment:          92.12
Total monthly payment:     34.37
```

That is certainly better than this:

```
printf("%f %f %f", princ, inter, total);
```

which displays

```
256.25 92.12  34.37
```

Put the same thought into every aspect of your program. It takes a little longer, but the results are worth it. Your programs appear more professional and are more useful to those using them.

Table 4.2 summarizes the output methods discussed in this chapter.

Table 4.2
Summary of Output Commands

Function or Keyword	Data Type	Comments
puts()	string type only	C and C++. Use for outputting strings only. Outputs literals in quotes, variables, and constants. May automatically move the cursor to the next line after displaying (but check your compiler documentation).
putchar()	single characters	C and C++. Use to output a character declared as either an *int* or *char* type. Does not automatically move the cursor to the next line after displaying (but check your compiler documentation). Use it to display a literal character in single quotes, a *char* constant or variable, a control code, or a special character.

Function or Keyword	Data Type	Comments
printf()	all data types	C and C++. Include a format specifier for each data item to be output. Can be used to output multiple arguments in one instruction. Does not automatically move the cursor to the next line—use \n code.
cout	all data types	Use with C++ only. Separate arguments with << characters. Does not automatically move the cursor to the next line. Format specifiers are optional.

Table 4.2
Summary of Output Commands
(continued)

Questions

1. What is output?

2. What three types of arguments can be used in a puts() parameter?

3. What three types of arguments can be used in a putchar() parameter?

4. What are control codes?

5. What is the difference between the \n and the \r control codes?

6. How would you display the quote symbol on the screen?

7. What are the two parts of the printf() instruction?

8. What are the advantages of printf() over puts()?

9. What is a format specifier?

10. How do you display the value of a numeric variable?

Exercises

1. Write the `puts()` instructions for printing your name and address.

2. Write the `printf()` instructions for printing your name and address.

3. Write the `puts()` instruction that centers the word Title on the screen. The screen is 80 characters wide.

4. Write the `printf()` instruction that displays the word Page on the far right side of the display.

5. Write one `printf()` instruction that outputs the values of the following variables:

```
float length, width, height, volume;
```

6. A program will display a person's name and age. Write a `printf()` instruction that displays the values of the variables:

```
char name[12];
int age
```

7. A program has these variables:

```
char item[] = "Floppy disk";
float cost = 3.55;
float markup = 0.75;
```

Write the `printf()` instructions that display:

```
Item Name:  Floppy disk
Item Cost:       3.55
Markup :         0.75
```

Note the alignment of the values.

8. A program has the following variable:

```
int count = 30;
```

Write the output instructions that sound a bell, then display the following, using the value of the variable count to display the number in the last line:

```
Warning! Warning! Warning! Warning!
An intruder has been detected.
You have 30 seconds to leave the premises.
```

Five

Input in C/C++

nput is the process of getting data into the computer for use by your program. When you input data, you input it into a variable. That is, the data a user types in response to an input prompt becomes the value of a variable, stored in memory. You then use the variable in whatever process your program performs. As Figure 5.1 shows, input can come from various sources.

Figure 5.1

Whatever the source of input, the computer stores it as a variable in memory.

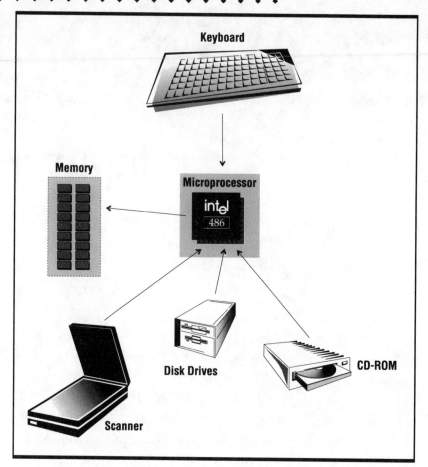

NOTE

As you will see, the word i n p u t is used in two different ways. When used as a verb, it refers to the process of entering data into the computer. Used as a noun, it means the data that is entered into the computer.

The proper input is critical to a program. As the old saying goes, *Garbage In, Garbage Out*. If the data input into your program is wrong, then your output will be wrong. The accuracy of your output can be no better than that of your input.

In this chapter, you will learn how to take data from the keyboard. You will learn how a program can read data from a disk file in Chapter 12.

You can only input data into a variable, not a constant. The constant will always contain the initial value you assign to it. When you input a value into a variable, you are placing the value in a memory location associated with that variable. If the variable already has a value, the new value you input (or assign to it with the equal sign) takes its place (Figure 5.2). The old value will be gone forever.

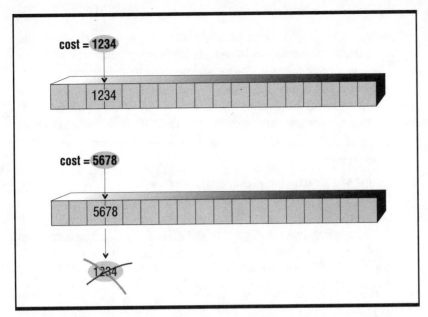

Figure 5.2
A variable's contents are
replaced when you input
another value.

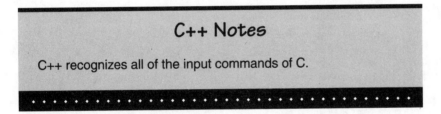

C++ Notes

C++ recognizes all of the input commands of C.

The gets() Function

The gets() function inputs a string into a variable. The parameter is the
variable name. For example, consider this program:

```
main()
{
    char name[15];
    gets(name);
    puts(name);
```

```
    }
```

The gets() command will assign up to the first 14 characters typed on the keyboard to the string variable called name. Remember that C sets aside the number of memory locations specified in the declaration. Because one space is reserved for the null terminator, you can enter one character less than the specified number. If you want to enter a 15-character name, for example, declare the variable with a maximum of 16, as in

```
    char name[16]
```

When a gets() instruction is executed, the program will appear to stop. It is waiting for the user to type something. Nothing typed actually becomes the variable's value until Enter (↵) is pressed. When that happens, the string the user typed is assigned to the variable and the cursor moves to the next line on the screen. The ↵ keystroke is not assigned to the variable, but C adds the null terminator \0 to complete the string.

Now look at another example in more detail:

```
    main()
    {
        char name[25];
        printf("Please enter your name: ");
        gets(name);
        printf("Confirming, your name is: %s", name);
    }
```

When you run the program, you'll see this prompt:

```
    Please enter your name:
```

Since a printf() command is used, without the \n code, the cursor remains immediately after the prompt. It will be one space away from the colon because the space was inserted between the colon and the closing quote in the printf() parameter. Now if you just sit there and watch the screen, nothing will happen. The program is waiting for some sort of input—for you to type your name.

As you type your name, the characters are echoed onto the screen. If you make a mistake, before you press ↵, you can press the backspace key to delete characters and retype them. Some systems let you press the Esc key to erase all of your characters at one time and start over.

When you press ↵, the characters you typed are assigned to the variable `name` and the null terminator is inserted. The second `printf()` command is then executed. The screen will look like this (if your name is Alvin Aardvark):

```
Please enter your name: Alvin Aardvark
Confirming, your name is: Alvin Aardvark
```

Remember, your name appears after the first prompt only because the characters were echoed from your input. They were not accepted into the program until you pressed ↵. They were displayed after the second prompt as a variable by the `printf()` command.

The `gets()` function is an excellent way to enter strings into your program.

The getchar() Function

The `getchar()` function inputs a single character from the keyboard. With most compilers, you can input the character as either a `char` or `int` type because of the way the K&R standard defines character variables. (Refer back to Chapter 4 for more information about the dual personality of characters.)

To input a character, use either of these formats:

```
int letter;              char letter;
letter = getchar();      letter = getchar();
```

Notice that `getchar()` is not called like the other functions you've learned so far. Instead of appearing at the beginning of a line, it is assigned to a variable with the equal sign (=). This format says "The value of the variable `letter` is assigned the results of performing the `getchar()` function." In effect, the function call `getchar()` is treated as a value itself (Figure 5.3). When the line is executed, the `getchar()` function is called, a character is input, and the result assigned to the variable. *This function does not take an argument.* That is, there is nothing passed to the function in the parentheses.

When the user presses a key, `getchar()` echoes the keystroke onto the screen. No follow-up ↵ keystroke is needed, because `getchar()` accepts only one character—the program continues immediately after one is entered. The character is assigned to the variable as soon as you press the key.

 NOTE

Some C and C++ compilers use the function `getch()` to input a character without the need to press ↵. With these compilers, the user may have to press ↵ after typing a character when you read it with `getchar()`. Check your compiler documentation.

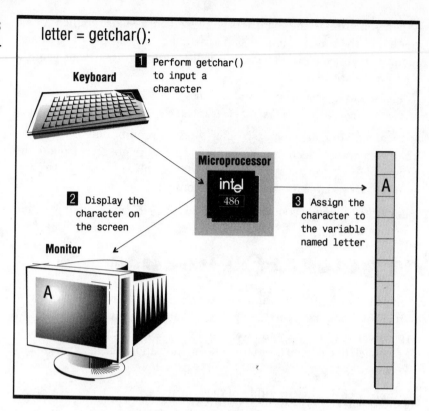

Figure 5.3
The getchar() function.

letter = getchar();

Keyboard

1 Perform getchar() to input a character

Microprocessor

intel
486

2 Display the character on the screen

Monitor

A

3 Assign the character to the variable named letter

A

Now why would you want to accept a single character? Certainly you've seen programs that want a Yes or No answer, or ask you to select from a menu of items. These are perfect applications for getchar() because it does not wait for a ↵ keystroke. Just pressing the key of your selection completes the input and continues the program.

With getchar(), even though the assigned type is an int, you can display the character using the putchar() function, or using the %c specifier in a printf() instruction:

```
/*getchar.c*/
main()
{
    int initial;
    puts("Please enter your middle initial.");
    initial = getchar();
    putchar('\n');
```

```
        putchar(initial);
        putchar('\n');
        printf("%c",initial);
}
```

This program inputs a character into the int variable named initial and then displays it using the putchar() and printf() functions. If you type the letter J in response to the prompt, your screen would display three J's on separate lines—once from being echoed as you typed it, twice more from output statements. On most systems, a new-line command is not automatically performed after you enter the character.

You can also output the character's ASCII value using the %d specifier:

```
/*ascii.c*/
main()
{
        int letter;
        letter=getchar()
        printf("The ASCII code of %c is %d\n",letter,letter);
}
```

In this example, the variable letter is input using a getchar() instruction. The printf() command displays the same variable in two formats. The %c specifier displays the character as it was typed on the keyboard. The %d specifier displays the variable as an integer, the ASCII code equivalent to the letter.

Even if you declare the variable as an int and enter a numeric digit, you cannot use the digit in a math operation. As long as you use getchar() to input the character, it is treated as a character, not a numeric value.

"Press Enter to Continue"

Use the getchar() function by itself to pause a program. For example, your screen can only display so many lines at one time—usually 25. If you use a series of puts() instructions to display more lines than can fit on the screen, the first ones displayed will scroll off the top. The user may not have enough time to read the instructions before others take their place.

Figure 5.4
Using getchar() to
pause the display.

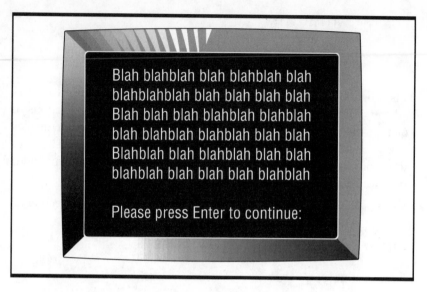

Blah blahblah blah blahblah blah
blahblahblah blah blah blah blah
Blah blah blah blahblah blahblah
blah blahblah blahblah blah blah
Blahblah blah blahblah blah blah
blahblah blah blah blah blahblah

Please press Enter to continue:

To solve this problem, write enough puts()—or other output commands—
to fill just a part of the screen, then add the instructions

```
printf("Press Enter to continue");
getchar();
```

The getchar() instruction, used here by itself and without a parameter,
will pause the program until a key is pressed (Figure 5.4). The key doesn't
really have to be ↵, but any other key will appear on the screen and may
confuse the user. When you use getchar() this way, no value is stored
in a variable. If you press the letter Y to continue, the Y is displayed on
the screen but is not assigned to anything.

The & Address Operator

You know that each variable used in a program takes up space in your
computer's memory. (The amount of space depends on the variable type;
see Chapter 3 if you need a refresher.) Every space in memory is numbered, from 0 up to the last location in your system. If your computer has
2 megabytes of memory, the locations are numbered from 0 to 2,097,151,
as shown in Figure 5.5. These numbers are known as memory *addresses*.

When you declare a variable, C sets aside enough memory locations to
store the value. If you declare an int variable, called count, for example,

C sets aside two memory locations to store count's value. The first of these memory locations is the variable's address.

In Figure 5.6, the variable count has a value of 2341. This value is stored in memory locations 21560 and 21561. So the address of count, not

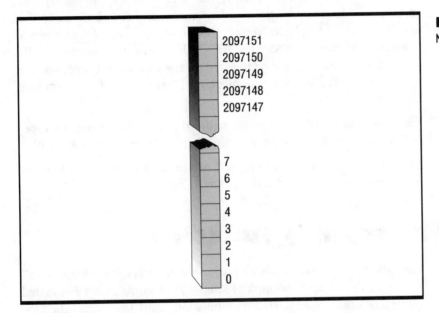

Figure 5.5
Memory addresses.

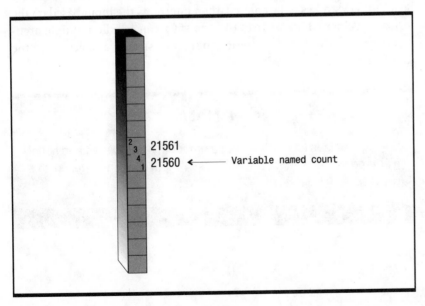

Figure 5.6
A variable and its address.

NOTE

The actual addresses of variables will be different with every computer and may even change each time you run the same program. We're using the address 21560 just as an example.

the value of count, is 21560. You only need to assign the first memory location as the address because C knows how many spaces each type of variable takes up. If count is an int variable, which takes up two memory locations, and it starts at 21560, then it must end at 21561.

When you want to refer to the value of a variable, perhaps to display it in an output command, use the variable's name. You can also refer to the variable's address by placing the ampersand (&) in front of the variable's name, as in &count. The & character is called the *address operator*. It tells C you are interested in the address where the variable is stored, not the value stored in the location. So while count has a value of 2341, &count has a value of 21560.

You do not use the address operator with string variables. Strings are a special class of variable, called an array, that you will learn about Chapter 10.

You need to understand the address operator because it is used to input numeric and char data with the scanf() function.

The scanf() Function

The scanf() function is an all-purpose way to get information of all types into the computer. Think of *scanf()* as meaning *SCAN Formatted* characters from the keyboard. The function scans (monitors) the keyboard for keystrokes to be entered, then interprets the input based on the format specifiers. Like printf(), scanf() can handle multiple arguments so you can input numeric, char, and string variables all at the same time.

C++ Notes

C++ recognizes all of C's input commands, but it has an additional all-purpose input function, cin. See "Input in C++" later in this chapter.

Also like `printf()`, `scanf()` takes a parameter with two parts, a control string and a data list. (See Figure 5.7.) The control string contains format specifiers indicating how the data input will be interpreted. In the `scanf()` function we call the specifiers *conversion characters*. The data list indicates the variables that will hold the input values.

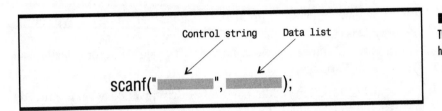

Figure 5.7
The `scanf()` parameter has two parts.

The format specifiers are the same as those used for `printf()`:

%d	inputs an integer number
%u	inputs an unsigned integer
%f	inputs a `float`
%e	inputs number in scientific notation
%g	inputs a decimal number in the shortest of decimal or scientific notation
%c	inputs a `char`
%s	inputs a string
%o	inputs an octal number
%x	inputs a hexadecimal number

When you input numeric or `char` data, you must use the address of the variable in the data list, not just the variable name itself:

```
main()
{
    float amount;
    scanf("%f", &amount);
}
```

The `scanf()` instruction will input a `float` value and insert it in memory where the variable `amount` is stored. When a value is placed in a variable's address, it is automatically assigned to the variable.

When a `scanf()` function is executed, the program waits for you to enter data. Your keystrokes appear on screen until you press ↵.

The scanf() function inputs data quite differently than gets() and getchar(). To understand how scanf() operates, we need to look at those differences in some detail.

Stream Input

When you enter data into a gets() command, everything you type until you press ↵ is assigned to the variable. When you enter a character using the getchar() function, the character you type is automatically assigned to the variable.

The scanf() function is different. Rather than just take what is entered and assign it to a variable, scanf() uses the format specifiers to interpret how the characters entered should be used.

scanf() is said to get its data from an *input stream*. A stream is a series of characters being input from some source. In the case of scanf(), the source is the keyboard. When you press ↵ after typing your input, everything you typed is sent to the scanf() function as a series of meaningless characters in the order you typed them. scanf() must then determine which characters agree with the type indicated by the format specifier, and which to ignore. The format specifiers are called conversion characters because they convert the raw characters in the input stream into data based on the specified types. Figure 5.8 illustrates the process.

Scanf() automatically ignores all whitespace characters—spaces, tabs, or the new-line command—except when the next data type is a char. Consider this program:

```
main()
{
    int count;
    puts("Please enter a number: ");
    scanf("%d", &count);
    printf("The number is %d",count);
}
```

You can press the spacebar as many times as you want before typing the number. C ignores the spaces and looks for first non-whitespace character. It then tries to fit the characters into the format expected by the specifier. If the characters match—in this case if they are numbers—scanf()

Figure 5.8

Scanf( ) reads the input stream to determine which data to accept and which to ignore.

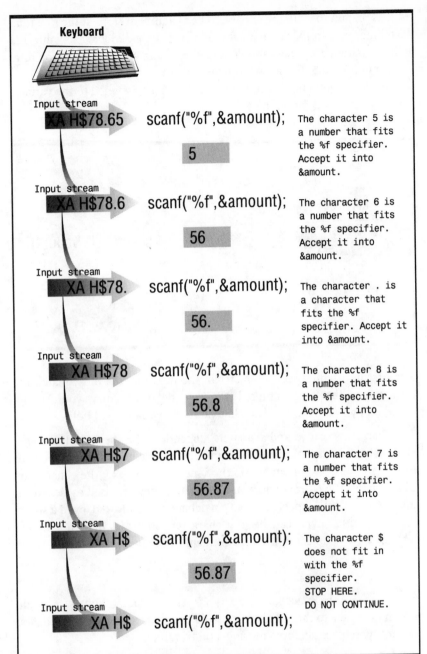

Keyboard

Input stream
XA H$78.65   scanf("%f",&amount);   The character 5 is a number that fits the %f specifier. Accept it into &amount.

5

Input stream
XA H$78.6   scanf("%f",&amount);   The character 6 is a number that fits the %f specifier. Accept it into &amount.

56

Input stream
XA H$78.   scanf("%f",&amount);   The character . is a character that fits the %f specifier. Accept it into &amount.

56.

Input stream
XA H$78   scanf("%f",&amount);   The character 8 is a number that fits the %f specifier. Accept it into &amount.

56.8

Input stream
XA H$7   scanf("%f",&amount);   The character 7 is a number that fits the %f specifier. Accept it into &amount.

56.87

Input stream
XA H$ scanf("%f",&amount);   The character $ does not fit in with the %f specifier. STOP HERE. DO NOT CONTINUE.

56.87

Input stream
XA H$ scanf("%f",&amount);

assigns the numbers to the variable. The assignment stops at the first non-matching, non-numeric character. So if you type *123abc*, the value 123 will be assigned to the variable and the letters abc will be ignored, as shown in Figure 5.9. The assignment will also stop at the first whitespace character—if you enter *12 3*, the value 12 will be assigned to the variable and the number 3 ignored.

Figure 5.9

Scanf() stops accepting data at the first non-numeric character.

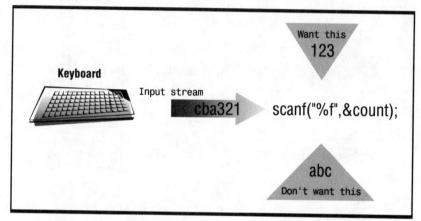

The first non-whitespace character in the input stream must match the format specifier. If you entered *ABC123*, the entire entry would be ignored and you'd have no idea what value the variable will hold.

The characters considered a "match" depend on the specifier. If the specifier is %d, for example, only the number characters and the hyphen (minus sign) are acceptable. If the specifier is %x, the characters 0123456789ABCDEF are acceptable because they are used as hexadecimal numbers. If the specifier is %c, any character is allowed, even a space. Because a char type can be any character, scanf() does not ignore whitespace characters in the input stream. If the instruction is

```
char letter;
scanf("%c", &letter);
```

and you press the spacebar before typing the character, scanf() would assign the space to the variable, ignoring the character that followed. You cannot type spaces before entering a char value.

When you enter a string, scanf() begins the assignment at the first non-whitespace character. It stops assigning input to the variable at the next white-space character. Look at this program:

```
main()
{
    char name[25];
    puts("Please enter your name: ");
    scanf("%s", name);
    puts(name);
}
```

Notice that the ampersand is not used with a string variable name. If you enter *Nancy* and press ↵, the characters are assigned to the variable name. But if you typed *Nancy Chesin* (as illustrated in Figure 5.10), scanf() would begin assigning characters at the first non-whitespace character and stop at the next whitespace character. Only the first name *Nancy* is assigned, and the last name *Chesin* is ignored. Because of the ways scanf() operates, if you want to enter a string that contains a space, you must use the gets() function.

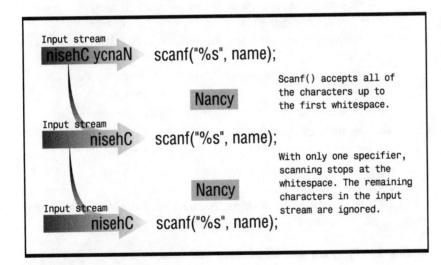

Figure 5.10
scanf() stops reading characters into a string at the first whitespace character.

Using scanf()

Now let's look at the scanf() function a little closer. Consider this program:

```
main()
```

```
    {
        int count;
        printf("Please enter an integer number then press Enter:
");
        scanf("%d", &count);
        printf("Confirming your entry: %d ", count);
    }
```

Here's what happens when you run the program:

1. The `printf()` instruction displays a prompt on the screen:

> Please enter an integer number then press Enter:

Because a new-line code is not included, the cursor remains at the end of the prompt.

2. The program waits for the user to enter a value.

3. You type an entry, then press ↵.

4. `Scanf()` looks at the input stream and determines which characters to accept and which to ignore. If it encounters numeric characters before any non-numeric characters, it continues scanning the line up to the first non-numeric or whitespace character. The numeric characters are converted to a number and stored in the address of the variable. If it encounters any non-numeric characters before a numeric character, the scan stops and the characters are ignored.

5. The cursor moves to the beginning of the next screen line.

6. The `printf()` instruction displays the value of the variable `count` following the message *Confirming your entry*.

You can use as many `scanf()` functions as needed to input your data. Listing 5.1, for example, shows a program that inputs four variables—an `int`, a `float`, a `char`, and a string. Notice that the address operator is used for all of the variables except the string.

Listing 5.1: Program that Inputs Four Variables

```
/* scanf3.c */
main()
{
    int count;
    float amount;
    char letter;
```

```
    char name[15];
    puts("Enter an integer and press Enter");
    scanf("%d", &count);
    puts("Enter a float and press Enter");
    scanf("%f", &amount);
    puts("Enter a character and press Enter");
    scanf("%c", &letter);
    puts("Enter a string and press Enter");
    scanf("%s", name);
    printf("%d  %6.2f %c  %s", count, amount, letter, name);
}
```

You can declare a character variable as an `int` type, but you must input it using the `%c` specifier. You cannot input it using the `%d` specifier (although you can *display* the character's ASCII value using the `%d` specifier in a `printf()` command).

Obtaining Proper Input

Because of the peculiarities of how `scanf()` operates, it is possible for input to be ignored. So it is critical that you prompt the user before each `scanf()` instruction.

For example, suppose you write a program that inputs the amount of a purchase:

```
main()
{
    float  amount;
    puts("Please enter the amount of the sale: ");
    scanf("%f", &amount);
    printf("\nYour purchase was %f", amount);
}
```

Since the value to be entered is a dollar amount, when someone runs the program they may enter it with a dollar sign, by typing *$45.65*. The dollar sign is included in the input stream. But because the dollar sign is not an acceptable character, and it is encountered first in the stream, the entire input is ignored. Not a very good way to do business.

To prevent this problem, include specific instructions before the scanf() command like this:

```
puts("Please enter the amount of the sale. Type the\n");
puts("amount only. Do not type a dollar sign or use\n");
puts("commas between thousands. This is valid: 4567.87\n"):
puts("This is not valid: $4,567.87\n");
puts("                    Thank you\n"):
```

It is possible, however, to accept input that includes characters you do not want to assign to the variable. Remember, in the printf() function, the control string can include more than format specifiers. Any literal text in the control string is printed, with values inserted at the positions of the specifiers. You can also include literal text in the control string of a scanf() instruction.

Suppose you write the scanf() instruction like this:

```
scanf("$%f", &amount);
```

The $ sign in the control string tells C to expect a dollar sign as the first non-whitespace character in the input. When the user enters $45.65, C is already expecting the dollar sign to be in the stream. It discards the sign, instead of terminating, then stores the numeric characters that follow in the address of amount.

However, any literal text in the control string *must be entered* into the input stream, and it must be in the exact position in relation to the input specifiers. If the characters are not where they are expected, all of your input from that point on is ignored. For example, with the $ in the format specifier, your input will be ignored if you do not type it with the entry. If you do use the literal character, make certain the user knows it must be entered:

```
puts("Please enter the amount of the sale. Start the \n");
puts("number with a dollar sign, as in $4567.87\n"):
puts("Do not use commas between thousands.\n"):
```

The dollar sign is not stored as part of the variable and will not be displayed when you use the variable in a printf() command. It only appears on screen as you enter the data because all characters are echoed. If you want to display a dollar sign with the number later on in your program, format the printf() instruction like this:

```
printf("Your purchase was $%f", amount);
```

The dollar sign is just another literal character displayed by `printf()`. It will display before the number inserted at the position of the `%f` specifier.

Because of the potential problems when using literals in `scanf()` functions, avoid them unless you absolutely need them or have a very special application.

Beware of scanf()

On many systems, characters being typed into the input stream are stored in an area of memory called the buffer. If `scanf()` terminates early, some characters will remain in the buffer instead of being assigned to variables. It is possible that the next input operation could start reading the characters still in the buffer from the last attempted input, rather than those you type in direct response to the next input.

Use `scanf()` with caution. Input one piece of data at a time and include prompts thoroughly explaining the type of input desired.

Input in C++

C++ compilers support the `gets()`, `getchar()`, and `scanf()` functions as you learned them in this chapter. In addition, C++ has another general-purpose input command for accepting data of all types. The `cin` command, combined with the *extraction* operator >>, inputs data from the keyboard. The instructions

```
int count;
cin >> count;
```

will input an `int` type from the keyboard into the variable `count`. With `cin`, you do not need to use the address operator for numeric and `char` variables—just use the variable name.

You also do not need to pass format specifiers to the function. `Cin` is *overloaded*, which means it can determine how to perform based on the data it receives. Because of overloading, most C++ programmers prefer to use `cin` rather than `scanf()`.

To input multiple arguments, separate each variable name with an extraction operator, as in:

```
cin >> amount >> count >> age >> name;
```

At first, you may have trouble remembering whether to use the extraction >> or insertion << operators. Figure 5.11 shows an easy way to remember. Picture the operators as arrows pointing away from << or to >> the variables in the data list.

Visualize the operator >> as arrows pointing toward the variables, signi-

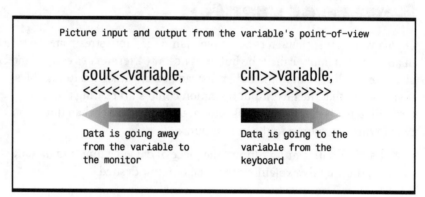

Figure 5.11
The insertion and extraction operators.

fying data going to them through input. When you use `cin` for input, use the operator that points toward the variables you are inputting data into.

Visualize the operator << as arrows pointing away from the variables, signifying data coming away from the variables to the monitor. When you use `cout` for output, use the operator that points away from the variables that are passing the data to the monitor.

Unassigned Variables

You might declare a variable in a program but never assign it any value. This can occur because a `scanf()` instruction terminates prematurely, or because you just forget to write an input command to get the value. If you use a variable that hasn't been assigned a value in an output command, no error message will appear, but the value displayed will be meaningless.

When you start your computer, memory locations that are not used by the operating system are filled with random data. When C assigns memory locations to a declared variable, it does not change whatever is in those memory locations until you assign an initial value or input a value. Thus, if you output a variable before assigning it a value, the random data already in the location will appear. But that's not the worst of it. If you try to use the variable in a calculation, you will not get an error message, but a totally meaningless result. If you are not aware of what occurred, you could assume the result was accurate.

To play it safe, some programmers assign initial values to all variables. You can assign zero to numeric variables, and a space to `char` and string variables, as in:

```
int count=0;
char initial=' ';
float rate=0.0;
```

Of course, your program logic may require other initial values.

NOTE

Most interpreters (such as for the BASIC language) and some compilers automatically assign zeros to numeric variables.

This way, if you display the variable before inputting or assigning it another value, at least you will not get nonsense on the screen. You'll learn later how to test the contents of variables, to check for valid values. Remember, *Garbage In, Garbage Out*.

Table 5.1 summarizes the input commands you've learned in this chapter.

Useful Input Algorithms

An *algorithm* is a way of performing a certain task. As you learn how to program, you are really learning how to develop algorithms—how to perform a task using the C language. It may seem that there are an unlimited number of algorithms. But actually, there is a core set of algorithms that you can use to develop 90 percent of your programs. Once you learn the most useful algorithms, you can design a program easily by using methods you already know.

One such algorithm is used to reassign the value of a variable. There are times when you want to input a value into a variable that already has a value. If you just use the variable name in an input command, the original value will be lost. But what if you don't want to lose the original value? Perhaps you want to compare the old and new values, as you'll learn how to do in Chapter 8.

The algorithm is simply to assign the value to another variable, as in

```
cache=amount
```

Table 5.1

Table appears next to this thing

Function	Data Type	Comments
gets()	String type only	C and C++. Use for inputting strings, including those with spaces. You must press ↵ after typing the string.
getchar()	Single characters	C and C++. Use to input a character declared as either an int or char type. You do not have to press ↵ after typing the character. Use without a parameter, as a variable (for example, letter = getchar()), or use by itself to pause a program.
scanf()	All data types	C and C++. Needs format specifiers for each data item to be input. Do not use to input strings that contain spaces. You must be careful to insure that the data is input and assigned correctly. Scanf() can be used to input multiple arguments in one instruction. Do not use a space before a char variable.
cin	All data types	Use with C++ only. Does not need format specifiers or address operators. Can input multiple arguments. Separate arguments with >>.

Here, the value in the variable amount is assigned to the variable cache. Until a new value is input or assigned to amount, both variables will have the same value. The second variable simply provides a useful place in memory to store the value until you need it again. When you do need the value, use the variable that serves as the storage location.

The program in Listing 5.2 shows an example of reassigning values. (You'll see more practical examples in chapters to come.)

Listing 5.2: Program that Reassigns a Value

```
/* storage.c */
main()
{
    int number, storage;
    puts("Enter the value of the number");
    scanf("%d", &number);
    storage=number;
    puts("Enter the value of the number");
    scanf("%d", &number);
    printf("The original value was %d\n", storage);
    printf("The new value is %d", number);
}
```

A value is input into the variable named number in the lines

```
puts("Enter the value of the number");
scanf("%d", &number);
```

The value in number is then saved in the variable storage with the instruction

```
storage=number;
```

Then a second value is input into the variable number, using a duplicate of the same instructions that input the first. Both values, the old and the new, can then be displayed. The original value was not lost, simply tucked away in another memory area, as illustrated in Figure 5.12.

Questions

1. What is the meaning of Garbage In, Garbage Out?

2. Why is it not necessary to press ↵ after a getchar() input?

3. What are two ways to use getchar()?

4. What is the address operator?

5. What are the advantages of using scanf() for input?

6. What are conversion characters?

7. When would you use gets() rather than scanf() to input a string?

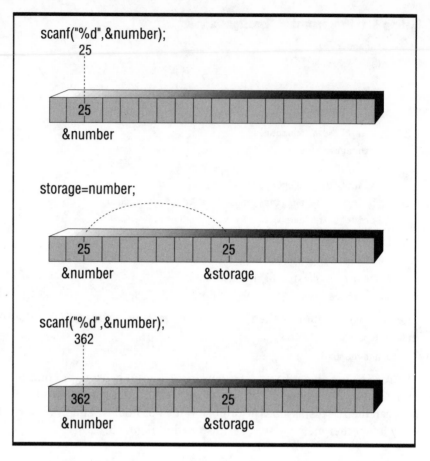

Figure 5.12
Effects of reassigning values.

8. What are the advantages and disadvantages of formatted `scanf()` input?

9. Is it necessary to assign initial values to all variables?

10. What problems can be encountered when using `scanf()` to input a `char` variable?

Exercises

1. Write a program that inputs your name and telephone number, then displays them on one line on the screen.

2. Write a program that inputs a number, then displays the address where the number is stored in memory.

3. Write a program that inputs three numbers, then displays the numbers in reverse order—the last number input is displayed first, etc.

4. Write a program that uses `getchar()`, `gets()`, and `scanf()`.

5. Explain what is wrong in the following program:

```
main()
{
    char initial;
    initial = gets();
    puts(initial);
}
```

110.00
× .05
5.50

110.00
+ 5.50
115.50

Six

Operators

• •

S omething's missing! In Chapter 5, you learned how to input data into the computer. In Chapter 4, you learned how to output data to the monitor. It's now time to learn what comes between—processing.

The processing phase of a program converts *data* that you input into *information* that is output. The difference between data and information is subtle, but important. Data is raw material, characters and numbers that are valuable but not in a form that can be used as a finished product. Information is the finished product; it's what you wrote the computer program to achieve.

The process of converting data into information takes many forms. When working with numbers, the process often involves some form of mathematical operation. For example, you may need to multiply the amount of an order by the sales tax rate, then add the tax to the order. The process, illustrated in Figure 6.1, involves two operations that can be described as:

sales tax = amount of order times tax rate

total order = amount of order plus sales tax

Figure 6.1

Process involved in a sales order.

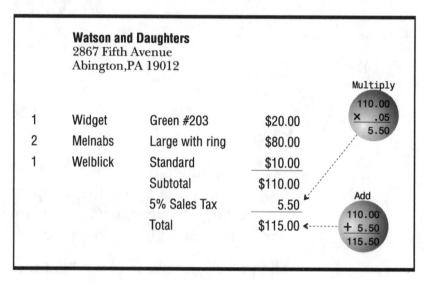

Operators are needed to perform the calculations that transform data into information. An operator is a symbol that tells the computer how to process the data. In this chapter, you will learn about arithmetic, incrementing, and assignment operators.

C++ Notes

C and C++ use mathematical operators the same way. C++, however, can apply certain operators to various data types because of *overloading*. In Chapter 10 you'll learn how to use the + operator in C++ to join two strings.

Arithmetic Operators

Use arithmetic operators to perform math. The arithmetic operators are:

Operator	Function
+	addition
–	subtraction
*	multiplication
/	division
%	remainder of integer division

Notice that the asterisk is used for multiplication (not the × character) and the slash for division—don't use the backslash (\).

Operators are often used in instructions that perform math and then assign the results to a variable. In our invoice example, it would make no sense to assign the sales tax an exact literal value, as in

```
sales_tax = 4500;
```

Instead, the value must be calculated. A variable is always on the left side of the equal sign, and an arithmetic operation on the right side:

```
sales_tax = amount * tax_rate;
price = cost + shipping + insurance;
per_unit = total / count;
```

These instructions tell the compiler to perform three operations:

- Let the variable `sales_tax` have the value of `amount` multiplied by the value of `tax_rate`.
- Let the variable `price` have the sum of three values—`cost` plus `shipping` plus `insurance`.
- Let the variable `per_unit` have the value of `total` divided by the value of `count`.

The computer performs the math specified on the right side of the equation, then assigns the resulting value to the variable on the left side. You can use any combination of variables, constants, and literal values on the right side of the equal sign:

```
sales_tax = amount * 0.06;
price = 56.90 + shipping + 7.87;
per_unit = 156.65 / 12.50;
```

Listing 6.1 shows how operators are used in a program. The program inputs the name and address of a customer and the amount of their order. It then computes a shipping charge (ten percent of the order) and a six percent sales tax. The `puts()` and `printf()` instructions display a complete invoice.

Listing 6.1: Program for Calculating and Displaying an Invoice

```
/*invoice.c*/
#define tax_rate 0.06
#define shipping 0.10
main()
{
    char name[15], address[20], city[15], state[3], zip[6];
    float order, total, tax, ship;
    printf("Customer name: ");
    gets(name);
    printf("Street address: ");
    gets(address);
    printf("City: ");
    gets(city);
    printf("State: ");
    gets(state);
    printf("Zip: ");
    gets(zip);
    printf("Order amount: ");
    scanf("%f",&order);
    tax = order * tax_rate;
    ship = order * shipping;
    total = order + tax + ship;
    puts("\n\n\n\n");
    puts("                    INVOICE\n");
    printf("%s\n%s\n%s, %s  %s\n", name, address, city,
state,zip);
    printf("\t\t\t\t%-10s\t%10.2f\n", "Order:",order);
    printf("\t\t\t\t%-10s\t%10.2f\n", "Tax:",tax);
    printf("\t\t\t\t%-10s\t%10.2f\n", "Shipping:",ship);
    printf("\t\t\t\t\t\t_____\n");
    printf("\t\t\t\t%-10s\t%10.2f", "Total:",total);
}
```

Integer Division

You use the % operator to calculate the remainder of dividing integers. If you use the division operator (/) with integer variables or numbers, the result will always be an integer. For example, dividing 12 by 5 (12/5) will result in 2, not 2.4. The remainder (0.4) is what is left over after dividing integer numbers.

It may be useful to know how much is left over after a division. But since we are dealing with integer numbers, we cannot use the value 0.4. That's a float value. Instead, we store the remainder as an integer. In this case, 5 goes into 12 two times, with 2 left over. So the remainder of 12/5, calculated with the operation 12 % 5, is 2. The remainder is always an integer number.

As an example, look at Listing 6.2. This program calculates how many twenty, ten, five, and one dollar bills are needed to make change. The most important thing this program demonstrates is the algorithm, the technique of using integer division to perform a task that would otherwise require more complex operations. Like all algorithms, it will seem quite simple once you grasp its concept.

Listing 6.2: Program using the remainder operator to make change

```
/*change.c*/
main()
{
int amount,twenties, tens, fives, ones, r20, r10;
printf("Enter the amount of change needed: ");
scanf("%d", &amount);
twenties= amount/20;
r20=amount % 20;   /* r20 represents remainder after twenties */
tens= r20/10;
r10=r20 % 10;      /* r10 represents remainder after tens */
fives= r10 / 5;
ones = r10 % 5;
putchar('\n');
printf("To make change for $%d give the following: \n", amount);
printf("%d twenty(ies)\n", twenties);
printf("%d ten(s)\n", tens);
printf("%d five(s)\n", fives);
```

```
    printf("%d one(s)\n", ones);
}
```

If you enter 57, the output will appear as

```
To make change for $57 give the following:
2 twenty(ies)
1 ten(s)
1 five(s)
2 one(s)
```

Figure 6.2 shows how the program works. The number of twenty-dollar bills is calculated by the instruction `twenties = amount/20`. Because the variables named `amount` and `twenties` are both integers, the result will be a whole number—the number of times 20 can be divided into `amount`. To the computer, the result is just a number to be stored in memory. But to us, the value of `twenties` is information because it represents the number of twenty-dollar bills in the amount.

Now that we know how many twenty-dollar bills are in `amount` (2), how do you determine the number of tens? Visualize how you would do this task in real life. After handing out the twenties, you would determine how much remains and how many tens it requires. The program does the same thing. To determine how much remains, use the remainder operator. The instruction `r20=amount % 20` sets the variable `r20` to what remains after dividing `amount` by 20. To us, this represents how much is left over after subtracting as many twenties as possible. After giving two twenty dollar bills, a total of $40, there is 17 left over.

We then repeat the same pattern—for `tens` and then `fives`. The number of `ones` is just how much is left over after dividing by `fives`.

Operators and Data Types

Normally, you use the same type of data (`int` or `float`) on both sides of the equal sign in an arithmetic operation. If you are adding two `float` values, for example, you would assign the results to a `float` variable, as shown in this program:

```
main()
{
    float cost, shipping, total;
```

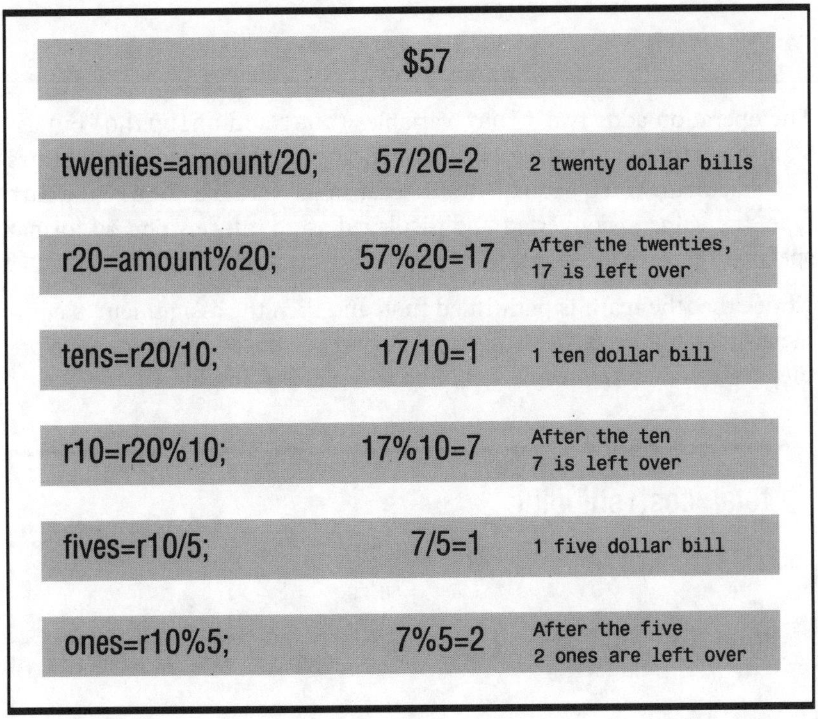

Figure 6.2
How the change program works.

$57		
twenties=amount/20;	57/20=2	2 twenty dollar bills
r20=amount%20;	57%20=17	After the twenties, 17 is left over
tens=r20/10;	17/10=1	1 ten dollar bill
r10=r20%10;	17%10=7	After the ten 7 is left over
fives=r10/5;	7/5=1	1 five dollar bill
ones=r10%5;	7%5=2	After the five 2 ones are left over

```
        cost = 56.09;
        shipping = 4.98;
        total = cost + shipping;
        printf("Your total bill is $%.2f", total);
    }
```

The output of this program is

```
Your total bill is $61.07
```

You can also have different numeric types on the left and right sides of the operation. The value displayed will depend on the type of the variable on the left side. For example, look at this modified version of the program:

```
main()
{
        int total;
        float cost, shipping;
        cost = 56.09;
        shipping = 4.98;
```

```
            total = cost + shipping;
            printf("Your total bill is $%d", total);
    }
```

The operation adds two `float` variables (`cost` and `shipping`) but assigns the sum to an `int` variable named `total`. If you added the values on a calculator you'd get 61.07. But because the variable `total` is an `int` type, the value is converted and displayed as an integer. The `%d` format specifier displays the result as 61.

Notice that the math is performed first, and then the assignment is completed (see Figure 6.3). If the values were converted to integers before they were added, the result would have been 60—56 plus 4.

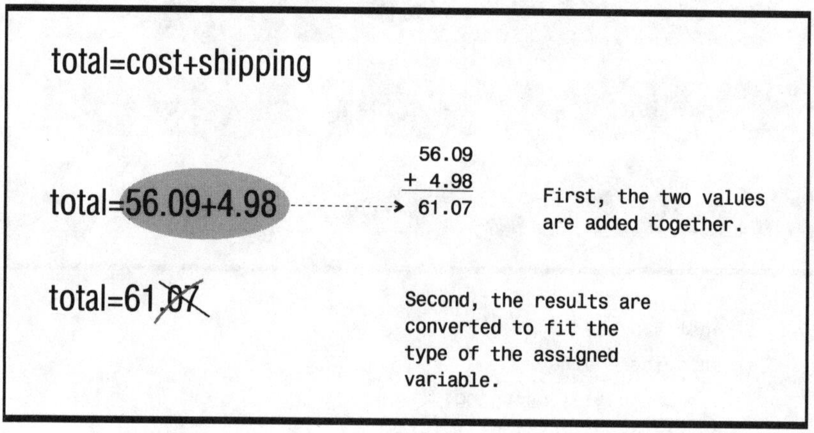

Figure 6.3

The math is performed before the data is converted to the variable type.

You can also add two integer numbers and assign them to a `float` type:

```
main()
{
    int cost, shipping;
    float total;
    cost = 56;
    shipping = 4;
    total = cost + shipping;
    printf("Your total bill is $%.2f", total);
}
```

In this case, a `float`-type number will be displayed because of the `%f` specifier and the variable type. But because the numbers added were integers, the decimal places will be all zeroes—60.00.

`Floats` and integers can be mixed on the right side of the equal sign as well. Again, with addition and subtraction, the results depend on the assigned variable's data type. For instance, look at these instructions:

```
main()
{
    int shipping;
    float total, cost;
    cost = 56.09;
    shipping = 4;
    total = cost + shipping;
    printf("Your total bill is $%.2f", total);
}
```

The operation adds a `float` and an integer number, and the result will appear as a `float`, 60.09.

The same rules apply to division. If you divide two numbers (literal values) and assign the result to a `float`, at least one must have a decimal place if you want to display an output with decimal places. This is demonstrated by the program illustrated in Figure 6.4. Here, the same calculation is performed three times. Each time the results are assigned to a `float` type. In the first calculation, however, neither of the literal values

```
main()
{
    float c;
    c=12/5;
    printf("%f\n",c);        Output

                             2.000000
    c=12.0/5;
    printf("%f\n",c);        2.400000
    c=12/5.0;
    printf("%f\n",c);        2.400000
}
```

Figure 6.4
Dividing literal types.

has a decimal place, so the result is incorrectly displayed with all zero decimal digits.

Expressions

An *expression* is the right side of an equation without a variable on the left side. Expressions are used in output instructions, as in:

```
main()
{
    int count;
    count = 5;
    printf("The number is %d", count + 19);
}
```

This program displays

```
The number is 24
```

The expression in the `printf()` instruction is `count + 19`. When the `printf()` function is called, the expression is evaluated (calculated) first. The result of the expression is then displayed by the `%d` specifier.

An expression does not change the value of the variable. In the example, after `count + 19` is calculated and 24 is displayed, the value of the variable count is still 5. Remember, the expression is just the right side of the equation. The calculated value is not assigned to any variable.

Expressions can include any combination of constants, variables, and literal values, and any operators:

```
printf("%d", count + number);
printf("%d", 16 - 4);
printf("%f", amount * tax_rate);
```

As a general rule, you can use an expression in any place you can use a variable. However, you should always carefully consider whether to use an expression or assign the results to a variable. For example, look at this program:

```
main()
{
    float cost, shipping;
    printf("Enter the cost of the item: ");
```

```
        scanf("%f", &cost);
        printf("Enter the shipping charge: ");
        scanf("%f", &shipping);
        printf("The total due is %f", cost + shipping);
    }
```

The instruction

```
    printf("The total due is %f", cost + shipping);
```

displays the same output as

```
    total = cost + shipping; /*total must be declared as a float*/
    printf("Amount due equals %f", total);
```

Both instructions display the amount due. In the first instance, using an expression, there is no need to declare a variable to store the results of the calculation, and there is no need to type an equation. The math is performed and the result output immediately in the `printf()` instruction. However, the result of the operation is never stored in your computer's memory. If you later need to display the amount due, you must again use the expression `cost + shipping`.

When you assign the calculation to a variable, as in the second set of instructions, you must declare the variable and write the equation. But this time, the results of the calculation are stored in memory. To use the value again, you only need to type the variable name, not the complete expression.

If you'll need to use the results of a math operation more than once, assign the results to a variable and write the equation. Use an expression when you'll only need the results one time.

Order of Precedence

When the computer encounters an equation, it does not automatically perform the math from left to right. It scans the line first, performing math operations based on the order of precedence of the operators. *Order of precedence* means that some operations are performed before others, even though they appear later in the equation. The order is multiplication and division first, then addition and subtraction. An easy way to remember the order is to use the mnemonic phrase My Dear Aunt Sally.

The computer scans the equation and performs any multiplication and division operations in the order it finds them. A division encountered before a multiplication will be performed first. Neither is assigned any additional preference. The computer assigns temporary locations to store the results, then returns to the beginning of the equation and performs any additions and subtractions as it finds them.

Consider this simple equation:

```
a= 1 + 4 / 2 * 5 + 3;
```

If you perform the math simply from left to right, as if using a calculator, the result will be 15.5 (Figure 6.5). The computer, however, remembers My Dear Aunt Sally and calculates the result as 14. (Figure 6.6 illustrates how the result is calculated.) In your programs, you must make certain the math is performed as you want it.

Figure 6.5

Performing math from left to right, as with a calculator.

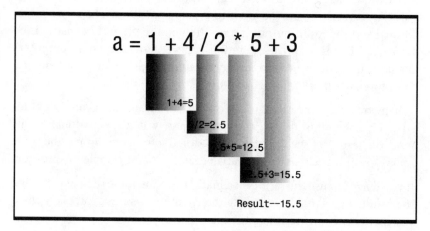

For example, the most common mistake beginning programmers make is when calculating averages. Listing 6.3 shows a program that attempts to input three numbers and calculate their average. We say "attempts" because the average displayed will always be wrong. Do you see why? The error is in this line:

```
average = number_1 + number_2 + number_3 /3;
```

When the computer performs the math, it does so in this order:

1. Divide number_3 by 3.

2. Add the result of the division to number_1 and number_2.

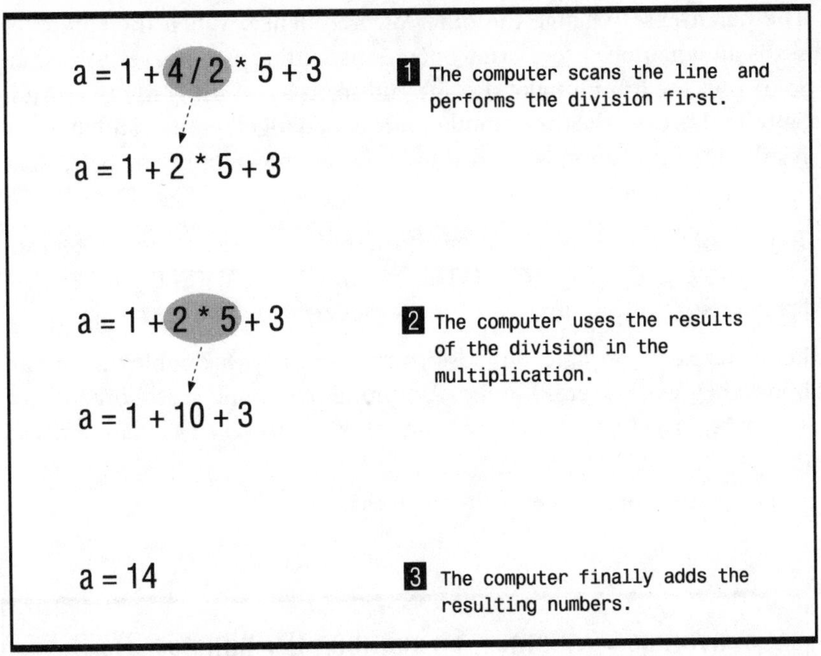

Figure 6.6

Performing math using the order of precedence.

$a = 1 + \boxed{4 / 2} * 5 + 3$

1 The computer scans the line and performs the division first.

$a = 1 + 2 * 5 + 3$

$a = 1 + \boxed{2 * 5} + 3$

2 The computer uses the results of the division in the multiplication.

$a = 1 + 10 + 3$

$a = 14$

3 The computer finally adds the resulting numbers.

Listing 6.3: An Incorrect Program to Calculate the Average of Three Numbers

```c
/*average.c*/
main()
{
    float number_1, number_2, number_3, average;
    printf("Enter the first number: ");
    scanf("%f", &number_1);
    printf("Enter the second number: ");
    scanf("%f", &number_2);
    printf("Enter the third number: ");
    scanf("%f", &number_3);
    average = number_1 + number_2 + number_3 / 3;
    printf("The average is %f", average);
}
```

If you entered a value of 100 for each input, the average would display as 233.33. To write the instruction correctly, use this form:

```c
average = (number_1 + number_2 + number_3) /3;
```

The parentheses change the order of precedence. When the computer scans an equation, it performs operations within parentheses first, then returns to the beginning of the line and scans again using My Dear Aunt Sally. In this case, the three numbers are added together first, and then the result of the operation is divided by three, as shown in Figure 6.7. Voila! The correct answer.

To control the order of operations further, you can use multiple levels of parentheses, as in Figure 6.8. The computer calculates the innermost levels first, working toward the outer levels..

Let's look at an example. Suppose you pay employees double time for all hours they work over 40 hours. Assuming that employees work at least 40 hours, or get paid for a minimum of 40 hours, the calculation needs these parts:

```
40 * rate        /* normal weekly salary
```

Figure 6.7
The correct formula for computing the average.

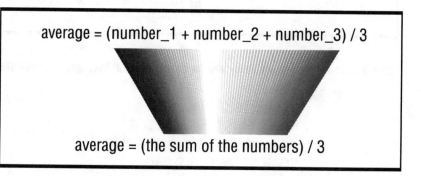

$$average = (number\_1 + number\_2 + number\_3) / 3$$

$$average = (the\ sum\ of\ the\ numbers) / 3$$

Figure 6.8
Multiple levels of parentheses

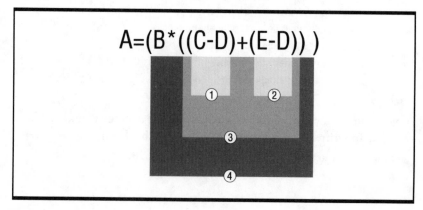

$$A=(B*((C-D)+(E-D)))$$

```
hours-40         /* overtime hours
rate * 2         /* double-time rate
```

The equation must multiply the overtime hours by the double-time rate, then add the result to the normal weekly salary. Ignoring the order of precedence, we could write the equation like this:

```
total = 40 * rate + hours - 40 * rate * 2
```

Now let's assume a person worked 48 hours at $10 per hour. Without parentheses, this equation would be calculated like this:

Operation	Result
40 * rate	400
40 * rate	400
400 * 2	800
400 + 48	448
448-800	-352

A paycheck of minus $352 certainly seems incorrect. To write the equation properly, use parentheses:

```
total = (40 * rate) + ((hours - 40) * (rate * 2))
```

The equation is now divided into two logical parts. (The program is shown in Listing 6.4). The items in the first set of parentheses represent regular hours. The items in the second set represent overtime hours. The overtime hours section has two levels of parentheses itself. C will perform the operations in the inner levels before the outer levels. So five operations are performed here:

40 * rate	400
hours - 40	8
rate * 2	20
8 * 20	160
400+160	560

Listing 6.4: Program for Calculating Salary with Overtime

```c
/*payroll1.c*/
main()
{
    float rate, hours, total;
    printf("Enter your hourly rate of pay: ");
    scanf("%f", &rate);
    printf("Enter the number of hours you worked: ");
```

```
        scanf("%f", &hours);
        total = (40 * rate) + ((hours - 40) * (rate * 2));
        printf("Your salary is %f", total);
}
```

If you find using parentheses confusing, break the equation down into separate variables. Listing 6.5 shows the weekly salary program written with a series of operations rather than one long equation. Because the results of each calculation are assigned to a variable, each result can be displayed separately to make the output more meaningful. This technique gives you more control over the process and will make it easier to find an error if one occurs.

Listing 6.5: Program with separate operations

```
/*payroll1.c*/
main()
{
        float rate, hours, total, regular, extra, d_time, overtime;
        printf("Enter your hourly rate of pay: ");
        scanf("%f", &rate);
        printf("Enter the number of hours you worked: ");
        scanf("%f", &hours);
        regular = 40 * rate;
        extra = hours - 40;
        d_time=rate * 2;
        overtime = extra * d_time;
        total = regular + overtime;
        printf("Your regular weekly salary is %.2f\n", regular);
        printf("You worked %.2f overtime hours\n", extra);
        printf("Your overtime pay is %.2f\n", overtime);
        printf("Your total pay is %.2f\n", total);
}
```

Useful Processing Algorithms

Some of the most useful algorithms in programming involve arithmetic operations. Many are used so frequently that most programmers don't

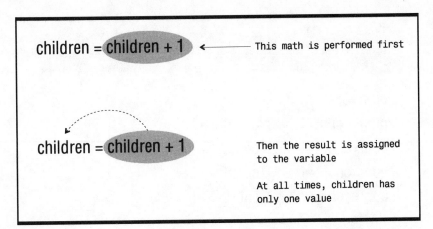

Figure 6.9

The counter algorithm.

children = children + 1 ← — This math is performed first

children = children + 1   Then the result is assigned
                             to the variable

                             At all times, children has
                             only one value

even think of them as algorithms. Of these algorithms, the two most important are counters and accumulators.

Counters

A *counter* is a variable that starts at an initial value and increases by one each time something occurs. The algorithm for a counter is:

```
variable = variable + 1
```

A math teacher would no doubt object to this formula, claiming that you cannot have the same variable on both sides of the equation. But this is perfectly legal in computer programming.

The computer evaluates (calculates) the expression on the right first, then assigns it to the variable on the left (see Figure 6.9). At no time does the variable have more than one value. Think of the counter as meaning this:

The new value of the variable is equal to the old value plus 1.

Let's run through the counter algorithm—follow along in Figure 6.10. We'll start with a variable called count and assign it an initial value of zero:

```
int count;
count=0;
```

Now apply the algorithm:

```
count = count + 1
```

The computer performs this instruction as:

```
count = 0 + 1
```

Figure 6.10

Performing the counter
algorithm.

Instruction	Math actually performed	Value of the variable count after the instruction
count=0;		0
count=count+1;	count=0+1	1
count=count+1;	count=1+1	2
count=count+1;	count=2+1	3
count=count+1;	count=3+1	4

The current value of count (0) is added to the literal value 1. The result of that calculation, 1, is then assigned to the variable count. Count has a new value.

Now let's perform the same instruction again:

```
count = count + 1;
```

The computer performs this operation:

```
count = 1 + 1
```

The current value of count (1) is added to the literal value 1. The result, 2, is then assigned to the variable count. Each time the operation is performed, count is incremented—increased—by one.

Of course, you can count by any number and begin the initial value at any number. If we assign count an initial value of 1, the instruction

```
count=count + 2
```

will increment in odd numbers—1, 3, 5, 7, and so on. You can count by fives using count=count+5; or by tens with count=count+10; or any number.

To count down (*decrement*), just change the algorithm to

```
variable=variable-1
```

Each time the operation is performed, the value of the variable will decrease by one.

Increment Operators

Counters are used so often that C provides special operators to increment and decrement a variable. The operator ++*variable* adds 1 to the value of the variable before the instruction is performed. The operation performs the same function as

```
variable = variable + 1;
```

Look at this program, as an example:

```
/*count.c*/
main()
{
    int count=0;
    printf("The first count is %d\n", count);
    printf("The second count is %d\n", ++count);
    printf("The last value of count was %d\n", count);
}
```

The output of the program is:

```
The first count is 0
The second count is 1
The last value of count was 1
```

Before the second `printf()` instruction is performed, the compiler increments the value of `count` by 1, exactly as if you had written the instructions like this:

```
count=count+1;
printf("The second count is %d\n", count);
```

By using the increment operator, you can perform the counter algorithm without having to write a separate instruction.

The increment operator actually changes the value of the variable. Make sure that you understand the difference between the increment operator `++count` and the expression `count+1` in the following line:

```
printf("The second count is %d\n", count+1);
```

The expression `count+1` does not change the value of the variable `count`. It simply results in an incremented value being displayed. A program using the expression is shown in Listing 6.6.

```
main()
{
    int count=0;
    printf("The first count is %d\n", count);
    printf("The second count is %d\n", count+1);
    printf("The last value of count was %d\n", count);
}
```

The program produces this output:

```
The first count is 0
The second count is 1
The last value of count was 0
```

The expression `count+1` is evaluated as 1, but it does not change the value of the variable `count`. When the variable is displayed by the third `printf()` instruction, it still has its original value.

You can use the incremental operator within `printf()` statements, as well as an expression on the left side of an equation. This instruction, for example, increments the variable `count` and then assigns the value to the variable `number`:

```
number = ++count;
```

It is equivalent to these two instructions:

```
count = count + 1;
number = count;
```

You can even use the ++ operator, with a variable name, as an instruction by itself:

```
++number;
```

If you place the ++ signs on the other side of the variable name, you increment the variable *after* the instruction is completed. The syntax is

```
variable++
```

Look at this modified version of the previous program:

```
main()
{
    int count=0;
    printf("The first count is %d\n", count);
    printf("The second count is %d\n", count++);
```

```
        printf("The last value of count was %d\n", count);
}
```

The `count++` operator increments the value *after* the second `printf()` instruction is performed. In the second `printf()` instruction, the original value is displayed, as shown by this output:

```
The first count is 0
The second count is 0
The last value of count was 1
```

The value of the variable is 0 when the first and second `printf()` instructions are performed. It is incremented to 1 before the third `printf()` function is carried out.

You can use this operator to reassign a variable's original value and increment it in one step, as in this program:

```
main()
{
        int number, storage;
        puts("Enter the value of the number");
        scanf("%d", &number);
        storage=number++;
        printf("The original value was %d\n", storage);
        printf("The new value is %d", number);
}
```

The command

```
storage=number++
```

first assigns the value of the variable `number` to the variable `storage`, then increments the value of `number` by one.

The decrement operators function in the same way, but they reduce the value of a variable by one. Their syntax is

`--variable`	Subtracts 1 from the value before the instruction is performed.
`variable--`	Subtracts 1 from the value after the instruction is performed.

Accumulators

An accumulator also increments the value of a variable. But instead of always increasing the value by the same amount, the increase is variable—it can change with each operation. The general syntax is:

```
variable = variable + other_variable
```

It is called an accumulator because the value keeps accumulating. For example, look at these instructions

```
int total, number;
total = 0;
scanf("%d", &number);
total = total + number;
```

Let's assume that you input 10 as the value of number. After the instruction

```
total = total + number;
```

total has a value of 10. The computer performed the instruction using these values:

```
total = 0 + 10;
```

Now suppose you perform the scanf() and accumulator instructions another time and enter 15:

```
scanf("%d", &number);
total = total + number;
```

This time, the computer will perform the instructions using these values:

```
total = 10 + 15;
```

You are accumulating the values of the variable number.

Listing 6.7 shows a program that inputs three numbers and calculates their average. A simple math expression could have been used to calculate the average:

```
average = (A+B+C)/3
```

We used an accumulator to total the numbers and a counter to count the entries to demonstrate how they are used. You'll learn a more powerful way to use these algorithms in Chapter 9.

Listing 6.7: Program Using a Counter and an Accumulator to Calculate the Average of Three Numbers

```
/*average1.c*/
main()
```

```
{
    float number, total, count, average;
    total = 0.0;
    count = 0.0;
    printf("Enter the first number: ");
    scanf("%f", &number);
    total += number;
    ++count;
    printf("Enter the second number: ");
    scanf("%f", &number);
    total += number;
    ++count;
    printf("Enter the third number: ");
    scanf("%f", &number);
    total += number;
    ++count;
    average = total/ count;
    printf("The average is %f", average);
}
```

Assignment Operators

The assignment operators are shortcut accumulators:

Operator	Example	Equivalent
+=	total += amount	total = total + amount
-=	total -= discount	total = total - discount
*=	total *= tax_rate	total = total * tax_rate
/=	total /= count	total = total / count
%=	total %= count	total = total % count

Each performs an operation using the assigned variable as the common element. To visualize how they work, look at Figure 6.11. Just picture an invisible copy of the variable and the arithmetic symbol from the left of

Figure 6.11

The assignment operator.

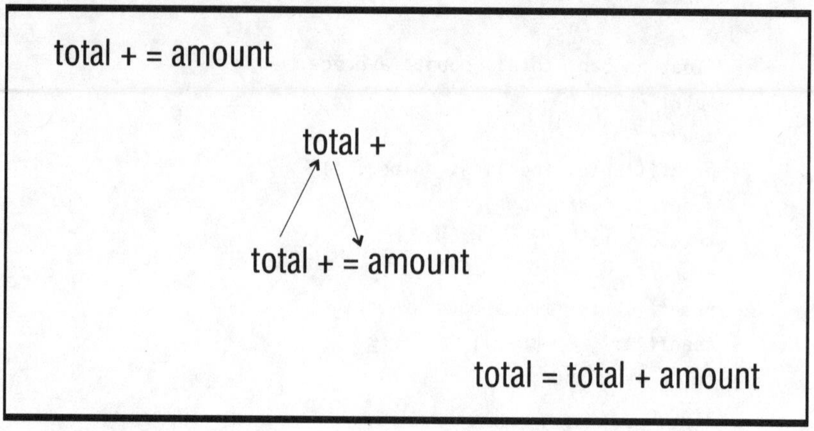

total + = amount

total +

total + = amount

total = total + amount

the equation moved to the right side. The instruction

```
total *= rate
```

is the same as

```
total = total * rate
```

Assigning Initial Values

It is crucial that you assign initial values to all counters and accumulators. Remember, both algorithms add (or subtract) something from the current value. If you do not assign an initial value, the amount added will be added to the unknown, random, contents in the variable's address. Assigning the initial value clears the contents, much like pressing the Clear button on a calculator.

For example, look again at Listing 6.7, the program that averages three numbers. Now suppose the address of the variable total contains the random value 1827. If the assignment

```
total = 0;
```

were not in the program, and you entered the number 75, the first accumulator would perform math like this:

```
total = 1827 + 75
```

Assigning an initial value of zero insures that the math is performed correctly, as

```
total = 0 + 75
```

Program Design

Now that you know how to perform mathematical operations using operators, the logic of your programs can be more sophisticated. You should take a little extra time to ensure that your program produces the correct results. Let's look at some examples.

Beware Logic Errors

Earlier in this chapter (Listing 6.4), we used an example of a program that calculated weekly salary. The program will compile without errors, and you could run the program for some time before discovering that it has what may be a major flaw—it assumes an employee works at least 40 hours, or gets paid for a minimum of 40 hours. If these assumptions are true, there is no problem. But what if a person works less than 40 hours and only gets paid for what they work? If you input less than 40 hours, the calculation will be incorrect. The problem is in the calculation:

```
total = (40 * rate) + ((hours - 40) * (rate * 2));
```

First, even if a person works less than 40 hours, 40 is still being multiplied by the rate in the calculation `40 * rate`. Second, the result of `hours - 40` will be a negative number. That negative value will be multiplied by the double-time rate and added to the regular salary. When a negative number is added, the value is really subtracted. So, the employee will lose two hours of pay for every hour under 40 worked.

The solution to this problem will be given in a later chapter. As far as we are concerned now, however, the solution is less important than understanding the problem.

Look For Patterns

When you program, look for patterns. Look for instructions that can be used more than once, perhaps with just minor changes. Seeing patterns makes it easier to understand how a program works, and therefore, easier to write a similar program at another time.

For example, there is a pattern in the program that uses integer division to make change (Listing 6.2). Look at this series of instructions for the pattern:

```
twenties= amount/20;
r20=amount % 20;
tens= r20/10;
r10=r20 % 10;
fives= r10 / 5;
ones = r10 % 5;
```

Notice that the variables on the right side of the equations are used twice—once with the / operator and once with the % operator. Also notice that the result of each remainder operation is used in the expression that follows it. Figure 6.12 illustrates this pattern.

You can easily extend the program by extending the pattern to other levels. For example, if you wanted to use fifty-dollar bills as well, you would modify the program like this:

```
fifties=amount/50;
r50=amount % 50;
```

Figure 6.12

Patterns in the make change program.

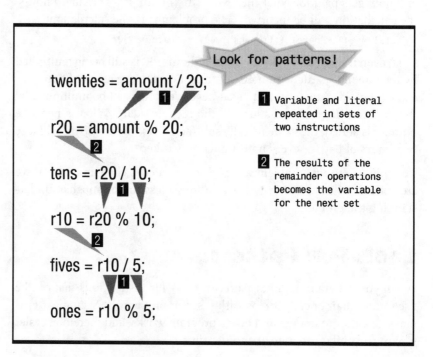

Look for patterns!

twenties = amount / 20;

r20 = amount % 20;

tens = r20 / 10;

r10 = r20 % 10;

fives = r10 / 5;

ones = r10 % 5;

1 Variable and literal repeated in sets of two instructions

2 The results of the remainder operations becomes the variable for the next set

```
twenties= r50/20;
r20=r50 % 20;
```

Two new instructions are added that follow the same pattern. The instructions that compute the number of twenties are just modified slightly.

Troubleshooting Problems

If you are not sure of the accuracy of your output, try adding extra `printf()` statements. Divide your process into as many discrete operations as possible. After each operation that changes the value of a variable, add a `printf()` statement that displays the variable's contents, even if you don't want to see the value in the finished program.

When you run the program, look at the output of these extra `printf()` statements and compare it with what you expected it to be. The first incorrect output will point your way to the problem. For example, if you saw this output from the salary program:

```
regular is 400
extra is -2
d_time is 40
```

you would immediately question the negative number for the variable `extra`. You can assume the problem is somewhere before the `printf()` statement that displayed the variable. Once you correct the problem, you can delete the extra lines.

Questions

1. What is the difference between the operators / and %?
2. Can you mix different types of data in the same operation? If so, how will it affect the results of the operations?
3. What is an expression?
4. Where can you use an expression?
5. Describe the order of precedence.
6. Why use parentheses in an operation?
7. Explain the difference between `count=count+1` and `count++`.

8. What is an accumulator?

9. Describe an assignment operator.

10. What is the difference between --count and count--?

Exercises

1. Write a program that tells a person how old they will be in the year 2000.

2. Write a program that calculates the square and cube of a number input on the keyboard.

3. Write a program that converts a fahrenheit temperature to celsius. The formula is celsius = (5.0/9.0)×(fahrenheit−32).

4. Modify the program in Exercise 3 to report how many degrees the input temperature is from the freezing point in both fahrenheit and celsius.

5. Explain what is wrong in the following program.

```
#define tax_rate 0.06
main()
{
        float cost, total;
        printf("Enter the cost of the item: ");
        scanf("%f", &cost);
        printf("Enter the shipping charge: ");
        scanf("%f", &shipping)'
        total = cost + cost * tax_rate + shipping;
        printf("The total is %f", total);
}
```

Seven

How Functions Function

• • • • • • • • • • • • • • • • • • •

f you throw all of your belongings together in a heap on the floor, you'll have a difficult time finding anything. To make life easier, you sort your valuables beforehand, dividing them neatly between the shelves. When you need to find something, you know exactly where it is.

Your programs can suffer from the same disorganization. As a program grows larger, working with it in one large `main()` function becomes more difficult. You can't put your program code on closet shelves, but you can divide it into functions.

A function is a block of instructions that together perform a specific task. You write your own functions and use them just as you use functions in a C or C++ library—you call the function to perform a task, even passing arguments back and forth.

Functions are particularly useful when you need to perform the same instructions more than once. For example, if your program displays a lot of information on the screen, you'll need to pause the display when the screen becomes full. Rather than typing the instructions that pause the screen every time the program needs to do that, you type them once in a separate function. Then, whenever you need to pause the screen, you just call the function, as illustrated in Figure 7.1.

Figure 7.1
Calling a function more than once.

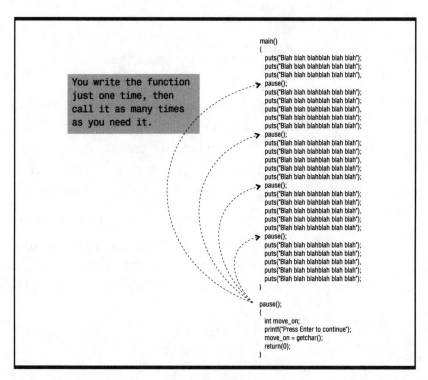

You can also use functions to help organize a difficult program. Try to divide the program into sections, each performing a separate complete task. If you have trouble writing a section, then subdivide it yet again. Continue to subdivide the program into smaller and smaller sections until you can write the instructions that perform each task. You place each section into its own function. Once you've written all of the individual functions and tied them together in `main()`, the program is done!

Using Functions

You place your own functions after the closing brace of `main()`. Each function has the same structure as `main()`, as shown in Figure 7.2. Just as in `main()`, the function name is followed by parentheses, with no closing semicolon. There are opening and closing braces surrounding the instructions.

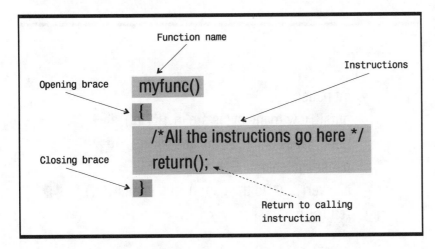

Figure 7.2
The structure of a function.

When you call a function, the computer performs the instructions in the function and then returns to the command that appears immediately after the function call. Depending on your compiler, the `return(0)` command may be optional—C would return anyway when the function is complete.

For example, Figure 7.3 illustrates a program that displays a question and an answer. The numbers indicate the program flow.

The instruction `answer()` in `main()` calls a function just as if it were in the C library. However, instead of being in the library, the code for `answer()` is in the program itself. After the first two `puts()` commands in

return() and the PCC Compiler

Remember, the PCC compiler on the disk provided with this book does not accept the syntax

```
return();
```

Instead, use either of these formats:

```
return;

return(0);
```

Figure 7.3
Calling a function.

```
main()
{
  int pause;
  puts("How many bytes are in 1K?\n");  1
  puts("Press enter for the answer\n");  2
  pause=getchar();  3
  answer();  /*Do the commands in answer() */  4
7 return(0);
}
answer()
{
  puts("These are the 1024 bytes in 1K.\n");  5
  return(0);  /*Go back to main() */  6
}
```

`main()`, the statement

```
answer();
```

calls the function. No parameters are passed to `answer()`, because the function has all of the information it needs to perform its task. The `puts()` instruction in `answer()` is performed, and then the `return(0)` command sends control back to the instruction immediately after the function call. The `return(0)` command in `main()` ends the program.

As far as the computer is concerned, the instructions are performed in this order:

```
puts("How many bytes are in 1K?");
puts("Press Enter for the answer");
pause=getchar();
answer();
puts("These are the 1024 bytes in 1K.");
return(0);
return(0);
```

You can call a function from anywhere in your program, even from within another function. When `return(0)` is encountered, control goes back to the line after the call. Listing 7.1 shows a program with two custom functions. The first function, `question()`, is called from `main()`. The second, `answer()`, is called from `question()`. The `return(0)` in `answer()` sends control back to `question()`, which then returns to the `main()` function. The output of the program, shown with the function that displays each line of output, is:

```
Welcome to the Sybex Challenge.          main()
Name a graphic interface from Microsoft. question()
Press Enter for the answer.              question()
The answer is Windows.                   answer()
Thanks for your patronage.               main()
```

Listing 7.1: Program Calling Two Functions

```
/*quiz2.c*/
main()
{
  puts("Welcome to the Sybex Challenge.\n");
  question();
  puts("Thanks for your patronage.\n");
```

```
        return(0);
    }
question()
{
    int move_on;
    puts("Name a graphic interface from Microsoft.\n");
    puts("Press Enter for the answer."\n);
    move_on=getchar();
    answer();
    return(0);
}
answer()
{
    puts("The answer is Windows.\n");
    return(0);
}
```

The best use of functions is to organize a program into distinct parts. In `main()`, you perform "housekeeping chores" of setting up the program and calling the functions. This is illustrated in Listing 7.2, an adaptation of the quiz program. Here, `main()` contains only function calls. The actual "work" of the program is performed in the functions following `main()`.

Listing 7.2: Program Using main() to Perform All Function Calls

```
/*quiz3.c*/
main()
{
    welcome();
    question();
    answer();
    the_end();
    return(0);
}
welcome()
{
    puts("Welcome to the Sybex Challenge.\n");
    return();
}
question()
```

```
{
    int move_on;
    puts("Name a graphic interface from Microsoft.\n");
    puts("Press Enter for the answer.\n");
    move_on=getchar();
    return(0);
}
answer()
{
  puts("The answer is Windows."\n);
  return;
}
the_end()
{
    puts("Thank you for your patronage.\n");
    return(0);
}
```

This structure makes it easy to find errors. For example, if a problem appears when the answer is displayed, you'd look for the error in the `answer()` function.

Functions are performed in the order they are called, not as they are listed in the program. So we could have placed the functions in Listing 7.2 in this order:

```
main()
answer()
welcome()
the_end()
question()
```

The output would still be correct because the functions are called in the appropriate order from `main()`.

Variables in Functions

When your programs have functions in addition to `main()`, you have to consider where and how to declare the variables. C has several types of variables. In this chapter, we'll look at automatic, external, and static variables.

Automatic (Local) Variables

Some functions need their own variables or constants. For example, let's consider the problem of pausing the screen after displaying a long series of messages. You can pause the screen using these instructions:

```
printf("Press any key to continue");
move_on = getchar();
```

And if you need to pause the screen several times in one program, place the instructions in a separate function. Then, when you need to pause the screen, you just call the function. Since `getchar()` requires a variable, you declare a variable within the function, like this:

```
pause()
{
    int move_on;
    printf("Press any key to continue");
    move_on = getchar();
return(0);


}
```

The variable `move_on` is part of the `pause()` function. Because it is declared within a function, it is said to be *local* to that function. A local variable is recognized only in the function where it was declared. In C, this type of variable is called *automatic*.

Think about that. If you declare a variable inside a function, it is only recognized in that function. This also applies to variables declared within `main()`. Look at this program:

```
main()
{
    int move_on;
    puts("Messages that fill the screen\n");
                        /* Here would be a series of messages
                           that fill the screen */
    pause();
}
pause()
{
    printf("Press any key to continue");
```

```
        move_on = getchar();
    return(0);
    }
```

The compiler would generate an error message because the variable move_on cannot be used in the pause() function. The variable is declared within main(), and so it is local to main() and only has meaning when used within main(). You need to declare the variable move_on within the pause() function instead.

Because an automatic variable is only valid in its function, you can use the same name for variables in different functions. In Figure 7.4, the variable named age is declared in both the main() and spouse() functions. Each variable is automatic, or local to the function in which it is declared. So this program has two variables with the same name. Each variable will contain its own value, stored in separate memory locations. The computer can distinguish which variable age you want to display by the function

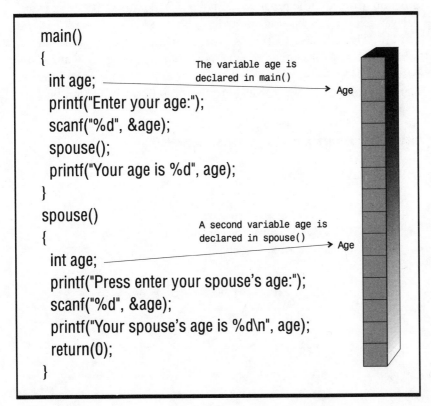

Figure 7.4

Local variables can have the same name in different functions.

in which the `printf()` command is located. When it executes the `printf()` instruction in the `spouse()` function, it displays the variable `age` automatic to that function. When it executes the `printf()` instruction in `main()`, it displays the variable `age` automatic to `main()`. The computer maintains two separate variables named `age`.

External (Global) Variables

An external variable is one that can be used by every function in the program. Some languages call these *global* variables. In order to be external, however, the variable must be declared before the `main()` function, like this:

```
int temp;
main()
```

Here, the variable `temp` is external so it can be used in any function in the program. Consider the program in Listing 7.3. Because `temp` is an external variable, it can be used in `main()`, `convert()`, `freeze()`, and `boil()`. The value is input in `main()`, then used for calculations in the other functions. One other variable is used in the program—`celsius`. Because `celsius` is only needed by the `convert()` function, it is declared in that function. It is local to that function and cannot be used elsewhere.

Listing 7.3: Program with an External Variable

```
/*f_to_c.c*/
int temp;
main()
{
    printf("Input a temperature :");
    scanf("%d", &temp);
    convert();
    freeze();
    boil();
}

convert()
{
```

```
float celsius;
celsius = (5.0/9.0)*(temp-32);
printf("%d degrees F is %6.2f degrees celsius\n",temp, celsius);
return(0);
}
freeze()
{
printf("It is %d degrees from the freezing point\n",temp-32);
return(0);
}
boil()
{
printf("It is %d degrees from the boiling point\n", 212-temp);
return(0);
}
```

If you have an external and a local variable of the same name, the local variable is used in the function. The function cannot use both.

Static Variables

An automatic (local) variable exists only while the function in which it is declared is being executed. When the function begins execution, a memory location is set aside and assigned to the variable. When the function ends, the memory location is released and the variable no longer exists.

If you perform a function more than once, the variable is created each time the function starts, and its address may change each time. The value stored in the variable is lost each time the function ends.

You can retain the value when the function ends by declaring the variable to be *static*. The declaration takes this form:

```
myfunc()
{
    static int count;
}
```

A static variable is assigned a permanent address space, as long as the program is running. When the function ends, the address space is not released, but stays assigned to the variable. The address will retain the value that it contained when the function ended. The next time the function is executed, the variable will have the same value. Keep in mind that the variable is still automatic and can only be used by the function.

Look at the program in Listing 7.4, which does not use a static variable. The function `doit()` is executed four times. Each time the function is called, the two variables are assigned an initial value of 0 and their values are displayed in a `printf()` statement. At the end of the function, the values of both variables are incremented by one. However, the variables are released after each execution and reassigned the initial value of 0 each time the function is executed, so the output is this:

```
autovar is 0     statvar is 0
autovar is 0     statvar is 0
autovar is 0     statvar is 0
autovar is 0     statvar is 0
```

Listing 7.4: Program Illustrating the Use of Local Variables

```
/*stat.c*/
main()
{
    doit();
    doit();
    doit();
    doit();
}
doit()
{
    int autovar = 0;
    int statvar = 0;
    printf("autovar is %d  statvar is %d\n", autovar, statvar);
    ++autovar;
    ++statvar;
return(0);
}
```

Now let's modify the declaration in `doit()` to create a static variable:

```
static int statvar = 0;
```

When you run the program with a static variable, the output is now

```
autovar is 0     statvar is 0
autovar is 0     statvar is 1
```

```
autovar is 0      statvar is 2
autovar is 0      statvar is 3
```

The first time the program is executed, the variable `statvar` is assigned the initial value of 0. The static declaration, however, tells the program to retain in memory whatever value the variable has when the function ends. After the function ends the first time, the value is 1—it was incremented by the `++statvar` operator. When the function starts the second time, the variable will still be 1; the assignment to 0 is ignored.

Each time the function is performed, the variable is incremented, and the incremented value is retained when the function starts again.

Passing Parameters

There are some tasks you can perform only by passing the function a parameter. When you pass a parameter to `puts()`, for example, you type the argument—the string you wanted to display—in the parentheses. You call the `puts()` function with a command like this:

```
puts("Hi there!");
```

The string "Hi there!" is sent to the library function `puts()`, telling it what data you want to display on the screen.

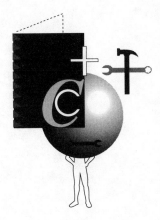

You pass a parameter to your own functions in the same way. Any data you want to send to the function must be in the parentheses. The list of variables being passed to a function is called an *argument list*.

Now consider what happens at the receiving end. The library function `puts()` has instructions that say "Display something on the screen." It expects a parameter to be passed to it—to fill in the "something." The function in the library needs a place to receive the argument—someplace to store the string passed to it, as shown in Figure 7.5. So it, too, has an argument list naming the variables that will store the received data. You can pass more than one argument, as long as the number of arguments in the function call, and their data types, match those expected by the function.

Now let's see how to pass an argument to your own custom function. Consider this program:

```
main()
{
```

Figure 7.5

An argument is needed to receive a passed value.

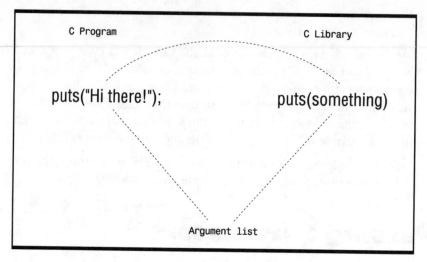

```
        int count;
        count = 5;
        doubles(count);
}
doubles(num)
int num;
{
        printf("%d", num * 2);
return(0);
}
```

The command `doubles(count);` in `main()` calls the function and passes to it the value of the variable count. The `doubles()` function receives the value of the argument into a variable named num. The variable num will have the same value as the variable count. Also notice that the variable num is declared *before* the starting brace in `doubles()`. This is called the *argument declaration,* and it tells the compiler what type of value will be received by the function. Only argument declarations can appear before the opening brace. If the function needs any other variables, they must be declared after the brace as usual.

Here's what happens in the program (refer to Figure 7.6 as you follow along):

1. The `doubles()` function is called and is passed the value of count.

C++ Notes

In C++, you can declare the arguments directly in the function argument list, like this:

```
doubles(int num)
```

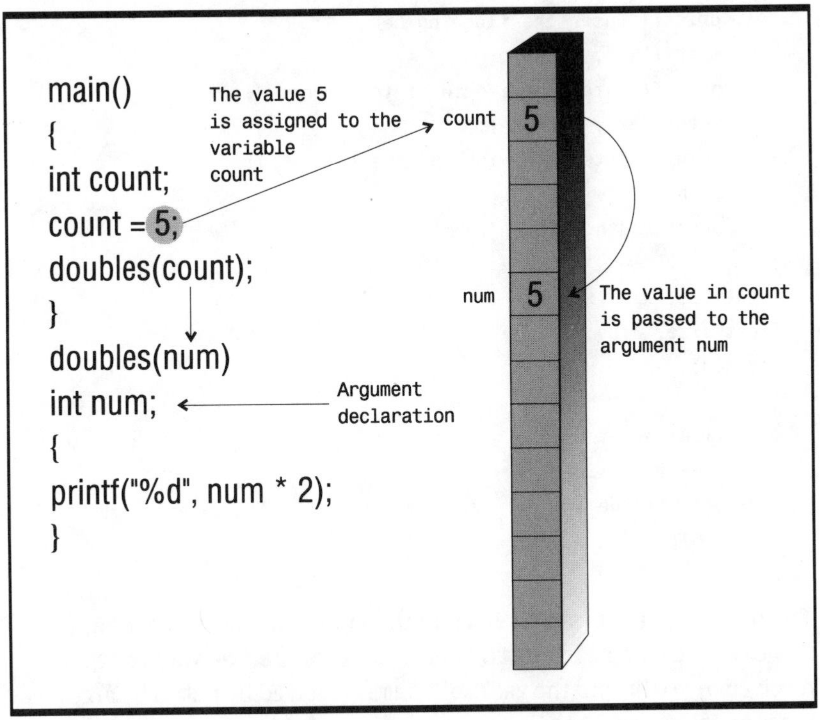

main()
{
int count;
count = 5;
doubles(count);
}
doubles(num)
int num;
{
printf("%d", num * 2);
}
The value 5 is assigned to the variable count
count
5
num
5
The value in count is passed to the argument num
Argument declaration

Figure 7.6
Passing a parameter.

2. The value of 5 is received by the argument named `num` in the function.
3. The function doubles the value and displays it in the `printf()` function.

You can pass as many items to the function as you need, of any type, as shown in the program in Listing 7.5. The function `area()` calculates the area of a floor. The length and width of the floor, and the floor's number, are input in `main()`, then passed to the function in the call

```
area(length, width, fnum);
```

Listing 7.5: Passing Multiple Parameters

```
/*area.c*/
main()
{
    float length, width;
    int fnum;
    printf("Enter the floor number: ");
    scanf("%d", &fnum);
    printf("Enter the length of the floor: ");
    scanf("%f", &length);
    printf("Enter the width of the floor: ");
    scanf("%f", &width);
    area(length, width, fnum);
}
area(size, wide, num)
float size, wide;
int num;
{
    float area;
    area=size*wide;
    printf("The area of floor %d is %.2f", num, area);
return(0);
}
```

The three arguments are received in the same order as they are passed. In this case, the value of `length` is received by `size`, the value of `width` is received by `wide`, and the value of `fnum` is received by `num`. The argument types match—two `floats` are received by two `floats`, and an `int` is received by an `int`.

The function `area()` also needs a variable to store the results of the calculation. The variable, also named `area`, is declared after the opening brace.

If you made a mistake and called the function like this:

```
area(width,length,fnum);
```

the value of `width` would be received by `size`, and the value of `length` would be received by `wide`. Because the types match, your compiler would not generate an error, and in this case the program would still generate the correct result—the order in which you multiply the numbers doesn't matter. But suppose you called the function using this argument list:

```
area(fnum, width,length);
```

The function would receive `fnum` into the argument `width`; `width` into `size`, and `length` into `num`. Two of the arguments do not match in type. If your compiler did not detect an error, the results would certainly be incorrect.

Now let's look at one more example, in Listing 7.6. The program inputs the cost of an item and a percentage discount. The variables `cost` and `discount` are passed to the function `price()` and received into the arguments `amount` and `mrkdown`. The variables `reduced` and `net` are needed within the function, so they are declared after the brace as automatic variables.

Listing 7.6: Passing Parameters

```
/*discount.c*/
main()
{
float cost, discount;
printf("Enter the cost of the item: ");
scanf("%f", &cost);
printf("Enter the percent discount as decimal number: ");
scanf("%f", &discount);
price(cost, discount);
}
price(amount, mrkdown)
float amount, mrkdown;
{
float reduced, net;
reduced = amount * mrkdown;
net = amount - reduced;
printf("The net cost is $%.2f", net);
return(0);
}
```

Price() multiplies the cost by the discount, subtracts the discount from the cost, and displays the net price. After running the program, your screen may appear like this:

```
Enter the cost of the item: 100
Enter the percent discount as decimal number: 0.05
The net cost is $95.00
```

Now suppose, by accident, you changed the function call to this:

```
price(discount, cost);
```

The compiler would not generate an error, because two float values are being received by two float arguments. Unfortunately, they are received by the wrong arguments. The value of discount is being received into amount and the value of cost into mrkdown.

If you enter an item cost of 100 and a discount of 0.05, the function reverses them. It calculates the item as costing five cents and the discount as 1000%. The cost of the item will be minus $4.95 (−4.95) instead of $95.00.

Returning Variables

A function can receive values and return them as well. Recall that the getchar() function uses this format:

```
key = getchar();
```

The instruction calls the getchar() function, which inputs a single character from the keyboard. When the getchar() function is performed, the character input is assigned to the variable named key. This is called *returning* a value.

Your own functions can return values to the calling function. When you want to return a value, however, you must add a few elements to the function. For example, look at this program:

```
main()
{
    char letter;
    letter = getlet();
    putchar('\n');
    printf("The character entered was %c", letter);
```

```
}
char getlet()
{
    printf("Enter a character: ");
    return(getchar());
}
```

The instruction

```
letter = getlet();
```

calls the function getlet(). This function inputs a character from the keyboard and returns the character to the variable letter in main().

When you want to return a value, you must tell the compiler the type of the value that will be returned. You do this by specifying the type before the function name, as in

```
char getlet()
```

The instruction tells C that the function getlet() will return a char value. The value to be returned is the argument of the return() function call. The instruction

```
return(getchar());
```

does the bulk of the work. Remember that getchar() is used where you would use an expression or value. In this program, getchar() inputs a character, and then return() passes the character back to the variable named letter and sends control back to main(), where the printf() instruction is performed.

"Void" Return Values

With C compilers following the ANSI standard, you must designate a function type, even if the function does not return a value. In these instances, the type is declared as "void," as in:

```
Void Myfunct()
```

This informs the compiler that the function will not return a value to the calling function. In C++, the void keyword is optional, but recommended.

Take time to study the `return()` function in this program. Make sure you understand how it and the `getchar()` function are used.

Now let's look at a program that both receives and returns a value. The program illustrated in Figure 7.7 inputs a value and then displays its square. The instruction

```
number = square(value);
```

calls the `square()` function, passing the contents of the variable named `value`.

The function definition `int square(num)` informs C that `square()` will return an `int` value, and that it will receive an argument into the variable `num`.

In this case, `return()` is the only instruction in the function. The instruction `return(num*num)` returns the value of the expression `num*num`, inserting it into the variable named `number`—the variable assigned to the function call in `main()`.

Figure 7.7

Program that returns a value from a function.

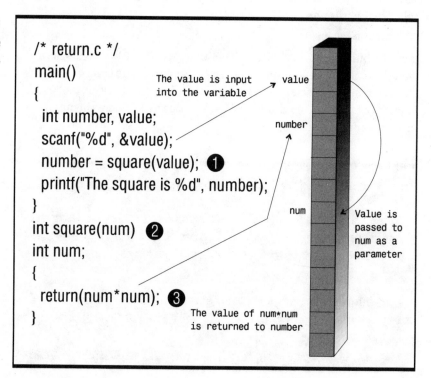

Returning Float Values

When a function is returning an int or char variable, placing the type before the function name is really optional. C was originally designed to handle nothing but int and char data, so if the type is missing, C will just assume you are returning an int or char.

If you are returning a float value, however, you have to do two things:

1. You must add the float type before the function name.

2. You must declare the function itself.

You declare the function as an external variable before the main() function, as shown in Figure 7.8. The instruction

```
float square();
```

sets up the compiler to handle a float function. Except for the function declaration and the float type, the program is the same as the one that squared an integer value.

With most compilers, you can also declare the function type within main(), like this:

```
main()
{
float number, value, square();
```

C++ Notes

Overloading is the C++ process that allows operators and functions to deal with more than one data type. You can use the same function name for several functions, as illustrated by these prototypes:

```
int doubles(int num);

float doubles(float num);
```

The program would then contain two functions named `doubles()`, one to double an integer number, another to double a `float` number.

Figure 7.8
Declaring a `float`-type function.

```
/* float.c */
float square();          ← Declares the function
main()                      as a float type
{
    float number, value;
    printf("Enter a number to be squared:");
    scanf("%d", &value):
    number = square(value);
    printf("The square is %.2f", number);
}
float square(num)        ← Defines the function
float num;
{
    return(num*num);
}
```

Defines the value returned as a float

Defines the value receives as a float

If your compiler doesn't allow this, declare the function before `main()` instead.

The return() Function in main()

Before going on, you may want to think about the 0 in the `return(0)` function in `main()`. If we use a parameter to send a value to a function, where are we sending the value 0 when we end a program? We are actually sending it to the operating system.

When you run a C program, think of the operating system as *calling* the `main()` function. When the program ends, the `return()` command reports back to the system. The parameter in `return()` tells the system whether an error has occurred and what the error is. The command `return(0)` tells the system that no error has occurred. Advanced programs can use other parameter values to inform the operating system of hardware or software errors, and to perform additional functions based on how the program ended.

Using Macros

You know that you can create a constant using the `#define` directive. If you use the command `#define PI 3.14`, C substitutes the value 3.14 when it encounters the constant name `PI` in your program.

The `#define` directive tells the compiler to replace the constant name with whatever follows it. If you follow the constant name with a complete instruction, the compiler will also make that substitution. For example, the following directive will substitute a `printf()` instruction for the constant named `ENTER`:

```
#define ENTER printf("Please enter a number:")
```

When you want to display the message named in the `printf()` command, you just use the instruction `ENTER`, like this:

```
#define ENTER printf("Please enter a number :")
main()
{
    int age, size;
    ENTER;
    scanf("%d", &age);
    ENTER;
```

```
            scanf("%d", &size);
    }
```

When you run the program, the prompt *Please enter a number:* will be displayed, just as if the `printf()` instruction appeared in `main()`, as shown in Figure 7.9.

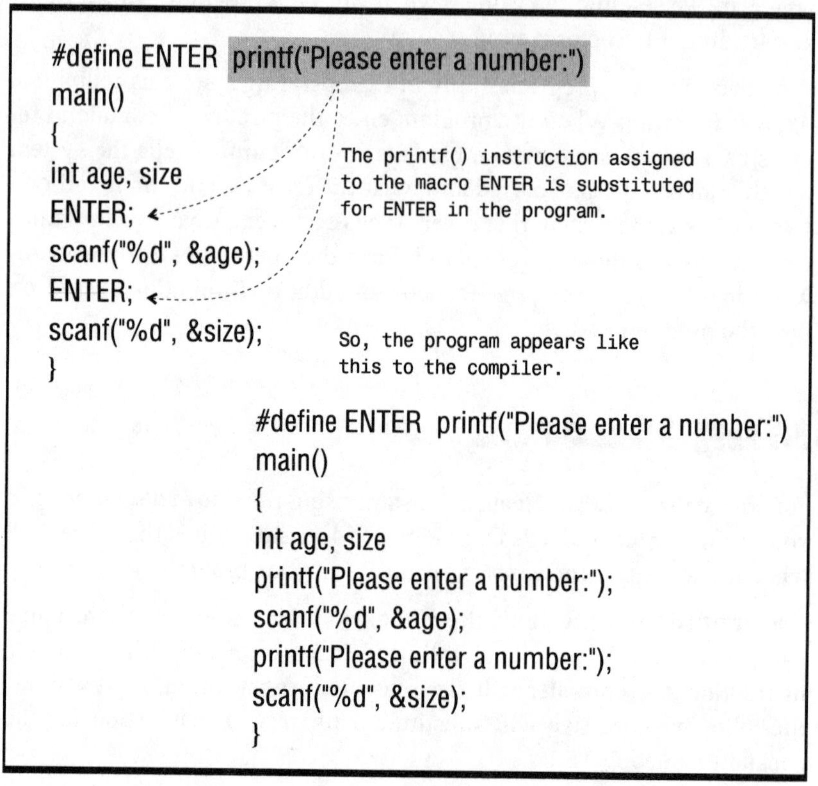

Figure 7.9

Defining a complete program
instruction.

```
#define ENTER  printf("Please enter a number:")
main()
{
int age, size
ENTER;  ◄------
scanf("%d", &age);
ENTER;  ◄------
scanf("%d", &size);
}
```

The `printf()` instruction assigned
to the macro ENTER is substituted
for ENTER in the program.

So, the program appears like
this to the compiler.

```
#define ENTER  printf("Please enter a number:")
main()
{
int age, size
printf("Please enter a number:");
scanf("%d", &age);
printf("Please enter a number:");
scanf("%d", &size);
}
```

Directives like this are called *macros*. They are powerful because they save you the trouble of retyping an instruction several times in the same program. You could use the ENTER macro, for example, every time you want to prompt for an entry. What makes macros even more powerful is that they can accept arguments, as functions can. This program, for example, uses a macro to convert fahrenheit temperature to celsius:

```
#define ENTER printf("Please enter a number: ");
#define CONVERT(temp)  (5.0/9.0)*(temp-32)
main()
```

```
{
    float climate;
    ENTER;
    scanf("%f", &climate);
    printf("it is %f\n", CONVERT(climate));
}
```

The second #define directive creates a macro named CONVERT that accepts one value as an argument. The argument that CONVERT receives is placed in the expression (5.0/9.0)*(temp-32) at the position of the word temp. You call the macro in the same way you would call a function, by using the value you want to convert as the calling argument, as in Figure 7.10. If you enter 212 in response to the input command, then the call CONVERT(climate) in the printf() command is calculated as the expression (5.0/9.0)*(212-32).

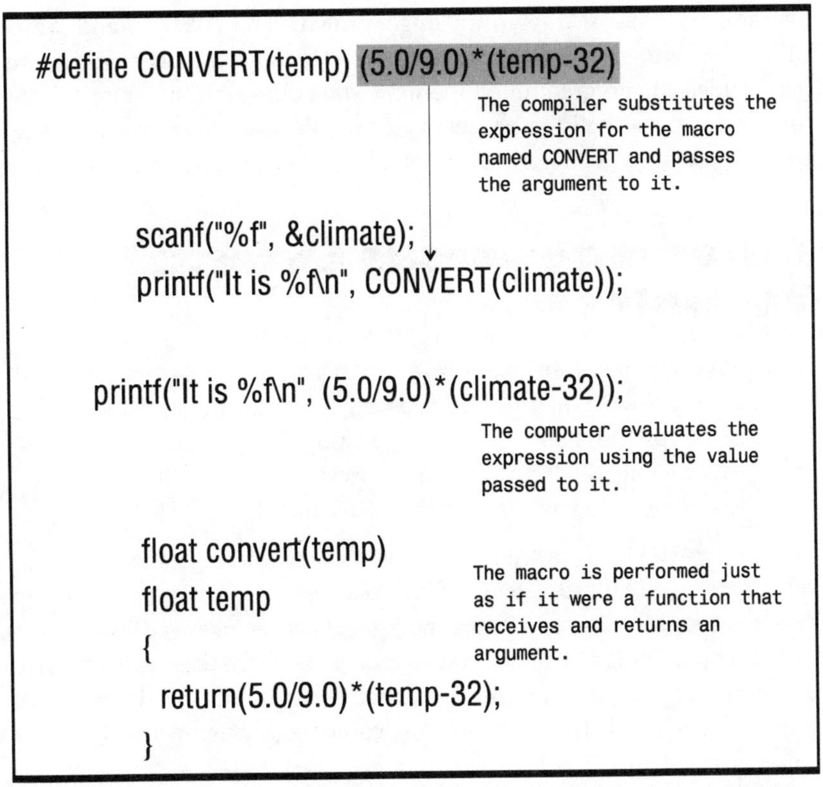

Figure 7.10
Defining an expression as a macro.

Inside the figure:

#define CONVERT(temp) (5.0/9.0)*(temp-32)

The compiler substitutes the expression for the macro named CONVERT and passes the argument to it.

scanf("%f", &climate);
printf("It is %f\n", CONVERT(climate));

printf("It is %f\n", (5.0/9.0)*(climate-32));

The computer evaluates the expression using the value passed to it.

float convert(temp)
float temp

The macro is performed just as if it were a function that receives and returns an argument.

{
    return(5.0/9.0)*(temp-32);
}

Using a macro has the same advantages as using a constant. If you decide to change your standard input prompt, for example, you'd only need to change the ENTER macro at the start of the program. If you made a mistake in the temperature conversion formula, you'd only have to edit one line, not every location where you used the macro.

Program Design

There are no precise rules to help you decide when to use functions and when to place all of your instructions in `main()`. As you gain experience, the decision will come naturally. If you are writing a short program, such as one that inputs a number or two, performs some math, and displays the results, then just use `main()`—it is really silly to divide a program of five or ten lines into functions unless necessary.

On the other hand, if you write a longer program all in `main()` and something goes wrong, where would you start to look for the problem? If you had divided the program into functions, you could start by asking "What function is most likely to be causing the problem?" You work your way from the most to the least likely source to solve the problem.

Automatic versus External Variables

New programmers often take the shortcut of using only external variables, hoping to save the trouble of passing and returning arguments. For instance, the program shown earlier in Listing 7.3 uses the external variable `temp` in four different functions. Because the variable is external, there was no need to pass its value as an argument.

While external variables seem easier to use, they can result in runtime errors that are difficult to detect and in inaccurate results. Not only can an external variable be used by all functions, it can be changed by them as well. If your results are incorrect, you'd have to search the entire program to determine where the mistake occurred. A small, innocuous statement buried deep in a little-used function could be changing the variable's value by accident.

Using automatic variables and passing values in arguments give you more control over the flow of the program. The value of an automatic variable can only be changed in the function where it is declared. If your results are incorrect, you add temporary `printf()` statements to each function displaying the values of local variables. You'll then be able to track down the offending instructions.

Invalid Input

The programs presented in this chapter were selected because they illustrate the concepts of using functions. They are not necessarily the best way to perform a task, nor are they error-proof.

For example, no matter how well you write your program, you cannot control the input typed on the keyboard. In the program shown earlier in Listing 7.6, the cost of an item and the discount rate are input using `scanf()` function. The calculations to compute the net costs are based on the assumption that the discount rate is entered as a decimal number, such as 0.05 for five percent. To help ensure the proper input, the `printf()` instruction prompts:

```
Enter the percent discount as decimal number:
```

The user, however, could still mistakenly enter 5 rather than 0.05. If they did, instead of reducing the item cost by five percent, the discount rate will be calculated at 500 percent. You'd be paying customers to buy from you!

In your own programs, don't assume that the input will be as expected. If anything, you have to learn to expect the unexpected. You'll learn how to prevent some of these possible errors in Chapter 8.

Questions

1. What is the difference between a function in the C library and a function you write yourself?

2. Must a function always be called from `main()`?

3. What occurs after a function is performed?

4. Explain the difference between automatic and external variables.

5. What are the relative advantages of using automatic and external variables?

6. When would you use a static variable?

7. How do you pass a value to a function?

8. How do you return a value from a function?

9. What is a macro?

10. How can you return a float value?

Exercises

1. Write a quiz program that asks four questions, each question and answer in a different function.

2. Write a program that inputs a number and then uses a function to calculate and display the number to the fourth power.

3. Convert the program in Exercise 2 so the calculation to the fourth power is made in a function, but the results are passed back to `main()` to be displayed.

4. Explain what is wrong with the following program:

```
dothis()
{
        puts("This is first");
        main()
        return;
}


main()
{
        puts("This is second");
        return(0);
}
```

>= 40000.00 && COST <= 60000.00

1 ..... 40,000 40,001 40,002 .... 60,000 60,001 60,002 .....

Eight

Letting the Computer Decide

• •

Starting with this chapter, your programming capabilities are about to take a giant leap forward. It's not that the topics of this and later chapters are any more difficult than what you've already mastered. They're not. But when you combine what you are about to learn with what you already know, you'll be entering a new plateau in programming sophistication.

Also starting with this chapter, we'll be paying more attention to the logic of program design. As your skills increase with the syntax and structure of C and C++, you'll notice a shift in emphasis. Rather than concentrating on each semicolon and brace, you'll be learning more about algorithms and problem solving. You'll learn that there is not just one "right" way to write a program—you could perform a task by writing a program several different ways.

In this chapter you'll learn how to have the computer make decisions. Rather than performing every instruction in the order you write them, your programs will decide, based on criteria you specify, which instructions to perform. In fact, you'll use the techniques you will learn here to correct most of the logic problems we've pointed out in earlier chapters.

The Big If

All of this magic is performed by the little `if` command—the small word with the big bang. You use the `if` command to decide whether an instruction should be performed. The structure of the command is:

```
if (condition)
    instruction;
```

The command says "if this condition is true, then perform the following instruction." (See Figure 8.1.) The computer performs the instruction, then continues normally, performing the instructions that follow the `if` command.

Figure 8.1

The structure of the `if` command.

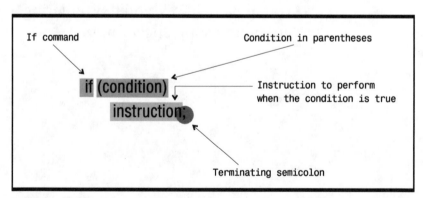

If the condition is false, however, the computer skips the instruction that is part of the `if` command, and moves on to the next instruction in the program. Writing an `if` command is easy as long as you remember these basic points:

- Place the condition in parentheses.
- There is no semicolon after the condition—it appears after the instruction.
- While we paraphrase the command by saying "If condition then do instruction," there is no *then* command in C.
- C is a free-form language, so the condition and instruction can be on the same line. Separating and indenting the condition, however, make a program easier to read.

Conditions

Conditions in `if` commands compare values—a variable or constant is compared with a literal or another variable or constant. The comparison is done with one of these operators:

Operator	Meaning	Example
==	equal	if (tax == 0.06)
>	greater than	if (hours > 40)
<	less than	if (hours < 40)
>=	greater than or equal to	if (salary >= 10000)
<=	less than or equal to	if (cost <= limit)
!=	not equal to	if (count != 1)

Note that when testing whether two values are the same, you must use the `==` operator, two equal signs in a row. If you use a single equal sign, your compiler will generate an error. The single = symbol is reserved for assigning value to variables.

A simple `if` construction can look like this:

```
if (time > 11)
    puts("Go home, it is after curfew.");
```

The instructions say "If the variable `time` is greater than 11, then display the following message." If the variable `time` were 11 or less, the message would not be displayed.

You can use `if` conditions to test numeric and `char` variables, but not strings. The following program segment, for example, would compile without a problem but it would not display the correct result:

```
gets(name);
if (name == "Adam")
 puts("Call home");
```

Strings are special variables discussed in Chapter 10.

Now look at Listing 8.1, a complete program that uses an `if` command. The program is a modification of one you saw in a previous chapter that computed the total of an order plus sales tax. In this program, a special luxury tax is added to items over $40,000. The calculation is performed in the command:

```
if (cost > 40000.00)
  luxury = cost * 0.005;
```

Listing 8.1: Sales Orders Program with Luxury Tax

```
/*luxury1.c*/
main()
{

    float  cost, tax, luxury, total;
    luxury = 0.0;
    printf("Enter the cost of the item: ");
    scanf("%f", &cost);
    tax = cost * 0.06;
    if (cost > 40000.00)
        luxury = cost * 0.005;
    total = cost + tax + luxury;
    printf("The total cost is %.2f", total);
}
```

The command says "If the value of `cost` is over $40,000, then assign the variable named `luxury` the value of `cost` times 0.5 percent." The last two instructions in the program are always performed, whether there is a luxury tax or not, because they come after the `if` command's terminating semicolon.

Notice that the variable `luxury` is assigned an initial value of 0 earlier in the program, but not the variable `tax`. The variable `tax` will always be assigned a value in the calculation `tax = cost * 0.06`, but `luxury` is only assigned a calculated value if the cost is over $40,000. If the condition is false, the calculation would not be performed and, if you did not assign an initial value, some unknown value would be added to the total. So as a general rule, it is wise to assign initial values to variables calculated in `if` statements, as well as to counters and accumulators.

When you use the greater-than or less-than operators, make certain they perform the condition you intend. In the previous example, the luxury tax is added only if the cost is at least one cent over $40,000, from $40,000.01 and higher. If the cost were exactly $40,000, no luxury tax would be charged. If the tax were imposed on items $40,000 and over, the proper condition would be

```
if (cost >= 40000.00)
```

The difference between > and >=, and between < and <=, is subtle but critical to the accuracy of your program.

Multiple Statements

The basic `if` statement performs one instruction. If you want to perform more than one instruction when the condition is true, you must use a second level of braces. The braces mark the beginning and end of a block of instructions performed when the condition is true.

For example, look at the program in Listing 8.2, where two instructions are performed when the condition is true. The brace after the condition marks the beginning of the block, and the brace after the second instruction marks the end of the block. Any instructions within the block will be performed only when the condition is true. The lines are indented to make it clear that they are part of the `if` command, but the indentation means nothing to the compiler.

Listing 8.2: Multiple Statements

```
/*luxury2.c*/
main()
{
```

```
float  cost, tax, luxury, total;
luxury = 0.0;
printf("Enter the cost of the item: ");
scanf("%f", &cost);
tax = cost * 0.06;
if (cost > 40000.00)
{
    luxury = cost * 0.005;
    printf("The luxury tax is %.2f\n", luxury);
}
total = cost + tax + luxury;
printf("The total cost is %.2f", total);
}
```

The if...else Command

When you use the `if` command by itself, you are only interested in performing instructions when the condition is true. You can also perform one set of instructions when the condition is true, and another set if the condition is false. For instance, suppose we wanted to print the message "There is no luxury tax for this item" for items under the luxury tax level. We could do so using two `if` commands, like this:

```
if (cost > 40000.00)
{
    luxury = cost * 0.005;
    printf("The luxury tax is %.2f", luxury);
}
if (cost <= 40000.00)
    puts("There is no luxury tax for this item");
```

However, there's a more efficient alternative. Both instructions can be combined into one because there are only two possible states involving the same variable—the cost is either above $40,000 or it is $40,000 or less. If one condition is false, then the other condition must be true. You combine the instructions using the `else` command:

```
if (condition)
  instruction;
```

```
else
    instruction;
```

The structure says "If the condition is true, perform the instruction that follows; else perform the instruction after the `else` command." The instructions following `else` are performed only if the condition is false. If you need to perform more than one instruction in either case, enclose the multiple instructions in braces. You need a semicolon after each instruction but not after the `else` keyword.

To print the message when no luxury tax is charged, you would modify the program as illustrated in Figure 8.2. Note that we no longer need to assign luxury an initial variable at the start of the program because the `if` command now accounts for all possible conditions.

Quiz Revisited

In Chapter 7, you saw several programs that displayed questions and answers. Because you had not yet learned the `if` command, you weren't able to keep score. Keeping score is really just a matter of comparing the correct answer with the response entered from the keyboard, as shown in the

```
if (cost > 40000.00)        If the condition is true,
{                           perform this block of
                            instructions

    luxury = cost*0.005;
    printf("The luxury tax is %.2f", luxury);
}
else  ←                     No semicolon
{

    puts(There is no luxury tax for this items");
    luxury = 0.0;
}
                            Otherwise, the condition is false,
                            so perform this block of
                            instructions
```

Figure 8.2
Modified instructions using the `else` keyword.

program in Listing 8.3.

This program uses a function to display the question, input the answer, determine whether the response is correct, and count correct and incorrect responses. Both the question and correct answer are passed to the function—the question as a string literal, the answer as an integer. The program is written so you can add additional questions by just inserting function calls, such as

```
ask("9 + 5 = ", 14);
```

Listing 8.3: Quick Program That Keeps Score

```
/*score*/
int correct, wrong;
main()
{
    char question[15];
    int answer;
    correct = 0;
    wrong = 0;
    ask("4 + 5 = ", 9);
    ask("6 + 2 = ", 8);
    ask("5 + 5 = ", 10);
    ask("4 + 7 = ", 11);
    printf("You answered %d question correctly.\n", correct);
    printf("You answered %d question incorrectly.\n", wrong);
}
ask(quest, ans)
char quest[15];
int ans;
{
    int guess;
    printf("%s", quest);
    scanf(."%d", &guess);
    if (guess == ans)
        ++correct;
    else
        ++wrong;
    return(0)
}
```

Logic Operators

The `if` conditions you have seen so far test only a single variable and a single value. That is, only one condition must be met for the statement to be evaluated as true. In the real world, programs often need to test for more than one value.

Look at the program in Listing 8.4, which assumes that not every item you sell is taxable. Instead of automatically adding a sales tax to every item, it asks whether the item is taxable, then if the item is taxable, adds a 6 percent sales tax.

Listing 8.4: Logic Based on User Input

```
/*iftax.c*/
main()
{
     int taxable;
     float  cost, tax;
     tax = 0.0;
     printf("Enter the cost of the item: ");
     scanf("%f", &cost);
     printf("Enter Y if the item is taxable, N if nontaxable: ");
     taxable=getchar();
     if (taxable == 'Y')
          tax = cost * 0.06;
     printf("\nThe total due is %f", cost + tax);
}
```

If the program looks correct to you, look at it again—it has a serious flaw. The program assumes the user will enter an uppercase letter Y if the item is taxable. If the user enters a lowercase y, the program would assume the item was not taxable because the `if` command tests only for an uppercase Y.

In situations like this, you should test for both possible inputs—Y or y. You could do this with two `if` commands. But instead, use the logical *or* operator—¦¦—like this:

```
if (taxable == 'Y' ¦¦ taxable == 'y')
```

Notes on getchar()

With some compilers (but not the PCC compiler provided with this book), the `getchar()` function is *buffered*. This means that the character input is stored in the computer's memory until the user presses the Enter key. If this is the case with your compiler, check your documentation for the `getch()` or `getche()` function. These are usually not buffered, so you can enter a single keystroke without the need to press ↵.

In addition, using the `getchar()` function after a `scanf()` input can cause a problem. As explained in Chapter 5, if you do not enter the proper data for a `scanf()` function, some characters could remain in the input buffer. The `getchar()` function could read one of those characters rather than the one you enter. You can avoid this potential problem by using a `gets()` command, or a non-buffered character input command such as `getch()` or `getche()`, if one is available in your compiler.

Another alternative is to empty the input buffer before the getchar() function. Add the command `#include <stdio.h>` at the beginning of the program. Then, insert the command `fflush(stdin)` before the `getchar()` statement. The `fflush()` command flushes (removes) any characters remaining in the standard input device buffer.

This instruction says "If `taxable` equals Y OR `taxable` equals y". So the item will be considered taxable if one or the other condition is true. If neither is true—you entered something other than Y or y—the item would be nontaxable. The entire condition is contained in one set of parentheses and the variable being tested—`taxable`—is repeated. The condition (`taxable == "Y' || 'y'`) would generate a compiler error.

There are three logic operators: `||` for OR, `&&` for AND, and `!` for NOT. When you use the OR operator, one or the other condition (or both) must be true for the `if` statement to be true. When you use the AND condition, both must be true. When you use the NOT operator the condition must be false.

You can use the `&&` and `||` operators to test the same variable against two values, as we just did, or two different variables. For example, suppose you need to write a program that inputs the user's income and number of dependents, as in Listing 8.5.

Listing 8.5: Testing Two Variables

```
/*twovars.c*/
main()
{
    int depents;
    float income;
    puts("Please enter your income");
    scanf("%f", &income);
    puts("Please enter the number of dependents");
    scanf("%d", &depents);
    if (income < 20000 && depents > 2)
        puts("You owe no income tax");
}
```

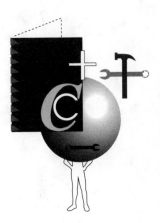

The `if` condition tests two variables, `income` and `depents`. The income must be less than $20,000 AND the number of dependents must be greater than two for the message to be displayed. If either condition were false, such as one dependent or $20,001 of income, the `puts()` instruction would not be performed.

Be very cautious when using the `&&` operator, to make sure it performs as expected. For instance, never use `&&` to test whether a variable has two values. The condition

```
if (taxable == 'Y' && taxable == 'y')
```

can never be true. It is impossible for a variable to be equal to two different values. However, you can test the same variable to determine whether it is within or outside a range of values.

As an example, suppose the luxury tax is only charged on items between $40,000 and $60,000. The condition to test for this is:

```
if (cost >= 40000.00 && cost <= 60000.00)
```

In order for the `if` to be true, both conditions must be met because of the *and* operator. For both to be true, the cost must be equal to or above $40,000 and less than or equal to $60,000 at the same time—inside the range, as illustrated in Figure 8.3.

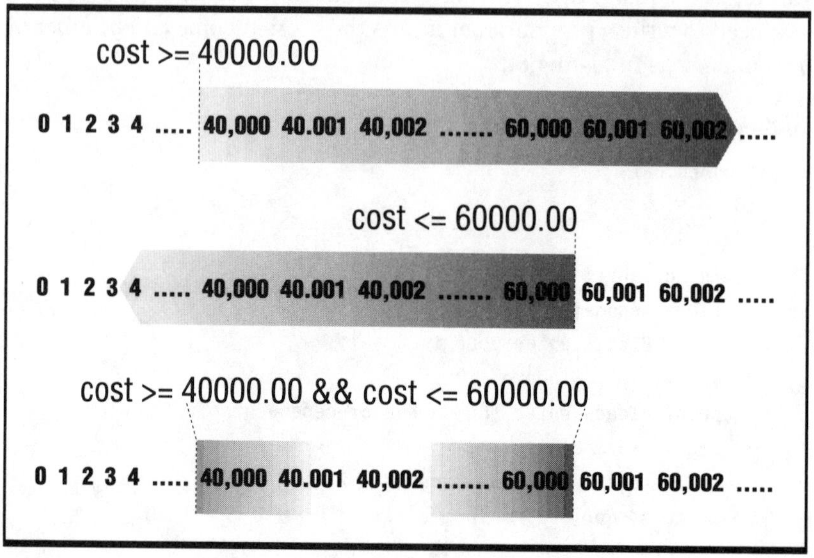

Figure 8.3

Logic for determining whether a value is within a range.

If you used the OR operator here, by mistake, every value of `cost` would be considered true. To test whether a value is outside the range, you must use the OR operator and change the placement of the greater-than and less-than operators. This statement tests whether a value is outside a range by asking if it is either below or above the range limits:

```
if (income <= 20000.00 || income >= 60000.00)
        puts("You are not middle class");
```

The NOT operator is called a *unary* operator because it works on only one item—either a variable or a constant name. A value of 0 is said to be false. A value other than zero—either a positive or negative value—is said to be true. These instructions, for example, will display the text "Count is false" because the variable count has a value of 0:

```
int count;
count = 0;
if (!count) puts ("Count is false");
```

The condition works the same as `if (count == 0)`. Likewise, these instructions will display the message "Count is true" because `count` has a value other than zero:

```
int count;
count = 1;
if (count) puts ("Count is true");
```

The condition is the same as `if (count != 0)`, a shortcut for testing a variable for a non-zero value. In chapters that follow, you'll learn how to use unary operators.

Nested if Statements

An `if` condition or `else` command can be followed by any type of instruction. The instruction can input or output a value, perform a mathematical operation, or call a custom function. The instruction can also be another `if` command. An `if` command that is contained within another is said to be *nested*. For example, in this instruction, the second `if` command is nested in the first:

```
if (income > 100000)
 if (status == 'S')
  taxrate = 0.35;
```

The second `if` condition is tested only when the first condition is true, so the variable `taxrate` is assigned only when both conditions are true. The same logic could be written as:

```
if (income > 100000 && status == 'S')
  taxrate = 0.35;
```

Both perform the same task, but the second example, using the && operator, is clearer. You don't have to decipher what each `if` statement does; just reading the statement explains its meaning—"If `income` is greater than 100,000 AND `status` is S, then `taxrate` is .35."

As a rule, any two consecutive nested `if` statements can be replaced by one statement with the && operator. Also as a rule, it's wise to avoid nested `if` statements because they can lead to ambiguous situations and difficult-to-read code. For example, look at this program:

```
main()
{
```

```
        float income;
        scanf("%f", &income);
        if (income >= 20000.00)
          if (income <= 100000.00)
           puts("Your tax rate is 22%");
        else
             puts("You earn less than $20,000 so your rate is 15%");
        }
```

The logic seems to be "If income is greater than $20,000 and below $100,000 then print one message, but if income is not over $20,000, then print the second message."

Unfortunately, the program would compile without error but not display the correct results. If you entered a value less than 20000, neither puts() instruction would be performed, and if you entered a value over 100000, the tax rate will be reported as only 15%.

The else command is linked with its nearest if, regardless of the indentation used to type the program. In this program, the indentation gives the impression that the else is connected with the first if condition, but in reality, the else is connected with the second if command—it is only performed when income is over 20,000 but not above 100,000.

If you want to follow the intended logic, write the statement like this:

```
        if (income >= 20000.00)
          {
          if (income <= 100000.00)
           puts("Your tax rate is 22%");
          }
        else
             puts("You earn less than $20,000 so your rate is 15%");
```

The second set of braces isolate the nested if command, forcing it to end at the closing brace. The else keyword is now associated with the first if command.

An even better way to write the statement is with only one if command, like this:

```
        if (income >= 20000.00 && income <= 100000.00)
           puts("Your tax rate is 22%");
        else
             puts("You earn less than $20,000 so your rate is 15%");
```

There is no ambiguity between nested if commands and multiple sets of braces.

Even though we've corrected the logic of the program, there is still a flaw. The program only displays a message if the income is $100,000 or less. A well-constructed program must take into account every possible situation. For instance, if you entered an income value of $150,000, no message would print. Does this mean you'd pay no income tax?

One solution is shown in Listing 8.6, which uses nested if...else commands to account for all income levels. Make sure you understand how these statements are nested. If the first condition is true (income < 20000.00) the first puts() is performed and the remainder of the instructions are skipped. The first else keyword is linked with the first if, so the second condition (income <100000.00) is not performed unless the first is false.

Listing 8.6: Use Nested if Statements to Account for All Conditions

```c
/*brackets.c*/
main()
{
    float income;
    printf("Enter your income: ");
    scanf("%f", &income);
    if (income < 20000.00)
        puts("Your tax rate is 15%");
    else
        if (income < 100000.00)
            puts("Your tax rate is 22%");
        else
            puts("Your tax rate is 35%");
}
```

Notice that there are three possible states but only two if conditions. When you use consecutive if...else combinations, you need one condition less than the number of possible states. If the first state is false, and the second state is false, then the third state must be true—there's no need to have an if statement to test it. If there were four possible states, you'd need three if...else combinations and a final fourth else.

The switch/case/default Construction

When you have four or more possible states, the logic of nested if...else commands can become confusing. An alternative is the switch command. Switch presents a menu-like structure, listing all of the possible states and the instructions to perform in each case, as shown in the program in Listing 8.7.

Listing 8.7: Program Using the switch Command

```
/*switch.c*/
main()
{
    int answer;
    puts("The C language is: \n");
    puts("1. A language spoken in the south of France\n");
    puts("2. Used only for writing large computer programs\n");
    puts("3. A compiled language easily ported to various
systems\n");
    puts("4. None of the above\n");
    puts("Enter your answer from 1 to 4\n");
    answer= getchar();
    putchar('\n');
    switch (answer)
    {
    case '1':
     puts("Sorry, you are incorrect.\n");
     puts("In the south of France, they speak Pascal\n");
     break;
    case '2':
     puts("Sorry. The C language can be used to write programs
\n");
     puts("of all types and sizes.\n");
     break;
    case '3':
     puts("Very good, you are correct\n");
```

```
        puts("The C language is compiled, and it can be used on
    a\n");
        puts("variety of computer systems.\n");
        break;
    case '4':
        puts("Sorry. Only number 3 is correct.\n");
        break;
    default:
        puts("You responded with a letter or a number other than 1
    to 4\n");
        }
    }
```

Switch has an argument containing an integer or char variable. Follow-ing the command is a block of instructions, within braces, consisting of a series of **case** commands. Each **case** performs instructions based on a possible value of the variable. The value must be expressed as an integer, a character literal in single-quotes, or as the name of an integer or char-acter constant.

The statement **case '1':**, for example, tells the compiler to perform the instructions that follow if the value of the switch variable is the character "1". If the value was not "1", the next **case** statement will be tested.

When the value matches a **case** condition, the statements following the **case** are executed. The **break** statement at the end of each **case** sends control to the end of the **switch**, so once a **case** is performed, the re-maining **case** statements are ignored and the **switch** ends.

If none of the **cases** are true, the instructions in the **default** section are performed. This makes it easy to account for all possible entries. You do not need a **break** command for the **default** condition, because it is al-ways the last section in the **switch** routine. Include a **default** section even if you think you can account for all possible conditions or inputs in the individual cases.

If you leave out a **break** statement, the computer will perform all of the instructions following the true case, up to the next **break**. You can use this to perform the same set of instructions for more than one case, as in:

```
case 'Y':
case 'y': puts("You responded with a yes");
        break;
```

```
        case 'N':
        case 'n': puts("You responded with a no");
               break;
```

Testing Floats and Strings

Because the value in a `case` statement must be an integer or character, you cannot have `case` statements such as `case 12.87:` or `case "Adam":`. Strings will be discussed in Chapter 10, but if you need to test for the values of a `float`, you must somehow convert the values into an integer or character literal format.

In most cases, you can use a series of `if...else` commands, as in Listing 8.8. The `if...else` commands assign an integer value to the variable named level based on the `float` value input into income.

Listing 8.8: Using Nested if Commands to Handle float Values

```
/*switchf.c*/
main()
{
    float income;
    char level;
    printf("Enter your income: ");
    scanf("%f", &income);
    if (income <= 20000.00)
      level = '1';
    else
      if (income <= 60000.00)
        level = '2';
      else
          if (income <= 120000.00)
            level = '3';
            else
            level = '4';
    switch (level)
    {
    case '1':
     puts("Taxrate = 15%");
     break;
```

```
case '2':
 puts("Taxrate = 28%");
break;
case '3':
puts ("Taxrate = 32%");
break;
case '4':
puts ("Taxrate = 36%");
break;
default:
puts("You entered an invalid entry");
}
}
```

At first glance it seems rather silly to use a series of if...else commands and a switch routine, when you could put all of the instructions in the if...else commands in the first place. With a simple program like this, you could just as easily do that. But when the instructions you have to perform for each case are more complicated, with nested if commands themselves, the switch structure is preferred. The case statements make it clear how many states are being tested, and what instructions are performed in each case. The housekeeping of assigning literal values with a separate series of if...else statements is well worth the extra work.

Program Design

As you can see, there may be several ways to write the same program—using multiple if statements, nested if statements, logical operators, or the switch command. The program in Listing 8.9, for example, shows how the quiz program (which previously used a switch command) can be performed with nested if...else instructions. Your own personal style will decide which you choose. No one can tell you that your way is wrong as long as your program does everything it is supposed to do. Of course, if your program gets incorrect results, then it is very definitely wrong, but not necessarily because you've selected the wrong structure.

Listing 8.9: Quiz Program Using Nested if...else Commands

```
/*quiz4.c*/
main()
```

```
{
    int answer;
    puts("The C language is: \n");
    puts("1. A language spoken in the south of France\n");
    puts("2. Used only for writing large computer programs\n");
    puts("3. A compiled language easily ported to various
systems\n");
    puts("4. None of the above\n");
    puts("Enter your answer from 1 to 4\n");
    answer= getchar();
    putchar('\n');
    if (answer=='1')
     {
     puts("Sorry, you are incorrect.\n");
     puts("In the south of France, they speak Pascal\n");
     }
    else
     if (answer=='2')
       {
        puts("Sorry. The C language can be used to write
programs \n");
        puts("of all types and sizes.\n");
        }
       else
         if (answer=='3')
          {
           puts("Very good, you are correct\n");
           puts("The C language is compiled, and it can be used
on a"\n);
           puts("variety of computer systems.\n");
           }
         else
            if (answer=='4')
                puts("Sorry. Only number 3 is correct.\n");
              else
     puts("You responded with a letter or a number other than 1
to 4\n");
    }
```

Select a method that you feel comfortable with, and that results in the clearest, least ambiguous program. Sometimes the best method requires the most instructions—the shortest program is not always the best. Whatever method you choose for a particular program, remember to always check for the correct input.

Check for Valid Input

Do not assume the user will enter a correct value or a character in either uppercase or lowercase. For example, Chapter 7 included a program that assumed you would enter a discount rate as a decimal number. The calculated results would be incorrect if you mistakenly entered 5, rather than .05 for 5 percent. One way to solve that problem is by adding the command

```
if (mrkdown > 1)
    mrkdown = mrkdown / 100;
```

The `if` command would convert the entry 5 to .05.

In Chapter 6 you saw a program that calculated a worker's salary. If you recall, the program actually subtracted money at double-time if the employee worked less than 40 hours. The program that corrects this flaw is shown in Listing 8.10. The `if` command contains two sets of instructions—one set when the number of hours is at least 40, the other set when it is more than 40. Every variable that will be displayed is assigned a value in one or the other set of instructions, so no unknown values will appear.

Listing 8.10: Corrected Salary Program

```
/*allhours.c*/
main()
{
    float rate, hours, total, regular, extra, d_time, overtime;
    printf("Enter your hourly rate of pay: ");
    scanf("%f", &rate);
    printf("Enter the number of hours you worked: ");
    scanf("%f", &hours);
    d_time=rate * 2;
    if (hours <= 40)
    {
```

```
            regular = hours * rate;
            extra = 0.0;
            overtime = 0.0;
            total = regular;
        }
        else
        {
            regular = 40 * rate;
            extra = hours - 40;
            overtime = extra * d_time;
            total = regular + overtime;
        }
        printf("Your regular weekly salary is %.2f\n", regular);
        printf("You  worked %.2f overtime hours\n", extra);
        printf("Your overtime rate is $%.2f\n", d_time);
        printf("Your overtime pay is %.2f\n", overtime);
        printf("Your total pay is %.2f\n", total);
    }
```

The overtime rate, represented by the variable dtime, is calculated before the if instruction because every employee has an overtime rate even if they didn't actually work any overtime hours for the current period. Since the calculation is not based on the condition being true or false, it is calculated outside the if commands.

These solutions to both problems, however, are not complete. You could still enter a negative number for the discount rate, or some outlandish number of work hours, such as 2500. You'll learn how to finally solve the input problem in the next chapter.

Questions

1. What is the difference between the = and the == symbols?

2. How do you perform more than one statement when a condition is true?

3. What is the purpose of the else command?

4. How do you test whether a number is within a range of values?

5. Explain the use of "nested" if statements.

6. How does the `switch` command differ from the `if` command?

7. How can you use a `float` value in a `switch` command?

8. Explain how an `if` command can be used to test for valid input.

Exercises

1. Write a program that inputs a number, then reports whether the number is odd or even.

2. Write a program that inputs a number, then reports whether the number is in the range from 1 to 100.

3. Write a program that inputs a integer number, then reports which range the number is in: below 0, from 0 to 50, 51 to 100, 101 to 150, or above 150.

4. Write a program that asks the user to enter numbers into the variables `lownum` and `highnum`. The value of `lownum` should be less than the value of `highnum`. If that is not the case, the program should exchange the numbers, placing the low value in `lownum` and the high value in `highnum`. Display the values to confirm the operation.

5. Explain what is wrong with the following program:

```
main()
{
int age;
printf(Enter your age);
scanf("%f", &age);
if age < 18 then
      puts("You cannot vote");
else
      if age > 18 then
            puts("You can vote");
}
```

Repetition

A program starts and a program ends, but that doesn't mean it has to perform a function only once. You may have more than one order to process, or several different calculations to perform. You may want to keep asking for an input until the user enters a value in the proper range.

C and C++ have three distinct structures, known as loops, for controlling repetition:

- the `for` loop
- the `do...while` loop
- the `while` loop

Any of these can repeat either an instruction, a series of instructions, or an entire program.

Using the for Loop

Use the `for` loop when you know the exact number of repetitions you want to perform. The structure of the loop is illustrated in Figure 9.1. Notice that you put the terminating semicolon after the instruction, not after the `for` parameter. The three elements within the parameter, however, must be separated by semicolons.

For example, this program uses a `for` loop to print the numbers 1 through 10 down the screen:

```
main()
{
    int repeat
    for(repeat=1; repeat <=10;repeat++)
        printf("%d\n", repeat);
}
```

Figure 9.1
Structure of the `for` loop.

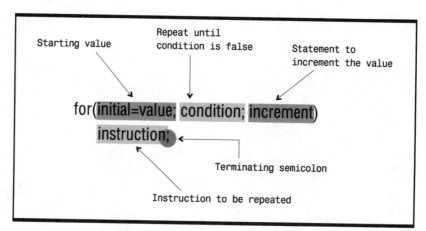

The loop is controlled by the variable named `repeat`, called the *index variable*. You can use any name for the index variable but it must be an integer type. The `for` parameter is divided into these segments:

`repeat = 1`	Initializes the starting value of the variable `repeat`.
`repeat <=10`	Sets the condition to repeat the loop as long as `repeat` has a value less than or equal to 10.
`repeat++`	Increments the value of `repeat` after each repetition.

With each repetition of the loop, the program displays the current value of the variable `repeat`.

C++ Notes

With C++, you can declare the index variable within the parameter, like this:

```
for(int repeat=1; repeat <=10;repeat++)
```

When this program first encounters the loop, it sets the value of `repeat` to 1. It then checks the condition to see if the value of `repeat` is less than or equal to 10. Since that condition is true, it will perform the instruction that is associated with the loop, displaying the value of the variable.

After performing the instruction, it increments the value by 1, and again checks the condition (as illustrated in Figure 9.2). Since the condition is still true, it performs the instruction a second time, displaying the current value of the variable. The process is repeated until the value is incremented to 11. The condition `repeat <= 10` is then false, so the instruction is not performed and the loop stops.

In the previous example, the value of the index variable was used in the instruction. You don't have to write the instruction that way:

```
main()
{
    int repeat
```

Figure 9.2

The condition is checked after
the end of each loop.

```
main()                          Repeat++ increments the
{                               value before the loop
                                is repeated
    int repeat
    for(repeat=1; repeat <=10; repeat++)
        printf("%d\n", repeat);
}
```

```
char letter
Puts("Please enter 10 characters");
for(repeat=1; repeat <=10;repeat++)
    letter=getchar();
}
```

This program performs the `getchar()` instruction ten times, once for
each repetition of the loop as the value of `repeat` is incremented from 1
to 11. The index variable is only used to determine the number of repetitions. You could have also written the `for` instruction this way, with the
same results:

```
for(repeat=101; repeat <=110;repeat++)
letter=getchar();
}
```

It, too, would input 10 characters, this time by incrementing the index
variable from 101 to 110. The exact value of the variable is only important
when you want to use it in the loop itself.

Pausing a Program

You can use a `for` loop without any instructions to place a timed pause
in a program:

```
for(delay=1; delay<=1000; delay++);
```

Even though there is no instruction, the loop is repeated 1000 times, as
the variable named `delay` is incremented and then checked against the
condition. This repetition pauses the program before executing the next
instruction.

Use this technique to pause the screen from scrolling and allow time to read instructions or prompts that appear. It is an alternative to asking the user to enter a key to continue.

You'll have to experiment to see how long a delay each 1000 repetitions will cause on your system. The length of the pause depends on the speed of your computer. A loop that pauses for one second on a fast computer may pause for two seconds on a much slower machine. Increase or decrease the number in the condition to find an appropriate length.

Multiple Instructions

To perform more than one instruction in the loop, enclose the whole series in braces. For example, here's a program that converts 101 consecutive temperatures (from 32 to 132) to celsius:

```
main()
{
  int temp;
  float celsius;
    puts("Fahrenheit\tCelsius\n");
    for(temp=32; temp<=132; temp++)
  {
      celsius = (5.0/9.0)*(temp-32);
      printf("%d\t\t%6.2f\n",temp, celsius);
  }
}
```

Two instructions are performed in each repetition of the loop. The value of the control variable determines both the number of repetitions and the values to be converted to celsius. Compare that program with the following one:

```
main()
{
    int temp, repeat;
  float celsius;
    puts("Fahrenheit\tCelsius\n");
    temp=10;
    for(repeat=1; repeat<=10;repeat++)
  {
```

NOTE

The printf() function formats and aligns the displayed values in columns. The two tab characters (\t\t) align the celsius temperatures with the column heading. The format specifier (%6.2) displays the temperatures with two decimal places, six characters wide.

```
        celsius = (5.0/9.0)*(temp-32);
                printf("%d\t\t%6.2f\n",temp, celsius);
                temp+=10;
        }
    }
```

Here the index variable only controls the number of repetitions. The temperatures to convert are based on the variable named `temp`, which is increased by 10 with each repetition—from 10 to 20, to 30, and so on up to 100.

Using Variables

If you do not know when you write the program how many repetitions will be needed, you can still use the `for` loop if you'll know the number when you run the program. You can input a value into a variable and use it in the condition. For example, this program asks the user to enter a range of temperatures to convert—in effect, the number of times they want the program to repeat:

```
main()
{
    int temp, start, end;
    float celsius;
        printf("Enter the starting temperature: ");
        scanf("%d",&start);
        printf("Enter the ending temperature: ");
        scanf("%d",&end);
        puts("Fahrenheit\tCelsius\n");
        for(temp=start; temp<=end; temp++)
    {
    celsius = (5.0/9.0)*(temp-32);
            printf("%d\t\t%6.2f\n",temp, celsius);
    }
    }
```

Here, you enter the starting and ending values that you want to convert. The variables are used in the `for` parameter to set the initial value of the index variable and to test for the condition. The loop stops when the value of `temp` is incremented past the ending variable. So if you enter 20 and 43, the program converts the temperatures from 20°F to 43°F into celsius, then stops—24 loops.

Nested Loops

When one `for` command is performed within another, they are said to be nested. The inside loop is completely repeated for each repetition of the outside loop. Picture nested `for` loops as being two-dimensional and single `for` loops as one-dimensional.

As an example, look at the following program:

```
main()
{
int row, column;
for(row=1;  row <=10;row++)
   {
        for(column=1;  column<=10;column++)
        printf("*");
      putchar('\n');   /*outside of second loop, inside first*/
   }
}
```

The program displays 10 rows of 10 asterisks. It uses two integer variables, `row` and `column`. The outer loop increments the value of `row` from 1 to 10. With each repetition of the loop, however, the inner loop is performed 10 times, incrementing `column` and displaying a row of ten asterisks. (Notice that the variable names help to make the logic clear.) Figure 9.3 shows this nesting. The inner loop is

```
for(column=1;  column<=10;column++)
printf("*");
```

So in total, 100 asterisks are displayed—10 inner loops (column positions) for each of 10 outer loops (rows). The values of the variables with each repetition are shown in Figure 9.4.

Notice where the instruction `putchar('\n');` is located. It is outside the inner loop, but within the braces of the outer loop. It is performed ten times, once for each outer loop, inserting a line feed after each row.

Listing 9.1 illustrates another example of nested loops. It performs ten outer and ten inner loops to create a multiplication table. Instead of merely displaying an asterisk, it displays the value of row multiplied by

Figure 9.3

Inner and outer loops.

```
main()
{
int row, column;
for(row=1; row <= 10;row++)                          Outer loop
  {
                                                     Inner loop
      for(column=1; column <= 10;column++)
      printf("*");
  purchar('\n');   /*outside of second loop, inside first*/
  }
}
```

Figure 9.4

Values of variables with each repetition.

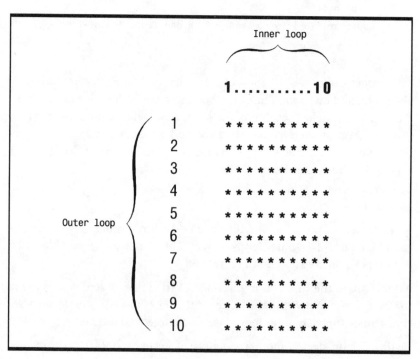

the value of `column`.

Listing 9.1: Multiplication Table Program

```
/*timestab.C/
main()
{
int row, column;
    puts("\t\tMy Handy Multiplication Table\n\n");
    for(row=1; row <=10;row++)
    {
        for(column=1; column<=10;column++)
        printf("%6d", row*column);
        putchar('\n');
    }
}
```

The output from timestab.c is shown in Figure 9.5.

Finally, consider this program:

```
main()
{
int row, column;
```

```
                My Handy Multiplication Table


    1     2     3     4     5     6     7     8     9    10

    2     4     6     8    10    12    14    16    18    20

    3     6     9    12    15    18    21    24    27    30

    4     8    12    16    20    24    28    32    36    40

    5    10    15    20    25    30    35    40    45    50

    6    12    18    24    30    36    42    48    54    60

    7    14    21    28    35    42    49    56    63    70

    8    16    24    32    40    48    56    64    72    80

    9    18    27    36    45    54    63    72    81    90

   10    20    30    40    50    60    70    80    90   100
```

Figure 9.5

Output from the multiplication table program.

```
for(row=1; row <=10;row++)
{
    for(column=1; column<=row;column++)
    printf("*");
    putchar('\n');
}
}
```

It displays the series of asterisks shown in Figure 9.6.

Figure 9.6
Output where repetition of inner loop is controlled by outer loop's value.

```
*
**
***
****
*****
******
*******
********
*********
**********
```

Each row of asterisks is a different length. Instead of the inner loop always repeating the same number of times, the number increases with each repetition of the outer loop—one asterisk on the first line, two asterisks on the second line, three on the third line, and so on. The number of repetitions of the column is the same number as the row. We do this by using the variable row in the condition of the inner loop.

With the first repetition of the outer loop, the inner loop is performed once, displaying one asterisk. With the second repetition of the outer loop, the inner loop is performed twice, displaying two asterisks. This process is repeated to create the pattern of asterisks.

Be cautious when writing programs that have two or more levels of for statements. A program that repeats 100 outer and 100 inner loops actually performs 10,000 repetitions!

Using the do...while Loop

Use a do...while loop when you do not know the exact number of repetitions but you do know you want to perform the loop at least once. The structure of the command is illustrated in Figure 9.7.

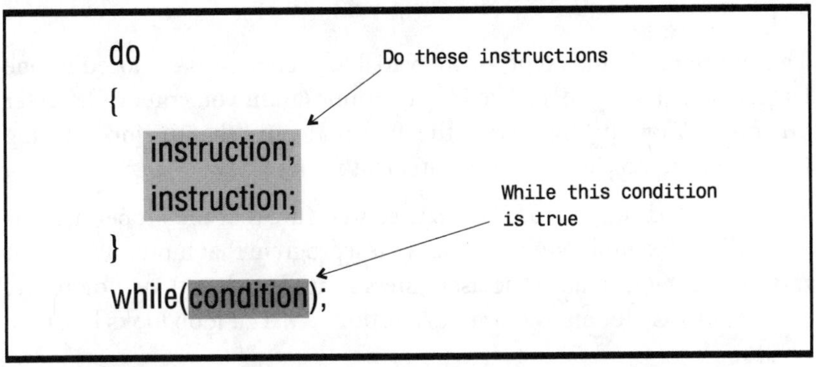

Figure 9.7
The structure of a do...while loop.

The instructions in the braces are performed repeatedly as long as the condition in the while statement is true. Because the condition isn't tested until the end of the loop, the loop will be repeated at least once—even if the condition is false when the loop first begins.

With the do...while loop, you have to make certain that the loop will come to an end. If the condition never becomes false, the loop will continue until you reset your computer or press the Ctrl+Break combination.

The do...while structure is often used to repeat a program until the user decides there is no more input:

```
main()
{
int temp;
float celsius;
char repeat;
 do
 {
printf("Input a temperature :");
scanf("%d", &temp);
```

```
celsius = (5.0/9.0)*(temp-32);
printf("%d degrees F is %6.2f degrees celsius\n",temp,
celsius);
printf("Do you have another temperature?");
repeat=getchar();
putchar('\n');
}
while (repeat== 'y' || repeat=='Y');
}
```

 NOTE

To avoid conflicts with the scanf() input, use a getch() or getche() command in place of the getchar() function, or use the fflush(stdin) command to empty the buffer. See Chapter 8 for additional information.

This entire program, excpt for the variable declarations enclosed in one large do...while block. The loop continues until you enter a character other than Y or y in response to the prompt. Notice that the input asking if you want to repeat is the last statement in the block.

The do...while structure is also used to insure that the proper input is entered. For example, suppose you write a program that inputs a discount rate in decimal format. If the user enters a rate less than 0, or 1 or above, you want to ask for another input. The do...while loop looks like this:

```
do
{
    printf("Please enter the discount: ");
    scanf("%f", &discount);
}
while(discount<0 || discount >=1);
```

The while condition uses the logical OR operator to test whether the value entered is outside of the range. The loop will repeat as long as the user enters an invalid number.

The routine is perfectly sound as long as the user eventually gets the idea and enters a correct number. If you're dealing with someone who doesn't understand what a decimal number is, however, the loop could go on forever. One solution is to add a counter to the algorithm, like this:

```
main()
{
    int count;
    float discount;
    count=0;
    do
```

```
   {
      printf("Please enter the discount: ");
      scanf("%f", &discount);
      count++;
   }
      while((discount<=0 || discount >=1) && count <20);
      if (count==20) puts("Stupid");
}
```

The user now has 20 tries to get it correct! The variable count is incremented with each invalid entry.

To perform just one instruction in a do...while loop, leave out the braces. This program, for example, lets you enter characters until you press the Y key:

```
main()
{
int a;
      do
            a = getchar();
      while(a!='y' && a!='Y');
}
```

Nested Do Loops

You can nest do...while loops to provide two levels of repetition. You can use an outer loop to repeat the entire program until the user decides otherwise, and inner loops to check for the proper input, as shown in Figure 9.8 The inner loop is used to enter a number between 0 and 100. When a valid entry is made, the loop ends and the remaining instructions in the outer loop are performed. The outer loop is repeated as long as this condition is true:

```
while (repeat== 'y' || repeat=='Y');
```

When you enter any other character than y or Y, the outer loop, and thus the program, ends.

Figure 9.8

Nested do...while loops

```
/* nest_do.c */
main()
{
char repeat;
int temp;
float celsius;
do
{
do
{
printf("Input a valid temperature:");
scanf("%d", &temp);
}
while (temp<0 II temp > 100);
celsius = (5.0/9.0)*(temp-32);
printf("%d degree F is %6.2f degree celsius\n", temp, celsius);
printf("Do you have another temperature?");
repeat= gerchar();
putchar('\n');
}
while (repeat=='y' II repeat=='y');
}
```

Outer loop repeats the entire program

Inner loop checks for proper input

Using the while Loop

Use a while loop when you do not know the number of repetitions and you may not want to perform the loop at all. The structure is:

```
while(condition)
```

```
   instruction;
```

An illustration of this syntax appears in Figure 9.9. For multiple instructions, use this format:

```
while (condition)
  {
   instructions
  }
```

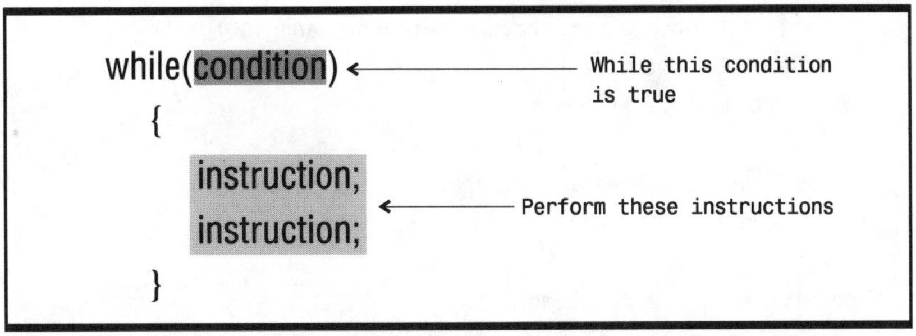

Figure 9.9
The structure of the while loop.

As in the do loop, the instructions will be performed as long as the while condition is true. But unlike the do structure, the condition is tested before the loop is performed even the first time. If the condition is false, the loop will not be performed even once.

To insure proper input, place the first input command outside the loop. You can then continue asking for input as long as the value is invalid, like this:

```
printf("Please enter the discount: ");
scanf("%f", &discount);
while(discount<0 || discount >=1)
    {
        printf("You got it wrong ");
        scanf("%f", &discount);
    }
```

Combining Loop Types

You can nest any combination of while, for, and do...while loops if the program logic requires it. The following program, for instance, nests a `while` loop within a `for` repetition to convert 10 temperatures, between 0 and 100, input from the keyboard:

```
/*mixed.C*/
main()
{
  int temp, count;
  float celsius;
  for(count=1; count<=10; count++)
     {
     printf("Enter a temperature between 1 and 100: ");
     scanf("%d",&temp);
  while (temp<0 || temp > 100)
  {
          printf("Invalid temperature, try again: ");
        scanf("%d", &temp);
  }
  celsius = (5.0/9.0)*(temp-32);
  printf("%d fahrenheit is %6.2f celsius\n",temp, celsius);
  }
}
```

The outer `for` loop will only be repeated 10 times. The inner loop will be repeated as long as you enter an invalid entry.

Program Design

Loops add yet another level of sophistication to program design. You have to study and test your algorithm carefully to insure that it works correctly.

The first step is to decide which structure to use—`for`, `do...while`, or `while`. Start by asking yourself:

- Do I know how many times I want the loop to repeat, or will I know it when the program runs?

If the answer is Yes, use a `for` loop. If the answer is No, ask yourself a second question:

- Do I want to perform the loop at least once?

If the answer is Yes, use the `do...while` loop. If the answer is No, use the `while` loop.

For example, suppose you want to compute the average of a series of numbers. Since you do not know how many numbers are in the series, you must use a `do...while` or `while` loop rather than the `for` loop. You might want to allow the user to abort the program after starting it, without performing the loop even one time. So you'll use a `while` loop.

But how do you stop the repetition? The user needs some way to tell the program they are done entering numbers and wish to stop. One way is to ask whether the user has an entry with each repetition, but that will require two entries with each loop—a number to be added and a Y or y to repeat.

A better way is to use an input value that will trigger the end of the routine, as shown in Listing 9.2. This program stops when a negative number is input. The first value is input before the loop, so you can stop the program immediately by entering a negative number as the first value. For each nonnegative number, it increments a counter and accumulates a total. Notice that the subsequent numbers are input just before the end of the loop, immediately before the `while` condition is tested at the start of the next repetition.

Notice the condition

```
If(count>0)
```

before the average is calculated. This is to prevent a division by zero, which would cause a runtime error on most computer systems.

Listing 9.2: A Program to Calculate Averages

```
/*average.C*/
main()
{
 float number, total;
 int count;
 total =0.0;
 count=0;
 printf("Enter a number, negative to end: ");
 scanf("%f",&number);
 while(number>=0)
 {
  count++;
  total+=number;
```

```
            printf("Enter a number, negative to end:");
            scanf("%f",&number);
        }
        If(count>0)
            {
            number=total/count;
        printf("Total=%.2f  Count=%d  Average=%.2f",number, count,
        total);
            }
    }
```

Now suppose you wrote the program getting all of the input within the loop, like this:

```
    while(a>=0)
    {
    scanf("%f",&a);
    count++;
    total+=a;
    }
```

When you input the negative number to stop the loop, it is incorrectly counted as an entry and added to the total before the while condition is tested again.

If you are using nested loops, you have to be very careful with counters or accumulators. For instance, suppose you decide to repeat the average program by simply enclosing it in another level of do...while, as in Listing 9.3. This program will not work correctly, because of the placement of the instructions:

```
    total =0;
    count=0;
```

Listing 9.3: Incorrect Placement of Assignment Operations

```
    /*ave_bad.C*/
    main()
    {
    char repeat;
    float number, total;
    int count;
    total =0.0;
```

```
count=0;
do
{
  printf("Enter a number, negative to end: ");
  scanf("%f",&number);
  while(number>=0)
    {
    count++;
    total+=number;
    printf("Enter a number, negative to end:");
    scanf("%f",&number);
    }
    If(count>0)
    {
  number=total/count;
  printf("Total=%.2f Count=%d Average=%.2f",number, count,
total);
  printf("Do you have another series of numbers?");
  repeat=getchar();
  putchar('\n');
    }
}
while (repeat== 'y' || repeat=='Y');
}
```

Because the assignment operations are outside the main loop, they are only performed once, when the program first starts. Each time the main loop is repeated for a new series of numbers, the counters and accumulators will retain their values. The result will be a cumulative average of all of the numbers entered. The instructions should appear within the outer loop, like this:

```
do
{
total =0;
count=0;
```

This will reset the counter and accumulator for each series of inputs. Notice that the program nests a while loop within a do...while loop.

Using Flags

A *flag* is an algorithm that informs the program that a certain condition has occurred—just as an actual flag on the moon signifies that astronauts have landed there. You assign a flag variable at the start of the program, or in an outer loop, and then later assign it another value to signify that some action has occurred or some value has been reached.

For example, the temperature conversion program uses a `do...while` loop to input values:

```
do
{
printf("Input a valid temperature :");
scanf("%d", &temp);
}
```

The same prompt appears with each repetition—for the first input and if you enter an invalid entry. Wouldn't it be nice to display a different message telling the user that they've entered an incorrect number? A program that does just that is shown in Listing 9.4.

Listing 9.4: Program Using a Flag Variable to Display Alternate Messages

```
/*flag.C*/
main()
{
 int temp;
 float celsius;
 char repeat;
 char flag;
 do
 {
   flag='n';
   do
   {
     if (flag=='n')
     printf("Input a valid temperature :");
     else
     printf("Input a valid temperature, stupid :");
     scanf("%d", &temp);
```

```
        flag='y';
    }
  while  (temp<0 || temp > 100);
  celsius = (5.0/9.0)*(temp-32);
  printf("%d degrees F is %6.2f degrees celsius\n",temp, celsius);
 printf("Do you have another temperature?");
  repeat=getchar();
  putchar('\n');
  }
  while (repeat== 'y' || repeat=='Y');
 }
```

A flag variable, conveniently called `flag`, is set to 'n' at the start of each outer loop. When the inner loop starts, it tests the value of the flag and displays one message if the value is 'n', or a second message if the value is anything else.

When the loop is first performed, the value is 'n' and the first message is displayed. When the user inputs a number, the flag variable is changed to 'y'. If the user's input was invalid, however, the inner loop would be repeated again. This time the condition (`flag=='n'`) is false so the second message is displayed.

Once the user enters a valid number, the temperature is converted, and the outer loop is repeated. The outer loop resets the value of the flag variable, so the user is given a new chance to enter a valid entry. As with the counter and accumulator, the flag is reset each time in the outer loop.

You can use any variable name for the flag variable, and any data type, although either a `char` or an `int` type are recommended. The flag values are also entirely up to you. The sample program used *n* to represent a valid entry, *y* for an invalid entry. You can pick any value that suits your fancy.

Using the break Statement

While the flag method does the job, it adds overhead to the program—another variable, several assignment lines, and an `if...else` structure. You can avoid this overhead, and accomplish the same job, by restructuring the program to use `while` loops, as shown in listing 9.5.

Listing 9.5: Using while Loops and a break Statement

```c
/*breaks.C*/
main()
{
int temp;
float celsius;
printf("Input a temperature or enter 555 to stop :");
scanf("%d", &temp);
while (temp != 555)
{
    while ((temp<0 || temp > 100) && temp != 555)
     {
     printf("Invalid temperature, try again: ");
     scanf("%d", &temp);
     }
    if (temp==555)
          break;
celsius = (5.0/9.0)*(temp-32);
printf("%d degrees F is %6.2f degrees celsius\n",temp,
celsius);
printf("Input a temperature enter 555 to stop :");
scanf("%d", &temp);
}
}
```

This program also prints two messages—one for a valid entry, and a second message on the repetition after an invalid input. Notice that this program does not ask if you have another temperature after each repetition. Instead, it ends when you type the value 555.

The entry condition considers a valid response to be a number between 0 and 100, or the number 555. The entry 555 immediately ends the program because of the instruction

```c
if (temp==555)
  break;
```

The **break** command ends the loop in which it is placed, just as if the **while** condition, or the condition in a **for** loop, became false.

All of the temperature conversion programs shown in this chapter are "correct." They each just use a different approach, or algorithm, to perform the same task. Asking the user if they have another entry doesn't require them to remember to enter a negative or special number to end the program, but it does require an additional keystroke with each repetition. Using a special number, such as 555, saves these keystrokes. The disadvantage is that you cannot use the same number as a valid response. For instance, if any negative number ends the program, you could not convert a temperature below zero.

The test of whether a program is "correct" or not is whether it runs without error, and continues running as long as you want it to.

Questions

1. What criteria do you use to select a `for`, `do`, or `while` loop?
2. What are the functions performed in a `for` parameter?
3. What stops a `for` loop?
4. What is a nested loop?
5. How do you use a flag?
6. What is the purpose of the `break` command?

Exercises

1. Edit the program shown in Listing 8.10 (Chapter 8) so that it repeats until the user has no additional input.
2. Write a program that displays a 6 percent sales tax table for sales from $1 to $50, in this format:

Cost	Shipping	Total
1	$ .06	$1.06
2	$ .12	$1.12

3. Write a program that inputs ten numbers between 0 and 25.

4. Write a program that displays this graphic:

```
* * * * *
* * * *
* * *
* *
*
* *
* * *
* * * *
* * * * *
```

5. Explain what is wrong with this program:

```c
main()
{
float row, column;
    puts("\t\tMy Handy Multiplication Table\n\n");
    for(row=1; row <=10;row++)
    {
        for(column=1; column<=10;column+)
        printf("%d", row*column);
    }
        putchar('\n');
    }
```

Arrays and Strings

· ·

The variables you've learned about so far can store only one value at a time. If you want to average 31 temperatures, for example, you can enter 31 different values in a variable one at a time, and total them using an accumulator. When you enter the second value, however, the first is lost; when you enter the third, the second is lost, and so forth. When you are done you'll have the total and average, but the original numbers will be lost.

If you wanted to enter the 31 values and save them for use later in the program, you'd need 31 different variables and 31 different input instructions.

In this chapter, you'll learn how to collect values in a special variable called an *array*. You will also learn more about working with string variables.

Arrays

Picture a group of people waiting in line at the movie theater. The only thing they have in common is that they are in the same line. The fact that a person is first in line doesn't tell us anything else about them—it doesn't mean that they are smarter, taller, or richer than the other people in line.

But while these persons are separate individuals, in no particular order, they are in the same collection. Because they are in a collection, they can be manipulated as a group. If the usher asks the line to shift to the left, to avoid blocking the popcorn stand, the line shifts over as a unit.

An array operates in the same way as the line. An array is a collection of values that can be dealt with as a group. Each element, or value in the array, is a separate variable and can be treated by itself. But because they are collected into an array, they can also be treated as a group. And just as the position of a ticket-holder in a line implies no other information about that person, the position of an array element has nothing to do with the value it holds.

You have already created and used some arrays in the form of strings. A string is really an array of individual characters. You've worked with arrays as groups by displaying strings with the `puts()` command. But you can also deal with each character individually.

You work with arrays in steps. First, you declare the array as a variable. Second, you enter values into the array. Finally, you can use the array to perform program logic.

Declaring an Array

You declare an array by designating the type of values it will store and the maximum number of elements, using the syntax shown in Figure 10.1. To create an array of 31 integer numbers, for example, use the declaration

```
int temps[31]
```

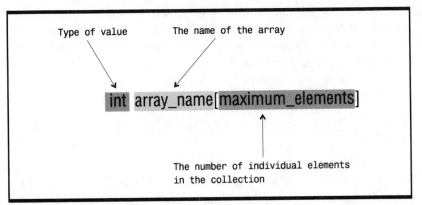

Figure 10.1
The syntax of an array declaration.

Note the use of square brackets, rather than parentheses or braces. As with any other variable type, you declare an array before `main()` to make it external (available to all functions), or inside `main()` or another function to make it automatic.

Declaring an array also creates the individual array elements, as shown in Figure 10.2. The first element of `temps` is referred to as `temps[0]`, the second element is `temps[1]`, the third element is `temps[2]`, and so on. Notice that the elements are numbered starting with 0, so the five-element array shown in the figure has elements numbered 0 to 4. There is no element `temps[5]`. The number in the brackets is called the `subscript`, and you refer to the elements as "temps sub 0," "temps sub 1," and so on.

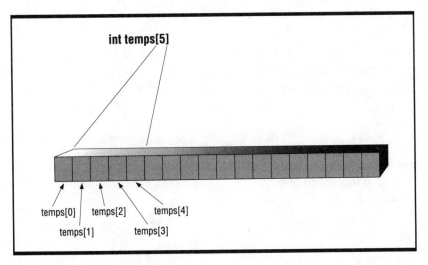

Figure 10.2
Declaring an array declares individual elements.

You cannot use a subscript number higher than one less than the declared number of elements. If you declare a 10-element array, you must make sure you never use a subscript number higher than 9. Your compiler won't pick up this potential problem during the compilation process. Instead, you'll either receive a runtime error when you execute the program, or get strange results.

When you declare a string, you are actually declaring an array of char variables:

```
char name[5];
```

But while you can input and output an entire array as a single unit, using gets() and puts(), with other data types you must perform these operations on array elements individually.

Entering Values into an Array

Once you declare an array, you can enter information into it. You can assign the array initial values when you declare it:

```
int temps[5] = {45, 56, 12, 98, 12};
```

This creates five elements with these values:

temps[0]	45
temps[1]	56
temps[2]	12
temps[3]	98
temps[4]	12

To initialize an array like this, enter the instruction before main(), or within main() or another function as a static variable:

```
int temps[5] = {45, 56, 12, 98, 12};
main()
{
static float prices[3] = {23.45, 34.56, 12.34};
```

You can also enter values by assignment, within main() or another function, as in this statement:

```
temps[0]=45;
```

If you want to assign values to every element, however, it is faster to use a loop. If you know the number of elements you want to assign, use a `for` loop:

```
main()
{
int temps[31];
int index;
for(index=0; index <31; index++)
    {
    printf("Enter temperature #%d: ", index);
    scanf("%d",&temps[index]);
    }
}
```

The variable `index` is used here to determine the number of repetitions. In this case, the loop is repeated 31 times, once for each element in the array. Each time the loop repeats, you'll see the prompt

```
Enter temperature #
```

followed by the subscript number of the element to be input.

Notice that the 31 repetitions are performed by incrementing the variable from 0 to 30, not from 1 to 31. This way, the variable `index` can also be used as the subscript number to designate the array elements, which are numbered from 0 to 30. When `index` has a value of 0, the element `temps[index]` is actually `temps[0]`. Thus, inputting a value into `temps[index]` using the `scanf()` function will insert a value into the first array element, `temps[0]`. As the `for` loop is repeated, the value of `index` is incremented, and with each repetition, the `scanf()` function inputs a value into another array element. Table 10.1 illustrates the process.

It is important that you distinguish between the value of the index variable, inside the brackets, and the value of the array element itself. The index variable only designates the position of the element in the array. It has no relation to the value of the element itself. Look at Figure 10.3. The subscript of the element shown is 0. The variable itself, `temps[0]`, has a value of 75.

Like the waiting line at the movie theater, the value of the subscript is not related to the value of the variable. The value of the next variable, `temps[1]`, can be higher, lower, or the same as the value of `temps[0]`.

Table 10.1

Using a Repetition to Increment the Array Subscript

Repetition	Value of Index	Element Being Input
1	0	temps(0)
2	1	temps(1)
3	2	temps(2)
4	3	temps(3)
5	4	temps(4)
6	5	temps(5)
.	.	.
.	.	.
.	.	.
26	25	temps(25)
27	26	temps(26)
28	27	temps(27)
29	28	temps(28)
30	29	temps(29)
31	30	temps(30)

Figure 10.3

Distinguish between the value of the subscript and the array element.

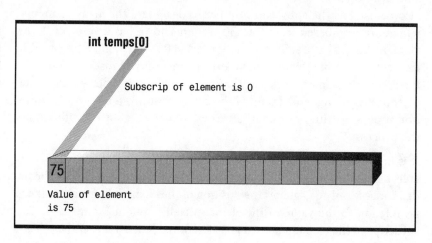

int temps[0]

Subscrip of element is 0

75

Value of element is 75

As with any variable, if you do not assign a value to an array element, it will contain some unknown value. You can quickly initialize an integer array to zero using this loop:

```
for(index=0; index <31; index++)
    temps[index]=0;
```

Using an array, you can input any number of elements by just changing the declaration and the loop condition.

Manipulating Arrays

You can use an array element in any instruction where you would use a variable—in input or output commands or in expressions. You always refer to the individual element by its subscript number.

The values stored in an array will be accessible whenever needed in the program. The program in Listing 10.1, for instance, uses an array in two different tasks. The values of the array elements are averaged, and then the array is used again to print a conversion chart. Each time, the array is accessed in a for loop that increments the index variable from 0 to the last array element.

Listing 10.1: Using an Array for Two Tasks

```
/*array1.c*/
main()
{
    int temps[31];
    int index, total;
    float average, celsius;
    total=0.0;
    /*load the array with values */
    for(index=0; index < 31; index++)
    {
        printf("Enter temperature #%d:", index);
        scanf("%d",&temps[index]);
    }

    /* read the values to average */
    for(index=0; index < 31; index++)
```

```
            total+=temps[index];
        average=total/31.0;
        printf("average is: %f\n\n", average);
        puts("Fahrenheit\tCelsius\n");

        /* read the values to convert */
        for(index=0; index < 31; index++)
        {
                celsius = (5.0/9.0)*(temps[index]-32);
                printf("%d\t\t%6.2f\n",temps[index], celsius);
        }
    }
```

The program assumes, however, that you will enter temperatures into all 31 array elements. If you were recording temperatures for November or February, the routine would not display accurate results. You don't actually have to use all of the array elements, as long as you make allowances in the program logic.

The program in Listing 10.2 can be used for any number of temperatures, up to 31. The `for` loops of the previous program have been replaced with `do...while` loops, and the instruction

```
    index=0;
```

is used before each loop to initialize the repetition to start with the first array element. A separate instruction like this isn't needed with a `for` loop, because the value is initialized in the loop parameter.

Listing 10.2: Using a do...while Loop to Load an Array

```
/*array2.c*/
main()
{
    int temps[31];
    int index, total;
    float average, celsius, count;
    total=0.0;
    /*load the array with values */
    index=0;
    do
    {
```

```
        printf("Enter temperature #%d -- 555 to quit:", index);
        scanf("%d",&temps[index]);
        index++;
    }
    while(index< 31 && temps[index-1] != 555);
    /*average the array*/
    index=0;
    do
    {
        total+=temps[index];
        index++;
    }
    while(index< 31 && temps[index] != 555);
    count=index;
    average=total/count;
    printf("average is: %f\n\n", average);
    puts("Fahrenheit\tCelsius\n");

    /* convert the values*/
    index=0;
    do
    {
        celsius = (5.0/9.0)*(temps[index]-32);
        printf("%d\t\t%6.2f\n",temps[index], celsius);
        index++;
    }
    while(index< 31 && temps[index] != 555);
}
```

The values are input until all 31 array elements have been entered or until you enter the flag value 555, using this condition:

```
while(index< 31 && temps[index-1] != 555);
```

Notice that one is subtracted from the variable index because the variable is incremented after the number is entered. If you do not enter all 31 elements, the number 555 that you enter to end the repetition is inserted into the array element after the last actual temperature.

The number 555 is used as a flag. The program logic will watch for that value to determine whether you stopped entering temperatures before the end of the array.

When the array is averaged, a `do...while` loop totals all of the values up to the end of the array or until it reaches the value 555. While the variable `index` contains the number of temperatures, it must be an integer to be used as an array subscript. To obtain a `float` value from a division operation, however, the values divided must be `floats`. So the program defines a `float` variable called `count` and assigns it the number of temperatures before using it to perform the math:

```
count=index;
average=total/count;
```

Because the last line of the loop increments the `index` variable, the value of `index` will actually be one more than the last array element that contains a valid temperature. If you enter values into array elements 0 through 4, for example, the value of `index` will be 5. That value, however, also represents the number of elements you entered—0 through 4 is five elements—so it is used as the count to compute the average.

If you follow the logic of the program carefully, you might see a potential problem in the second and third `while` conditions. When you do enter all 31 temperatures (0 to 30), the value of `subscript` is incremented to 31, and used in the condition as `temps[31]`, one more than the maximum subscript allowed. You will not get an error, however, because of the order of conditions in this statement:

```
while(index< 31 && temps[index] != 555);
```

To speed program execution, when most compilers examine an AND expression, they automatically stop evaluating the expression after finding the first false condition (as shown in Figure 10.4). Since the AND operator means that every condition in the statement must be true, there is no need to look past the first false statement.

Figure 10.4

Shortcut condition evaluation.

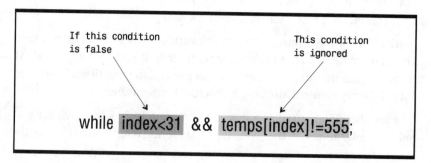

If this condition is false

This condition is ignored

```
while index<31 && temps[index]!=555;
```

After you enter all 31 array elements, the first condition in the expression (`index< 31`) will be false. When this occurs, the program doesn't even bother looking at the second condition, and thus never notices that its subscript is out of range.

You could easily test this by changing the order of the conditions to

```
while(temps[index] != 555 && index< 31);
```

If you then run the program and enter all 31 values, you would receive a runtime error because the computer would examine the array element with an out-of-range subscript.

There may be some compilers that do not use this shortcut. With these, you'll get a runtime error with the logic given. The solution is to declare the array with 32 elements but only use the first 31.

Examining an Array

By using repetition, you can scan the array elements, comparing the values in the array or searching for a specific value. Consider this routine:

```
/*highlow*/
high=temps[0];
low=temps[0];
index=1;
while(index< 31 && temps[index] != 555)
    {
    if(temps[index]>high)
        high=temps[index];
    if(temps[index]<low)
        low=temps[index];
    index++;
    }
printf("low is %d\n",low);
printf("high is %d\n",high);
}
```

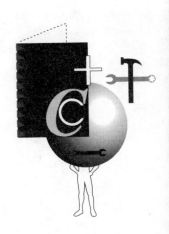

Assuming you've declared `low` and `high` as integer variables, this routine examines each element in the array to determine the lowest and highest values. The key is to assign the first array element initially to both the `high` and `low` variables. If you only looked at one element, it would naturally be both the highest and the lowest. This "seeds" the variables, which are then compared against the other array variables. If an array value is greater than the current value of `high`, then it becomes the new highest value. If it is less than the current value in `low`, it becomes the new lowest value. Figure 10.5 illustrates the first several cycles through the loop.

Figure 10.5
Variable values during the repetition.

Array Element	Value of Element	Value of High	Value of Low	Program Instruction Changing Value
temps[0]	65	65	65	high=temps[0] low=temps[0]
temps[1]	95	95	65	high=temps[1]
temps[2]	75	95	65	
temps[3]	34	95	34	low=temps[3]

Searching an Array

We often need to search an array for a specific value. This involves checking each element of the array to see if it is equal to a specific value. If you are just checking for any occurrence of the value, you can stop the search after the first matching value is found. If you have a thousand-element array, and you find a match in the first element, there is no need to continue searching the remaining 999 values.

Here is a routine to find a value in our sample temperature array:

```
/* found.c*/
printf("Enter the value to search for: ");
scanf("%d", &num);
index=0;
found=0;
while(!found && index< 31 && temps[index]!=555)
{
    if(temps[index]==num)
        found=1;
    else
        index++;
```

```
      }
    if(!found)
          puts("That number is not in the list");
    else
    printf("The number is in position %d\n", index);
```

The routine assumes you've declared a integer variable named `found`. The variable is used as a flag; it indicates that a match has been found, and so we can stop looking at the remaining array elements.

We use `found` as a unary operator. The expression

```
  while(!found)
```

means "while not found." This statement is true when `found` has a zero value. Since we assign `found` an initial value of 0 outside the loop, the condition is true for the first repetition, and the program examines the first array element (number 0) for a match.

When a match is located, the `if` condition assigns `found` the value of 1. This means that "while not found" is no longer true, and the loop ends. The final value of the variable `index` will contain the element number in which the match was located.

The final `if` condition prints an appropriate message depending on whether the match was found.

Notice that the `while` statement contains three conditions with AND logic operators. The loop will repeat as long as a match has not been found, the end of the array has not been reached, and the value 555 is not located.

Passing an Array

You can pass an entire array from one function to another, although C and C++ handle a passed array very differently than other types of variables. When you pass a variable other than an array, C makes a copy of the data and places it in a memory location associated with the receiving variable. There are two copies of the data, and changing the variable in the receiving function does not change the original variable.

When you pass an array, you are actually passing the address of the array. C does not make a copy of the entire array but merely assigns the same address area, and thus its data, to a second array name. Listing 10.3 shows how to pass an array as an argument. Notice that only the array name is used in the calling argument, without a subscript:

```
convert(temps)
```

Listing 10.3: Passing an Array

```
/*arr_pass.c*/
#define COUNT 31
main()
{
    int temps[COUNT];
    int index;
    float celsius;
    /*load the array with values */
    for(index=0; index < COUNT; index++)
    {
        printf("Enter temperature #%d:", index);
        scanf("%d",&temps[index]);
    }
    /* pass array to convert */
    convert(temps);
}


    /*convert function*/
    convert(heat)
    int heat[];
    {
        int index;
        float celsius;
        for(index=0; index <COUNT; index++)
        {
          celsius = (5.0/9.0)*(heat[index]-32);
          printf("%d\t\t%6.2f\n",heat[index], celsius);
        }
    }
```

Because you are actually passing the address of the array, you do not have to specify the number of elements in the receiving argument; just use empty brackets to indicate an array:

```
convert(heat)
int heat[];
```

Passing an array by its address rather than duplicating it saves memory, but it can have some side effects. Changing an array element in the receiving function will also change the value of the passed array. If the `convert()` function assigns new values to the `heat` array, the new values will also be applied to the `temps` array, as illustrated in Figure 10.6. In this program, the function `convert()` adds 1 to every element of the `heat` array. The `heat` array occupies the same memory address as the `temps` array, so every element in `temps` is also incremented.

Figure 10.6

Changing the value of an array
in a function.

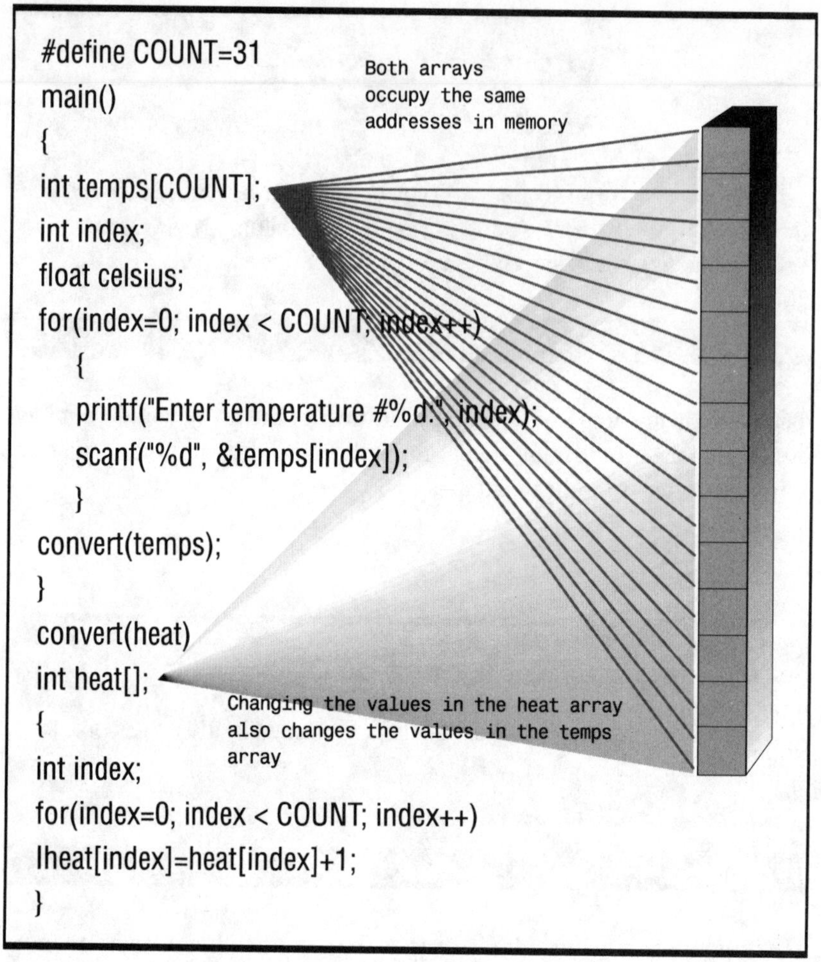

```
#define COUNT=31
main()
{
int temps[COUNT];
int index;
float celsius;
for(index=0; index < COUNT; index++)
    {
    printf("Enter temperature #%d:", index);
    scanf("%d", &temps[index]);
    }
convert(temps);
}
convert(heat)
int heat[];
{
int index;
for(index=0; index < COUNT; index++)
Iheat[index]=heat[index]+1;
}
```

Both arrays
occupy the same
addresses in memory

Changing the values in the heat array
also changes the values in the temps
array

An Array Exercise

As an example of using arrays, suppose you run the convention office in a hotel. You have ten meeting rooms, each with a specific legal capacity of persons. You would like a program that performs these three functions:

- Displays a chart showing the number and maximum occupancy of each room.
- Displays the occupancy limit of a specific room.

- Displays a list of rooms that have a specific maximum occupancy.

There are several ways to construct such a program. You can use one 20-element array that contains both the room number and occupancy amounts, like this:

```
int room[20]={102, 12, 107,43.....
```

The array is initialized with each room number followed by its occupancy. Room 102 can hold 12 persons, room 107 can hold 43 persons, and so on. If you locate the room number in the array, you know that its occupancy limit is stored in the next element.

Another option is to use a double-dimension array. We'll take a look at double-dimension arrays later when we discuss strings.

A third alternative is to use two parallel arrays. Parallel arrays are two independent arrays that can be related. You can visualize parallel arrays as two lines of graduates at a commencement exercise. As the two lines approach the entrance to the auditorium, individuals from each line are placed side-by-side. The first person in the right line will walk in with the first person in the left line, and so on. If you position the graduates in the lines randomly, there is no relation between those in the left line and those in the right line. But you can match the lines so that you have specific pairs combined when the lines meet.

When you use parallel arrays, you create two independent arrays whose orders of elements are coordinated. The first item in one array is somehow related to the first item in the other array, and so on.

The program shown in Listing 10.4 illustrates a solution to our room-management problem using parallel arrays. The room array contains a list of the ten room numbers that you have available. The max array contains the occupancy limits of the ten rooms. If we find the room number in element 5 of the room array, we know that its occupancy limit is in element 5 of the max array.

Listing 10.4: Using Two Parallel Arrays

```
/*rooms.c*/
int room[10]={102, 107, 109, 112,115,116,123,125,127,130};
int max[10]={12,43,23,12,20,15,16,23,12,15};
main()
{
```

```c
        int index, choice, num, rooms, flag, found;
        rooms=10;
        puts("1. Occupancy by room number\n");
        puts("2. Occupancy of specific room\n");
        puts("3. Find rooms with occupancy\n");
        printf("Enter choice 1 to 3: ");
        scanf("%d", &choice);
        if(choice==1)
        {
             for(index=0;index <rooms; index++)
             printf("Room %d  %d maximum\n",room[index],max[index]);
        }
        if(choice==2)
        {
             printf("Enter room number: ");
             scanf("%d", &num);
             index=1;
             found=0;
             while(!found && index<rooms)
                  if(room[index]==num)
                        found=1;
                  else
                        index++;

             if(!found)
                  puts("That room number is not for class use\n");
                else
        printf("Room %d holds %d persons\n", room[index],max[index]);
        }
        if(choice==3)
        {
            flag=0;
                printf("Enter the minimum number of persons: ");
              scanf("%d", &num);
              for(index=0; index<rooms; index++)
                 if(max[index]>=num)
                       {
                       flag=1;
        printf("Room %d holds %d persons\n",room[index],max[index]);
```

242   *Chapter 10: Arrays and Strings*

```
        }
     if(flag==0)
          puts("There are no rooms that large\n");
    }
  }
```

The program assigns the maximum array subscript to the variable `rooms`, and then displays a menu of options. Your choice determines which function is performed, in a series of three `if` statements. The program could have been written using a `switch` statement or nested `if...else` instructions instead.

The first `if` routine uses a `for` loop to print a table listing the room numbers and their occupancy limit. Only one subscript variable is needed, and it is used as the subscript for both the `room` and `max` arrays.

The second `if` routine inputs a room number and then searches the array for a match.

The third routine inputs an occupancy amount and lists all rooms that can serve that number. Rather than stopping when it locates the first match, it scans the entire array to print a table of all rooms that can serve the purpose. It uses the variable named `flag` to indicate when no rooms are located.

Strings

A string is an array of characters. When you declare a string, you give it a name and specify the maximum number of characters it can hold. The last array element, however, is reserved for the null terminator (\0), so you need to declare the array as one element larger than the maximum number of actual characters.

C and C++ let us input and output a character array as one entity—a string. But each character is really a separate array element, as shown in Figure 10.7. For instance, you can input a string and then display its individual characters, like this:

```
main()
{
char name[20];
int index;
```

Figure 10.7

Each character in a string is really a separate array element.

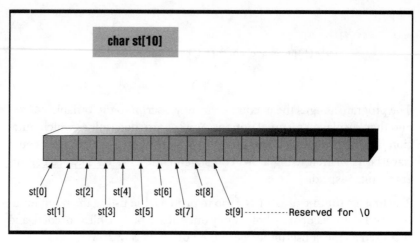

```
char st[10]
```

st[0] st[2] st[4] st[6] st[8]
   st[1] st[3] st[5] st[7] st[9]----------Reserved for \0

```
printf("Enter your name: ");
scanf("%s", name)
for(index=0, index<20;index++)
    printf("%c\n",name[index]);
}
```

If you do not enter all 20 characters, those after the null terminator will contain unknown values.

If C did not have a `gets()` function, you could also input a string by entering a series of characters and assigning them to the individual array elements, as shown in Listing 10.5.

Listing 10.5: Simulating the gets() Function

```
/*getstr.c*/
main()
{
    char name[10], letter;
    int index;
    index=0;
    puts("Enter a name, press Enter when done\n");
    do
    {
        letter=getchar();
        name[index]=letter;
        index++;
```

```
    }
    while(letter !='\r' && index<9);
    name[index]='\0';
    putchar('\n');
    puts(name);
}
```

Fortunately, C recognizes that strings are a different class of array by letting us input and output the array as a unit. Aside from that, C was not created with many other special functions for dealing with strings. But because strings are so useful in programming, most C and C++ compilers include special functions for working with strings. While you can perform the same functions by writing your own instructions, the built-in functions are more efficient. Table 10.2 lists some typical string functions found in C++ libraries.

Function	Description
strcat	Adds the character of one string to the end of another.
strchr	Returns the position of a specified character in the string.
strcmp	Compares two strings.
strcmpi	Compares two strings; not case sensitive.
strcpy	Copies one string, or string literal, to another.
strcspn	Returns the position of a character in the string from a specified character set.
strdup	Duplicates a string.
strlen	Calculates the string length.
strlwr	Converts a string to lowercase.
strncat	Appends specified characters from one string to another.
strncmp	Compares specified characters of two strings.
strcmpi	Compares two strings, not case sensitive.
strncpy	Copies specified characters from one string to another.
strnset	Changes specified characters in a string to another character.
strrev	Reverses the characters in a string.
strstr	Finds one string within another.
strupr	Converts a string to uppercase.

Table 10.2

String-Handling Functions

As an example, we'll look at some string-handling functions and see how you can perform them yourself.

Comparing Two Strings

In C and C++, you cannot directly compare the value of two strings in a condition like this:

```
if(string1==string2)
```

Most libraries, however, contain the strcmp() function, which returns a zero if two strings are equal, or a nonzero number if the strings are not the same. The syntax of strcmp() is shown in Figure 10.8 and used in this program section:

```
if(strcmp(name1,name2)==0)
      puts("The names are the same");
      else
      puts("The names are not the same");
```

Some compilers return a negative number if the first string is alphabetically "less than" the second, and a positive number if the first string is greater than the second.

If your compiler does not have a strcmp() command, you can write your own function that compares two strings element-by-element, like parallel arrays, stopping when you find a pair that do not match:

```
main()
{
```

Figure 10.8

The syntax of the strcmp() function.

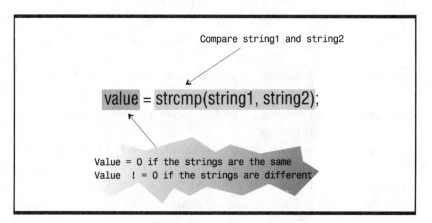

Compare string1 and string2

value = strcmp(string1, string2);

Value = 0 if the strings are the same
Value ! = 0 if the strings are different

```
int index, flag;
char name[10], name1[10];
gets(name);
gets(name1);
flag=0;
for(index=0;index<10;index++)
if(name[index]!=name1[index])
{
    flag=1;
    break;
}
if(flag==1)
puts("the strings are not the same");
else
puts("The strings are the same");
}
```

Determining String Length

The length of a string is not necessarily the same as the size of the array. For instance, you may declare a 20-element array called name but enter a name of less than 20 characters. Most C and C++ compilers use the strlen() function to determine the actual number of characters in the string, as shown here:

```
gets(name);
count=strlen(name);
printf("The string %s has %d characters", name, count);
```

The function will assign the number of characters in the input string (name in the example above) to an integer variable (count). To perform the same function manually, use a routine like this:

```
main()
{
int index;
char name[10];
gets(name);
for(index=0;index<10;index++)
{
if(name[index]=='\0') break;
```

```
        }
        printf("the length is %d", index);
        }
```

This routine searches the character array for the null terminator. The position of the terminator represents the number of characters in the string.

As an example of how to use the string-length function, here's a program that displays a string in reverse:

```
main()
{
char name[10];
int index, count;
gets(name);
count=strlen(name);
for(index=count;index>0;index--)
    putchar(name[index-1]);
putchar('\n');
}
```

It uses the length of the string as the starting index in a for loop that is decremented with each repetition. If the string is 5 characters long, the loop repeats 5 times, counting down from 5 to 1. Since the array elements are numbered from 4 to 0, the index number is decreased by one to result in the subscript number.

Assigning Strings

C does not allow you to assign characters to a string directly, as in this statement:

```
name="Sam";
```

Instead, use the strcpy() function found in most compilers. The syntax of the function is illustrated here:

```
strcpy(name,"Sam");
strcpy(name, name1);
```

In the first example, the characters *Sam* are assigned to the string called name. In the second example, the characters already assigned to the variable name1 are assigned to the variable called name.

To perform the same function yourself, you must assign characters to the individual elements of the array:

```
char name[]="Alan";
main()
{
char person[10];
int count, index;
count=strlen(name);
for(index=0;index<=count;index++)
     person[index]=name[index];
puts(person);
}
```

The routine assigns the characters in one array to the corresponding elements in another array.

Combining Strings

When you combine two strings, you add the characters of one string to the end of another string, moving the null terminator to the very end. The process is called *concatenation*. The K&R standard defines the `strcat()` function illustrated in Figure 10.9. The characters in the second parameter are added to the end of the first parameter.

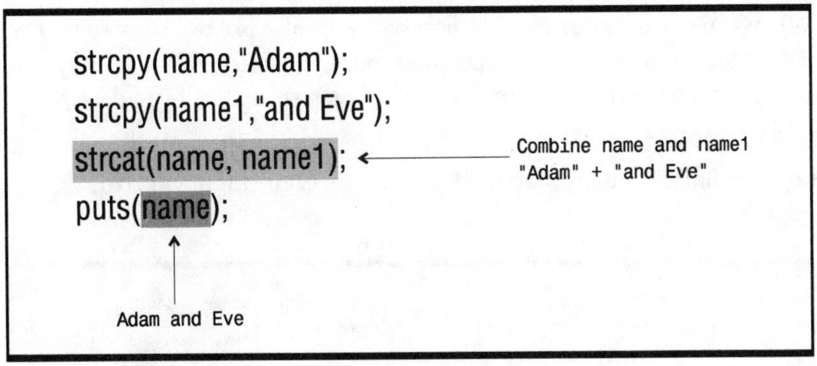

```
strcpy(name,"Adam");
strcpy(name1,"and Eve");
strcat(name, name1);  ←——  Combine name and name1
puts(name);                 "Adam" + "and Eve"

    Adam and Eve
```

Figure 10.9

The syntax of the strcat() function.

String Arrays

You can have an array of strings, just as you can have an array of any other data type. But an array of strings is really an array of arrays of characters. An array whose elements are arrays is called a two-dimensional array.

You can picture a two-dimensional array as a spreadsheet with rows and columns. You must define such an array with two subscripts—one specifies the number of rows in the spreadsheet; the other represents the number of columns. The following instruction declares an array of 10 rows and 20 columns, with 200 integer variables in all:

```
int table[10][20]
```

Visualize each element as an integer value in its own cell of the 10×20 spreadsheet. The element `table[0][0]` is in the top-left cell, and element `table[0][1]` is in the cell to its right.

When you declare an array of strings, you must also use two subscripts. The first subscript represents the maximum number of strings in the array; the second represents the maximum length of each string. So if you declare

```
char names[10][20];
```

you can have ten names up to 19 characters each (Figure 10.10).

Figure 10.10
Declaring a string array.

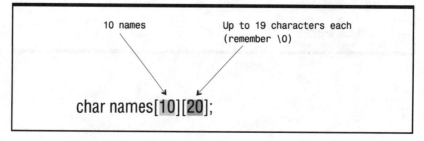

10 names   Up to 19 characters each
                        (remember \0)

char names[10][20];

If you had to enter strings as individual characters, you'd need nested loops. The outer loop would repeat 10 times, once for each string. The inner loop would repeat up to 19 times to input the characters of each string, as shown in Figure 10.11. The program inputs 10 names into an array, then uses a `for` loop to display all ten names.

Figure 10.11

Programming a string array.

```
/* sarray.c */                          Outer loop inputs 10 names
main()
{
char name[10][20], letter;
int index, index2;
for(index=0;index<10;index++)            Inner loop
{                                        inputs up to
index2=0;                                19 characters
puts("Enter a name, press Enter when done\n");   for each name
do
{
letter=getchar();
name[index][index2]=letter;
index2++;
}
while(letter !='\n' && index2<19);
name[index][index2]='\0';
putchar('\n');
}
for(index=0;index<10;index++)
puts(name[index]);
putchar('\n');
}
```

To assign a character to a string, you must use both subscripts:

```
name[index][index2]=letter;
```

The first subscript indicates which string within the array you want; the second subscript represents the position of the character within the string. For example, in Figure 10.12, element name[0][3] is the fourth character (*m*) in the first string (*Adam*) in the array of names. To display the entire string, only one subscript is needed to indicate the string itself:

```
puts(name[index]);
```

Figure 10.12

Strings and elements in a string array.

	name[0][0]	name[0][1]	name[0][2]	name[0][3]	name[0][4]
name[0]	**A**	**d**	**a**	**m**	**\0**

Fortunately, you can input entire strings as units, with only one loop, repeated once for each string in the array:

```
main()
{
char name[10][20];
int index;
for(index=0;index<10;index++)
gets(name[index]);
for(index=0;index<10;index++)
puts(name[index]);
}
```

Program Design

Since you must declare the maximum size of an array at the start of the program or function, this size is one of the first decisions you'll have to make. If you declare an array smaller than you'll actually need when you run the program, you'll get a runtime error or inconsistent results.

On the other hand, you should avoid declaring the array with some immense number in an attempt to "play it safe." Arrays, especially float and string arrays, are real memory hogs. As your programs grow larger and more complex, declaring huge arrays that you really don't need could lead to out-of-memory runtime errors.

Plan the size of the array carefully. Give yourself just enough allowance to make certain that the subscript number never exceeds the maximum element number.

Questions

1. What is an array?
2. Can an array store more than one type of variable?
3. How do you declare an array?
4. What is a two-dimensional array?
5. How do you declare an array?
6. What is the relationship between the value of the subscript and the value of the array element?
7. How do you compare two strings?
8. How do you assign a value to a string variable?

Exercises

1. Write a program that uses arrays to store the names, addresses, and telephone numbers of 20 persons. Store the names in first name, last name order.
2. Modify the program in Exercise 1 to input a name, and then search the arrays for the person's telephone number.
3. Explain what is wrong with this program:

```
main()
{
int temps(31);
int index, total;
for(index=0; index < 31; index++)
    {
    printf("Enter temperature #%d:", index);
    scanf("%d",&temps(index));
```

```
                          }
                high=temps(0);
                low=temps(0;
                index=1;
                while(index< 31)
                    {
                    if(temps(index)>high)
                        high=temps(index);
                    else
                    low=temps(index);
                    index++;
                    }
                printf("low is %d\n",low);
                printf("high is %d\n",high);
                }
```

Eleven

Structures and Pointers

• •

All of the variables you've used up to now have been of a single type: either character, string, integer, or `float`. Even an array, whether single or two-dimensional, can only store one type of variable. The variables have been simple, meaning that you can assign them a value by merely using their names in input or assignment statement.

In this chapter, you will learn about two classes of variables that are more multifaceted. A structure variable is a collection of other variables comprising different types. Pointers are variables which refer to the memory locations of other variables.

Structures and pointers provide a platform for developing more sophisticated applications.

Using Structures

A computer program usually represents some real-world situation in which information needs to be organized and processed systematically: an accounting system, an engineering problem, a student record system, or some other set of operations that can be performed through program algorithms.

In programs, we represent each piece of information in a variable, assigning it to a `float`, `int`, `char`, or string. But in real life, we often deal with objects that contain more than one type of information. For example, suppose you catalog your CD collection. You have a group of index cards, each card containing the name, description, cost, musical category, and index number of a CD in your storage rack (Figure 11.1).

Figure 11.1
Non-computerized record keeping.

C++ Notes

In C++, a structure can also be used to define a *class*. A class is a structure that contains member variables as well as functions. By defining the function within a class, you link it to the structure variables, as in this program segment:

```cpp
struct square {
    float   number;
    void assignnumber(double);
    float   squareit(void);


} amount;


void square::assignnumber(float num)
{
    number = num;
}


void square::squareit(void)
{
    float toreturn;
    toreturn = number*number;
    return (toreturn);
}


square.assignnumber(25.0);
cout << "The square of the number is " <<
square.squareit();
```

The :: symbol in the function definitions is called a *scoping* operator, and it associates the function with the class.

You could easily computerize the catalog by assigning each of these elements to a variable:

```
char name[20], description[40], category[12];
float cost;
int number;
```

But in the real world we don't deal with these five pieces of information individually, we store them as a group on a index card. While each bit of information on the card is different, together they represent one entity—one CD in the collection.

If you want a program to truly represent this real-world situation, you need some way of dealing with different types of data as a collection. Fortunately, C and C++ provide a way to collect different types of data together into one entity, a computer version of an index card, called a *structure*.

Defining a Structure

The first step in creating a related collection of variables is to define the structure. When you define a structure, you are really defining your own data type. You give the structure a name and tell the compiler the name and the type of each piece of data you want the structure to contain, as shown in Figure 11.2.

Figure 11.2
The elements of a structure.

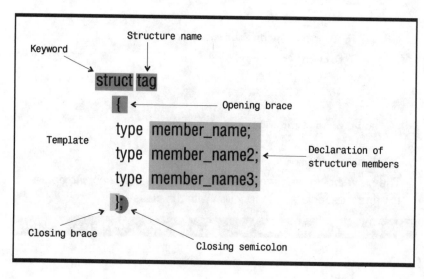

The definition must start with the keyword `struct`, followed by the name of the structure, called the *tag*. The pieces of data that make up the structure are called *structure members*, and they are placed in a group between opening and closing braces.

You declare structure members using the same syntax you use to declare variables. You must specify the data type of each member, and the size of any strings or arrays. Place semicolons at the end of each member declaration, and at the end of the structure.

The list of structure members is called the *template*. The structure doesn't actually declare any variables. Structure members are not themselves variables; they are components of one or more variables (called *structure variables*) that will be declared as belonging to the structure type. The template defines these components and tells the compiler how much memory to set aside for each structure variable.

You could define your CD collection using this structure:

```
struct CD
    {
    char name[20];
    char description[40];
    char category[12];
    float cost;
    int number;
    };
```

This creates a new data type called `CD`, which contains five pieces of information: three strings, a float, and an integer. The structure sets aside an area in memory 78 addresses wide (Figure 11.3).

Assigning a Structure Variable

Defining the structure doesn't give you access to the memory locations. Remember, before you can use any type of data, you need to declare a variable of the data type. You can't use a `float`, for instance, until you declare a `float` variable. Likewise, you can't use a structure until you declare a variable of the structure's type, using the syntax shown in Figure 11.4.

Figure 11.3

A structure sets aside memory
space for its members.

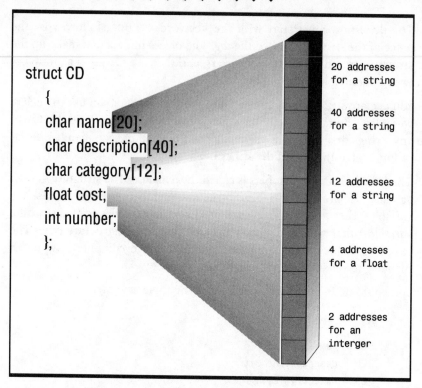

```
struct CD
    {
    char name[20];
    char description[40];
    char category[12];
    float cost;
    int number;
    };
```

20 addresses
for a string

40 addresses
for a string

12 addresses
for a string

4 addresses
for a float

2 addresses
for an
interger

Figure 11.4

Declaring a structure variable.

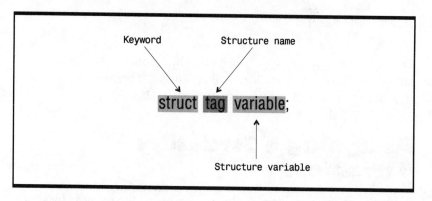

Keyword   Structure name

struct tag variable;

Structure variable

The keyword struct tells the compiler you are referring to a structure
type, and then the structure tag identifies the template that the variable
will follow. Following the tag is the name of the variable that you will
use in the program. For example, we could access the CD collection

by defining a variable like this:

```
struct CD disc;
```

We now have a variable named disc that is a collection of five elements. Like all variables, disc represents an area in memory. But because disc is a structure variable of the type CD, it represents a space in memory 78 addresses wide that will contain three strings, a float, and an integer (Figure 11.5).

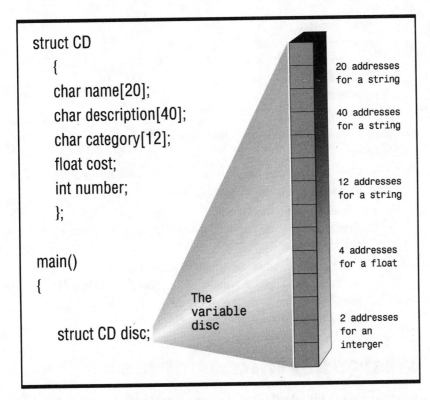

Figure 11.5
The components of a structure variable declaration.

If you need more than one variable of the same type (for example, to maintain the same information about your CD-ROMs), you can declare them in one instruction:

```
struct CD disc, cdrom;
```

The instruction declares two variables (disc and cdrom) that are of the CD structure type. However, if you have more than one structure type defined, you must declare the variables of each type separately. For example, if you have defined the CD structure and another structure called VIDEO, you might declare your variables like this:

```
struct CD disc, cdrom;
struct VIDEO movies, vacation;
```

You can also create the structure and declare the variable in one step. Place the variable name (or names) between the structure's closing brace and semicolon, as in:

```
struct CD
    {
    char name[20];
    char description[40];
    char category[12];
    float cost;
    int number;
    } disc;
```

To help make the terminology clear, let's review each element in the declaration:

- CD is the *structure tag*. It is the name of a new data type, a collection of items called a structure.

- The elements that make up the structure are called *structure members*. They are declared using the same syntax as a variable declaration.

- Disc is the variable name that you'll use in your program. It is a variable of the CD type, which means it contains all the members declared as part of the structure. It is sometimes called a *structure variable*.

Assigning Initial Values

If you know the initial values of the structure members, you can assign the values when you declare the variable. If you are only creating one variable of the structure type, you can initialize it as part of the structure definition:

```
struct CD
    {
    char name[20];
    char description[40];
```

```
char category[12];
float cost;
int number;
} disc = {"Best Hits","Tiny Tim","pop music", 12.50, 12};
```

This creates the CD structure, declares the disc variable, and assigns an initial value to each of the five structure members (Figure 11.6).

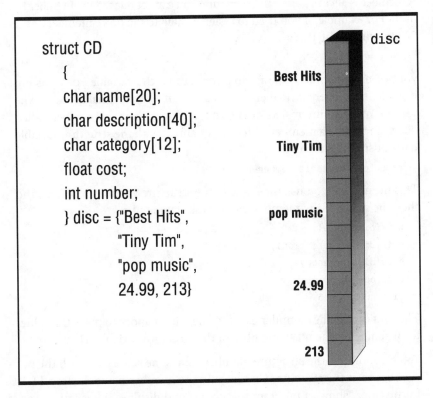

Figure 11.6
Initializing a structure variable.

As an alternative, you can initialize the members when you declare the variable:

```
struct CD disc = {"My Life and Times","B. Gates biography",
          "book on disc", 24.99, 213};
```

Because C is a free-form language, you can divide the assignment on several lines, as long as you do not divide a quoted string.

You can define a structure globally before the main() function, or locally within main() or another function. However, if you want to assign initial values to a structure that contains strings, you must declare it before `main()` or as a static variable:

```
static struct CD
```

Using a Structure

A member is always part of the structure. You cannot refer to the member by itself. For example, if you tried to assign a value to the `cost` member of the CD structure using this syntax:

```
cost = 23.13;
```

your compiler would generate an error because the variable `cost` has not been defined. There is no memory set aside under that variable name. The variable you are interested in is `disc`, and it contains a member called `cost`. To refer to a member, you must qualify it with the structure variable name, using this format:

```
structure-variable.member-name
```

This means that you use the name of the structure variable, a period, and then the name of the member, as in these statements:

```
gets(disc.name);
gets(disc.description);
gets(disc.category);
disc.cost = 16.95
disc.number = 5
```

The syntax tells the compiler exactly where in memory to place the value; for instance, in the `name` member of the structure variable `disc`.

You must output the structure member values the same way, with the period between the structure variable and the member name. Listing 11.1, for instance, shows a program that inputs and displays information on a CD. At no time are the member names used without a reference to the structure variable.

You can input and output the structure elements in any order; you do not have to use them in the order they are defined in the structure template.

Listing 11.1: Using a Structure with Input and Output

```
/*CD1.C*/
struct CD
```

```
    {
    char  name[20];
    char  description[40];
    char  category[12];
    float cost;
    int   number;
    } disc;


main()
{
    puts("Enter disk information\n\n");
    printf("Enter the name:");
    gets(disc.name);
    printf("Enter the description:");
    gets(disc.description);
    printf("Enter the category:");
    gets(disc.category);
    printf("Enter the cost:");
    scanf("%f", &disc.cost);
    printf("Enter the slot number:");
    scanf("%d", &disc.number);
    puts("The information on the CD is:\n\n");
    printf("Name:          %s\n",disc.name);
    printf("Description:   %s\n",disc.description);
    printf("Category:      %s\n",disc.category);
    printf("Cost:          %6.2f\n",disc.cost);
    printf("Location:      %d\n",disc.number);
}
```

Structure Arrays

So far we have worked only with the equivalent of a single index card; but we defined the structure so that we could maintain information about all the CDs in the collection. We need to use an array rather than a single variable. When you create an array of a structure, you are creating an array of the entire template. Declare the array using a subscript with the structure variable:

```
struct CD disc[10];
```

This sets aside ten sections of memory, each large enough to store a complete structure (Figure 11.7). Refer to the array element by subscripting the structure variable, not the member name:

```
gets(disc[0].name);
gets(disc[1].name);
```

Figure 11.7

An array of a structure

```
struct CD
    {
    char name[20];
    char description[40];
    char category[12];
    float cost;
    int number;
    };
    struct CD disc[10];
```

disc[0]   78 addresses
disc[1]   each element
disc[2]   Total of 780
disc[3]   addresses
disc[4]
disc[5]
disc[6]
disc[7]
disc[8]
disc[9]

The program in Listing 11.2, for instance, uses a structure array to represent the real-world task of filling out a series of index cards for the CD collection.

Listing 11.2: Programming a Structure Array

```
/*CD2.C*/
struct CD
    {
    char  name[20];
    char  description[40];
    char  category[12];
    float cost;
```

```
        int  number;
        } disc[10];


main()
{
int index, repeat;
char flag;
flag =  'Y';
index = 0;
do
  {
      printf("Enter disk # %d\n",index);
      printf("Enter the name:");
      gets(disc[index].name);
      printf("Enter the description:");
      gets(disc[index].description);
      printf("Enter the category:");
      gets(disc[index].category);
      printf("Enter the cost:");
      scanf("%f", &disc[index].cost);
      printf("Enter the slot number:");
      scanf("%d", &disc[index].number);
      index++;
      if(index<10)
       {
      printf("Do you have another? Y or N");
  scanf("%C", &flag);
       }
  }
while (index <10 && (flag == 'Y' || flag == 'y'));
puts("Name           Slot Number");
for(repeat=0; repeat<index;repeat++)
printf("%s     %d\n",disc[repeat].name,  disc[repeat].number);
}
```

A 10-element array of disc is declared as part of the structure definition:

```
} disc[10];
```

The variable flag is declared to indicate when the user is done entering information, if they have fewer than 10 CDs. The do loop inputs the array elements: five pieces of data (structure members) for each array element

(CD in the collection). The variable `index` will be used as the subscript number.

After each array element is entered, the user is asked whether they have another CD. The question isn't asked, however, if the user has already entered all 10 array elements.

The `do` loop uses this condition:

```
while (index <10 && (flag == 'Y' || flag == 'y'));
```

The AND condition means that both must be true: `index` is less than ten and the variable `flag` is Y or y.

Without the nested parentheses, C would combine the first two conditions and internally interpret the instruction as an OR condition (as shown in Figure 11.8). The loop would continue even after all ten elements are entered, if the flag had the value of y from the last input.

Figure 11.8
Interpretation without nested parentheses

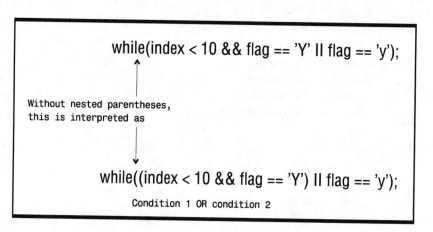

When the last CD is entered, the variable `index` is one more than the number of array elements. The variable is used in the `for` loop to print a list of CDs and their locations.

Note that every reference to a structure member includes the variable name. The array subscript follows the variable name.

Structures and Functions

The original K&R definition of C limited the use of structures. Structures could only be passed as arguments using special pointers, which you will learn about later in this chapter. In addition, you could not directly assign one structure to another, such as

```
CDROM = disc;
```

Today's modern C++ and C compilers have corrected the oversight. You can directly assign one structure to another, and pass an entire structure to or from functions.

With most C++ and ANSI C compilers, for example, you can pass and return an entire structure. Listing 11.3, for example, shows how to pass a structure to a function. The member values are input in `main()`, then the entire structure is passed to the `putdisc()` function for output. The structure variable is used in the function call:

```
putdisc(disc);
```

This passes the entire structure to the function. The function contains a variable that will receive the passed structure, and declares the variable as the same structure type, as

```
putdisc(disk)
struct CD disk;
```

The function now recognizes a separate structure variable, called `disk`, that contains the passed members of the `disc` structure. Within the function, the members are referenced with the `disk` tag, the name of the receiving structure.

Listing 11.3: Passing a Structure

```
/*CD3.C*/
struct CD
    {
    char   name[20];
    char   description[40];
    char   category[12];
    float  cost;
    int    number;
    } disc;
main()
```

NOTE

The PCC compiler provided with this book will report a warning when a program passes a structure between functions. You can ignore this warning, and it will not appear in later releases of the compiler.

```
                   {
                   puts("Enter disk information\n\n");
                   printf("Enter the name:");
                   gets(disc.name);
                   printf("Enter the description:");
                   gets(disc.description);
                   printf("Enter the category:");
                   gets(disc.category);
                   printf("Enter the cost:");
                   scanf("%f", &disc.cost);
                   printf("Enter the slot number:");
                   scanf("%d", &disc.number);
                   putdisc(disc);
                   }


                   putdisc(disk)
                   struct CD disk;
                   {
                   puts("The information on the CD is:\n\n");
                   printf("Name:         %s\n",disk.name);
                   printf("Description:  %s\n",disk.description);
                   printf("Category:     %s\n",disk.category);
                   printf("Cost:         %6.2f\n",disk.cost);
                   printf("Location:     %d\n",disk.number);
                   }
```

Listing 11.4 illustrates how to return a structure from a function. The members of the structure are input into the getdisc() function, then passed back to main() in the command

```
return(inputdisc);
```

Note that the structure tag (CD) is used in both the function declaration and in the variable declaration of getdisc(). When you are returning a type other than an int or char, you must specify the type in the function declaration. The type being returned is the structure CD, so the function is declared as

```
struct CD getdisc()
```

The structure used in the function is also of the type CD, so it is declared as

```
struct CD inputdisc;
```

Also note that the `getdisc()` function is declared globally as a structure variable along with the variable `disc`. This type of declaration is required in order for a function to return a structure.

Listing 11.4: Returning a Structure

```
/*CD4.C*/
struct CD
    {
    char   name[20];
    char   description[40];
    char   category[12];
    float cost;
    int   number;
    } disc, getdisc();
main()
{
disc = getdisc();
puts("The information on the CD is:\n\n");
printf("Name:          %s\n",disc.name);
printf("Description:   %s\n",disc.description);
printf("Category:      %s\n",disc.category);
printf("Cost:          %6.2f\n",disc.cost);
printf("Location:      %d\n",disc.number);
}


struct CD getdisc()
{
    struct CD inputdisc;
    puts("Enter disk information\n\n");
    printf("Enter the name:");
    gets(inputdisc.name);
    printf("Enter the description:");
    gets(inputdisc.description);
    printf("Enter the category:");
    gets(inputdisc.category);
    printf("Enter the cost:");
```

```
        scanf("%f", &inputdisc.cost);
        printf("Enter the slot number:");
        scanf("%d", &inputdisc.number);
        return(inputdisc);
    }
```

Understanding Pointers

While you can pass to a function as many arguments as you want, including an entire structure, you can only include one parameter in the return() command. That is, you can only pass back one value to the calling routine in the program. One solution would be to use global variables. However, you then lose some control over the structure of your program and make it more difficult to detect and find errors. If you want a function to pass back more than one value, use pointers.

You can refer to a variable in either of two ways. When you use the name of the variable, you refer to the value stored in the memory location. When you use the address operator (&), you refer to the address in memory where the variable is stored.

If you assign a value to a variable, such as

```
    tax = 35;
```

you are inserting a *value* into a memory location. The memory address assigned to the variable tax will contain the value 35. You can also display the *memory address* of a variable, using the & operator. The instruction

```
    printf("%d", &tax)
```

will display the address where the variable `tax` is stored, not the value stored in that location. However, the address operator, as in `&tax`, can only be used in an expression. It is not a variable, because it only represents an integer number; an instruction such as

```
    &tax = 25;
```

is not valid.

A *pointer* is a variable that contains the memory location of another variable. If `tax` is stored in location 21260, then a pointer to the variable `tax` will contain 21260.

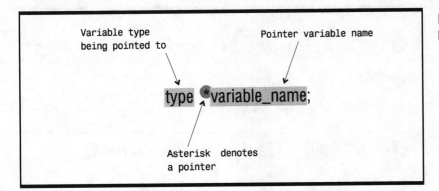

Figure 11.9

Declaring a pointer.

To create a pointer variable, use the syntax shown in Figure 11.9. You start by specifying the type of data stored in the location identified by the pointer. The asterisk tells the compiler that you are creating a pointer variable. Finally, you give the name of the variable. For instance,

```
int *taxptr
```

creates a pointer-type variable (indicated by the asterisks), named `taxptr`, that will contain the address of an integer type variable. The instruction

```
float *net
```

creates a pointer named `net` that will contain the address of a `float` variable.

Once you declare a pointer variable, you must point it to something. You do this by assigning to the pointer the address of the variable you want to point to, as in:

```
taxptr = &tax
```

This places the address where `tax` is stored into the variable `taxptr` (as illustrated in Figure 11.10). If `tax` is stored in memory address 21260, then the variable `taxptr` has the value 21260.

For example, look at this program:

```
main()
{
int *taxptr;
int tax;
```

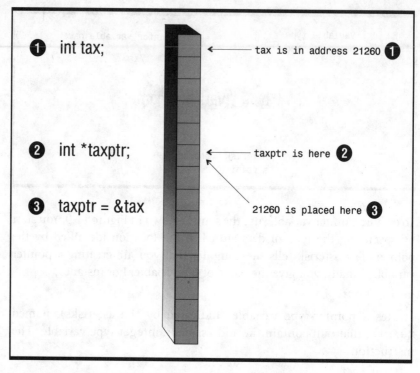

Figure 11.10

Assigning an address to a pointer.

1 int tax;

tax is in address 21260 **1**

2 int *taxptr;

taxptr is here **2**

21260 is placed here **3**

3 taxptr = &tax

```
    taxptr=&tax;
    tax=35;
    printf("tax is %d\n", tax);
    printf("the tax pointer is %d\n", taxptr);
}
```

Using our sample data, the output will be

```
tax is 35
the tax pointer is 21260
```

You might be saying "So what?"—after all, you could get the same result by assigning the address of `tax` to a regular integer (nonpointer) variable. The benefit is that you can also refer to the pointer variable as `*taxptr`. The asterisk tells the compiler that you are interested in the *contents of the memory location stored in the pointer*. You are not interested in the value 21260, but in the value stored in that memory location. While the value of `taxptr` is 21260, the value of `*taxptr` is 35.

You can only assign an address to the variable `taxptr`. The instruction

```
taxptr = 21260
```

would generate a compiler error because it is attempting to assign an integer value to the pointer. The only assignment you can make to the variable `taxptr` is the address of a variable, using the address operator, as

```
taxptr=&tax
```

However, you can assign a value to the pointer *taxptr, as in

```
*taxptr = 35
```

This means "place the value 35 in the memory address pointed to by the variable `taxptr`." Since the pointer contains the address 21260, the value 35 is placed in that memory location. And, since this is the location of the variable `tax`, the value of `tax` also becomes 35 (Figure 11.11).

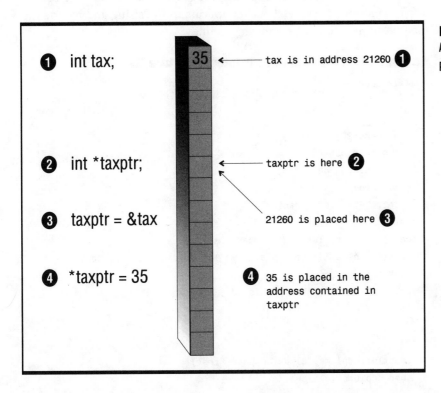

Figure 11.11
Assigning a value to the pointer.

This certainly seems like a long way to go to change the value of a variable. It would be easier to assign `tax` a new value. The real power of pointers, however, lies in their use as arguments to functions.

Pointers and Functions

Without a pointer, you must pass an argument to a function by value. That means that the value of the calling parameter is passed to the receiving parameter. A copy of the value is placed in a separate memory location. Changing the value of the receiving parameter does not change the value of the sending parameter.

When you pass a parameter by its address, to a pointer, you are not making a duplicate copy. Instead, you are creating a second variable that points to the same location in memory. So if you change the value of the pointer variable, you are changing the value of the sending variable as well.

The program in Listing 11.5 inputs a string and a character. It then counts the number of times the character appears in the string and reports the first position where the character is found.

Listing 11.5: A Program using Pointers to Return Values

```
/*letcount.c*/
main()
{
char name[20], letter;
int number, start;
puts("Enter a name\n");
gets(name);
printf("Enter a character");
letter=getchar();
countlet(name, letter, &number, &start);
printf("\nThe letter %c is in %s %d times\n",letter, name,
number);
printf("Starting position is %d", start);
}


countlet(ndplume, alpha, count, first)
char ndplume[], alpha;
int *count, *first;
{
    int index, flag;
    *count=0;
```

```
    index=0;
    flag=0;
    *first=0;
while(ndplume[index] != '\0')
{

    if(ndplume[index]== alpha)
    {
        *count=*count+1;
            if(flag==0)
    {

            *first=index+1;
            flag=1;
    }
}
    index++;


}
}
```

After the string and character are input, we pass four variables to the function `countlet()`: the string, the character, and the addresses of the variables `count` and `start`, indicated by the ampersand before the variable names.

The function assigns the addresses to receiving pointer variables: the address of `number` is stored in `*count`, and the address of `start` is stored in `*first` (Figure 11.12). The variables are initialized at zero, and then a `while` loop is initiated:

```
while(ndplume[index] != '\0')
```

The `while` loop will examine each character in the string and continue as long as the character is not the null terminator. When it finds a null terminator, the loop ends.

The placement of the braces in the `while` loop is critical; one `if` instruction is completely nested within the other (as illustrated in Figure 11.13). The first `if` condition tests whether the character being examined is equal to the character you want to count. If so, the counter is incremented by 1. In this case the counter is a pointer variable:

```
*count=*count+1;
```

Figure 11.12

Passing addresses to a function.

```
countlet(name, letter, &number, &start);
printf("\n The letter %c is in %s %d times\n",letter, name, number);
```

The address of
number is stored
in the pointer
named "count"

The address of
start is stored
in the pointer
named "first"

```
countlet(ndplume, alpha, count, first)
char ndplume[], alpha;
int *count, *first;
```

This adds 1 to the value stored in the address contained in the pointer. Because the pointer contains the address of the variable number, the variable number is incremented by 1, even though it is a local variable in the main() function. Note that you cannot use the syntax

```
*count++
```

This would change the actual address that the pointer is referring to, not the contents of the address.

The next if condition tests the value of the variable flag. If flag is zero, this is the first occurrence of the matched letter. The pointer variable *first is assigned the position of the character in the string, plus 1. (Adding one to the index references the position from the first character, which makes more sense to most people that counting from zero.) The value of flag is then set to 1, so the starting position will not be changed when the next matched character is located in the string.

After the if conditions, the index is incremented so that the next character of the string is examined in the following repetition. It is important to make sure the instruction index++ appears after the closing brace of the outer if instruction, and before the final two closing braces: one ends the while instruction, the other ends the function. If the instruction were anywhere else, the function would not work properly.

Figure 11.13

Placement of braces to group
the instructions.

```
countlet(ndplume, alpha, count, first)
char ndplume[], alpha;
int *count, *first;
{
    int index, flag;
    *count=0;
    index=0;
    flag=0;
    *first=0;
while(ndplume[index] != '\0')
{

    if(ndplume[index]== alpha
    {
        *count=*count+1;
    if(flag==0)
    {
      *first=index+1;
      flag=1;
    }
    }
    index++;

}
}
```

If the character
matches, the counter
is incremented

Sets the first
position variable
when the character
matches

Index++ is performed
with each repetition

When the function ends, control is passed back to main(), where the string,
character, number of occurrences, and starting position are displayed.

Note that the function does not return an argument in a `return()` call. Instead, the values of `number` and `start` have been assigned through pointers. By assigning values to the pointers in the function, the program "returns" the values to the variables in the calling argument.

You could write this program without using pointers by declaring the variables `number` and `start` as global variables. They could then be referenced in `main()` and in `countlet()` instead of being passed as arguments. However, using pointers gives you more control. Your variables are still local, but you can choose to have them altered by passing their addresses.

You'll need to use a pointer to work with disk files and to send your output to a printer rather than the screen display; these operations are the subject of Chapter 12.

Questions

1. When should a structure type be used?
2. How is a structure declared?
3. What is the difference between the structure tag and a structure variable?
4. How do you refer to a structure element?
5. Can you have an array of a structure?
6. Can a structure contain elements of the same type?
7. What is a pointer?
8. If a program contains the declaration `float *num`, what's the difference between the variables `num` and `*num`?
9. Why are pointers used in C programs?
10. How is a pointer passed to a function?

Exercises

1. Write a program that inputs product inventory information into a structure. The information includes the product name, cost, quantity, and the supplier name.

2. Modify the program in Exercise 1 to input information into a 20-element array of the structure.

3. Modify the program in Exercise 2 to display the total value of the inventory.

4. Write a program that inputs two `float` variables local to `main()`, then uses a function to square both numbers.

5. Explain what is wrong with the following program:

```
main()
{
struct CD
    {
    char  description[40];
    char  category[12];
    char  name[20];
    float cost;
    int  number;
    } disc;
    puts("Enter disk information");
    printf("Enter the name:");
    gets(name);
    printf("Enter the description:");
    gets(description);
    printf("Enter the category:");
    gets(category);
    printf("Enter the cost:");
    scanf("%f", &cost);
    printf("Enter the slot number:");
    scanf("%d", &number);
    puts("The information on the CD is:");
    printf("Name:          %s\n",name);
    printf("Description:   %s\n",description);
    printf("Category:      %s\n",category);
    printf("Cost:          %6.2f\n",cost);
    printf("Location:      %d\n",number);
}
```

Twelve

Outputting to the Disk and Printer

• •

Simply displaying information on the screen is useful, but limited. Even if you pause the program to give yourself time to read the screen, once information has scrolled out of view, you have to run the program again to read it.

In addition, your program retains the value of variables only as long as the program is running; the information that you input will be lost when you stop the program. So, for instance, if you enter your entire CD collection into an array of a structure variable, you'd only have to enter it again the next time you turn on your computer.

For a permanent record of the information, or to distribute your program's output to others, you need to print it on paper. To enter information only once, and retrieve it when you need it later, you can store your information on a disk.

Understanding Files

Data that you output does not go directly to the disk or to the printer when you issue an output command. Instead, it goes into a temporary storage area in memory called a *buffer*. When the buffer becomes full, the data is transferred to the disk or printer (see Figure 12.1). Data that you input from a disk also goes into the buffer; it is held there so it can be assigned to a variable or displayed on the screen.

Figure 12.1

Data is stored temporarily in a buffer.

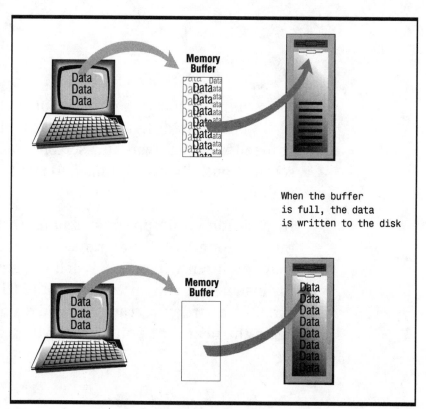

Memory Buffer

When the buffer is full, the data is written to the disk

Memory Buffer

In order to transfer information in and out of the buffer, you need a communications link between your program and your computer's operating system. This link is a file.

When your program creates a file, it sets up a special structure in memory, containing information that your program and your computer need to output or input information from the file, or to print information on the printer.

For example, the structure contains the address of the file's buffer, so your computer knows where to find the information you want to output to the disk, or where to place data that you want to input from the disk. The structure keeps track of the number of characters remaining in the buffer, and the next character position—to be either output or filled with input (see Figure 12.2).

Almost all C and C++ compilers maintain information about files in the header file stdio.h. This file contains several constant declarations that are

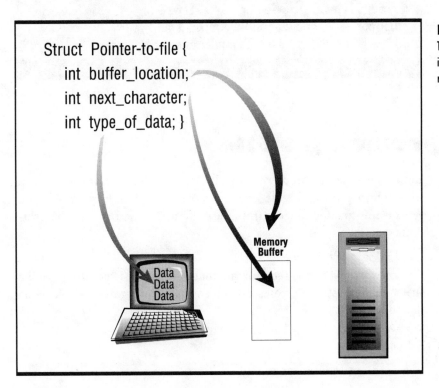

```
Struct  Pointer-to-file {
    int  buffer_location;
    int  next_character;
    int  type_of_data; }
```

Memory
Buffer

Data
Data
Data

Figure 12.2
The file structure stores information needed during runtime.

needed for file operations, and it may hold the template of the file structure. To use file functions and commands, start your program with this command:

```
#include <stdio.h>;
```

This makes the file constants and structure template available to the compiler when you compile and link your program.

When you input data from a disk file, you are making a copy of it in the computer's memory. The information remains on the disk unchanged. For that reason, programmers refer to input as *read* operations. When you output data to the disk, you are putting on the disk a copy of data that is in memory. This is called *writing* to the disk, or a *write* operation.

C++ Notes

Many C++ compilers have additional header files for special file functions. These may be named `iostream.h`, `fstream.h`, or another name depending on their functions and your compiler. Consult your compiler documentation for additional information.

Declaring a File

You create a file as a pointer to the file's structure in memory. When you write information to the file, or read information from it, your program gets the information it needs from the structure. To declare a file, use this syntax:

```
FILE *file_pointer;
```

The keyword FILE tells the program that the variable is pointing to a file structure. The asterisk creates a pointer variable, using the variable name that follows it.

If you plan to use more than one file simultaneously, you need a file pointer for each. For example, you will need two file pointers if you are writing a program that copies the contents of one file to another, or you want to read information from a disk and print it on your printer:

```
FILE *infile, *outfile;
```

Opening a File

The link between your program, the file, and the computer is established with the fopen() function, using the syntax shown in Figure 12.3.

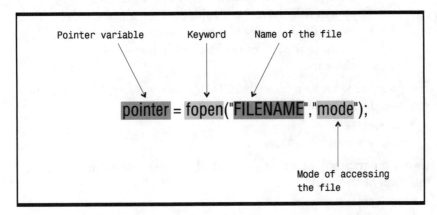

Figure 12.3
The syntax of the fopen()
function.

The function assigns the address of the file structure to the pointer variable. The parameter includes the file name, which must follow the file-naming conventions of your computer: in DOS, it can be up to eight characters with an optional three-character extension. To print output, rather than send it to a disk file, use the filename "PRN", in quotation marks. This will automatically send your output to your printer.

The mode argument specifies the type of operation you will be performing. In C and C++ commands, you also enclose the mode argument in

quotation marks. It can be:

r	Indicates that you are going to *read* information from the file into the computer. If the file doesn't already exist on your disk, your program will report a runtime error.
w	Indicates that you will be *writing* data to the disk or to the printer. If the file does not already exist, your operating system will create it. If the file is already on the disk, however, all existing information in it will be erased.
a	Indicates that you want to *append* (add) information to the end of a file. Your operating system will create the file if it does not already exist. If it does exist, the data you output will be added to the end of the file, without erasing its contents.

For example, to create a file called CD.DAT to store your CD collection, you would use a command such as this:

```
FILE *cdfile;
cdfile = fopen("CD.DAT","w");
```

If your program will be reading from the file, instead of writing to it, use this form of **fopen()**:

```
FILE *cdfile;
cdfile = fopen("CD.DAT","r");
```

Notice that the name of the file and the mode are in quotation marks because they are passed to the **fopen()** function as strings. You can also input the name of the file from the keyboard as a string variable, and then use the variable name as the argument without quotation marks.

If you want to print information about your collection, use a command such as this one:

```
FILE *cdfile;
cdfile = fopen("PRN","w");
```

You can only use the w mode when sending information to a printer.

How Files Work

C keeps track of your position in a file using a special pointer.

When you are reading information from a file, the pointer indicates the next data to be read from the disk. When you first open a file with the r mode, the pointer is placed at the first character in the file. After each read operation, the pointer moves to the next data that will be read. The amount of movement depends on how much information you are reading at one time (Figure 12.4). If you are just reading a character at a time, the pointer moves to the next character. If you are reading an entire structure, the pointer moves to the next structure. Once you read the last information in the file, the pointer is moved to a special code, called the end-of-file-marker. You'll get a runtime error if you try reading past the end of the file.

NOTE

C++ and many ANSI C compilers allow you to open a file for both reading and writing at the same time. These are indicated by the r+, w+, and a+ modes.

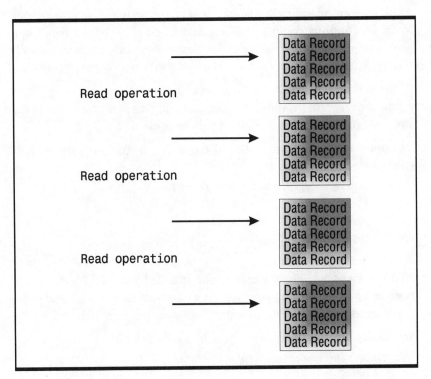

Figure 12.4

A pointer keeps track of the current file position.

When you open a file in the w mode, the pointer is also placed at the beginning of the file, so the first data you output is inserted at the beginning of the file. When you close the file, the operating system places the end-of-file-marker after the last data. If the file already exists when you open it in w mode, the data in the file will be overwritten by the new information that you write to it. Any data not overwritten will appear after the new end-of-file marker, so it will never be accessed in read operations. That's why opening an existing file in the w mode erases its contents—even if you open the file and then close it without writing any information.

When you open a file in the a mode, the pointer is placed at the end-of-file-marker. New data that you append to the file will be inserted, and then the end-of-file-marker added.

Avoiding Runtime Errors

At times, your operating system may not be able to open the file you specify in the fopen() command. There may be no room left on the disk, or you may be trying to read from a file that doesn't exist. You may also be trying to print when your printer is not turned on or is out of paper.

If you attempt to use a file that did not open, your program will stop with a runtime error. To prevent this from occurring, use an if command that stops the program when the file cannot be opened.

You open a file and test whether it has been opened properly in an if structure:

```
if ((cdfile = fopen("CD.DAT","w")) == NULL)
    {
    puts("Unable to open the file");
    exit();
    }
```

NULL is a special value defined in the stdio.h header file. If there is an error in opening the file, your system will return the NULL value rather than the address of the file structure, and your program will end.

You can use the same test when writing to the printer:

```
if((cdfile = fopen("prn","w")) == NULL)
    {
```

```
        puts("Turn on the printer, then run this again");
        exit();
        }
```

If the printer is not turned on, the prompt will appear so that you can pre-
pare your printer and run the program again. You can also place the condition in a `while` loop to give the user time to correct the problem:

```
while((cdfile = fopen("prn","w")) == NULL)
        {
        puts("Turn on the printer, then press Enter");
        flag = getchar();
        }
```

Note that this may not work with some systems. If your printer is not ready,
the operating system will display a message giving you the options to abort
(stop the operation) or retry. Turn your printer on; then press R to retry.

C++ Notes

C++ offers special `stream` file operations that can read and write
files using the >> and << operators. For instance, with some compilers, open a file for reading using the syntax

```
ifstream file_pointer(file_name)
```

For writing, use the syntax

```
ofstream file_pointer(file_name)
```

You may need to use a special header file for these operations.
Check your documentation for the name of the header file and how
to use it.

Closing a File

When you are done writing to or reading from a file, you must close the
link between it and your computer. Use this syntax:

```
fclose(file_pointer)
```

Closing the file ensures that all information in the file buffer has actually been written to the file. If you end your program before closing the file, any unwritten information still in the buffer may not be output and will be lost. The end-of-file marker may not be inserted correctly, and your operating system may not be able to access the file at a later time.

In addition, closing the file releases the file pointer so that you can use it for another file, or to perform another operation on the same file. For example, suppose you want to create a file, then confirm that the information was recorded correctly. Your program might use the structure shown in Listing 12.1.

Listing 12.1: Using One File Pointer for Two Operations

```
FILE *cdfile;
if ((cdfile = fopen("CD.DAT","w")) == NULL)
    {
    puts("Unable to create the file");
    exit();
    }


Instructions for writing to the file


fclose(cdfile);
if ((cdfile = fopen("CD.DAT","r")) == NULL)
    {
    puts("Unable to open the file");
    exit();
    }


Instruction from reading from the file


fclose(cdfile);
```

The file is first opened in the w mode, and then the data is written to it. The file is closed, and then opened again in the r mode so that the data can be read and displayed on the screen.

Some compilers let you make sure that all data has been written to the file by flushing the buffer with this command:

```
flush()
```

Chapter 12: Outputting to the Disk and Printer

This forces the data in the buffer to be written on the disk, or to be printed, even when you do not close the file.

Input and Output Functions

You can transfer data to and from files in several ways:

- To write data to a file or to a printer a character at a time, use `putc()` or `fputc()`.
- To read data from a file a character at a time, use `getc()` or `fgetc()`.
- To write data to a file or to a printer a string (line) at a time, use `fputs()`.
- To read data from a file a string (line) at a time, use `fgets()`.
- To write formatted characters, strings, and numbers to a disk or printer, use `fprintf()`.
- To read formatted characters, strings, and numbers, use `fscanf()`.
- To write an entire structure, use `fwrite()`.
- To read an entire structure, use `fread()`.

Working with Characters

Transferring data one character at a time is the most basic form of file operation. While it is not the most practical way to deal with information, it can illustrate how to use files. The following program, for example, writes characters to a file until you press the ↵ key:

```
/*fputc.c*/
#include "stdio.h"
main()
{
    FILE *fp;
    char letter;
    if((fp = fopen("MYFILE","w"))==NULL)
```

```
        {
            puts("Cannot open the file");
            exit();
        }
        do
        {
            letter=getchar();
            fputc(letter, fp);
        }
        while(letter!='\r');
        fclose(fp);
    }
```

The file is opened in the w mode—if the file MYFILE does not exist, it will be created. The do loop inputs a series of characters using the getchar() function, and it writes them to the file using putc(). The syntax for putc() is

```
putc(char_variable, file_pointer);
```

You can also use the fputc() instruction with the same arguments.

The repetition continues until you press the ↵ key, which inputs the return (\r) character, and then the file is closed.

Buffered getchar() Input

With compilers that use buffered input for the getchar() function, use the getche() function in its place to input individual characters for writing to a disk file. Replace the do...while structure with this do loop:

```
while((letter=getche())!='\r')
        fputc(letter, fp);
```

Reading Characters from a File

To read a character from a file, use the `getc()` or `fgetc()` function with the syntax

```
char_variable = getc(file_pointer);
```

For example, to input a character from a file pointed to by the pointer `fp`, use the instruction

```
letter = getc(fp);
```

Here is a program that reads the file created with the previous example:

```
/*fgetc.c*/
#include "stdio.h"
main()
{
    FILE *fp;
    int letter;
    if((fp = fopen("MYFILE","r"))==NULL)
    {
        puts("Cannot open the file");
        exit();
    }
    while ((letter=fgetc(fp)) != EOF)
        printf("%c",letter);
    fclose(fp);
}
```

We open the file in the `r` mode, and then read the characters in a `while` loop. Most of the work is done within the `while` parameter. The instruction

```
letter=fgetc(fp)
```

assigns a character in the file to the variable `letter`. The loop continues only as long as the variable does not equal `EOF`, a special constant that stands for *end-of-file*. When the pointer reaches the end of the file, the value returned to `letter` will equal the EOF value, which is declared in the stdio.h header file.

The sample programs just shown use the same file pointer and variable names to both write and read the data from the file. This doesn't have to be the case. You can write and read the files using different pointer and variable names, as long as the filename is the same in both operations.

Working with Lines

Instead of working with individual characters, you can read and write an entire line of text—a string—using the fputs() and fgets() functions.

The fputs() function has this syntax:

```
fputs(string_variable, file_pointer);
```

The function writes an entire string to the file or printer at one time, but it does not add a new-line command to the end of the string. If you want each line stored separately on the disk, or printed on a separate line, you must output the new-line command yourself. For example, this program creates a file of names:

```
/*fputs.c*/
#include "stdio.h"
main()
{
FILE *fp;
char flag;
char name[20];
if((fp = fopen("MYFILE","w"))==NULL)
    {
    puts("Cannot open the file");
    exit();
    }
flag = 'y';
while(flag!='n')
{
    puts("Enter a name");
    gets(name);
    fputs(name, fp);
    fputs("\n",fp);
    printf("Do you have another name?");
    flag=getchar();
    putchar('\n');
}
```

```
        fclose(fp);
    }
```

The `while` loop repeats until you enter the letter *n* in response to the prompt. The loop inputs a name using the `gets()` function; it then writes the name to the disk file using the `fputs()` command. The new-line code is then output, and you are asked if you have another name to enter.

If your compiler has a `strlen()` function, you can simplify the input repetition, like this:

```
printf("Please enter a name: ");
gets(name);
while(strlen(name) > 0)
{
    fputs(name, fp);
    fputs("\n",fp);
    printf("Please enter a name: ");
    gets(name);
}
```

The string you type is assigned to the variable `name`, then the length of the string is compared to 0. If you press ↵ without typing a name, the string will have a length of 0 and the loop will end. If you enter at least one character, the string and the new-line code are written to the disk.

On some compilers, you can shorten the algorithm even further, this way:

```
printf("Please enter a name: ");
while(strlen(gets(name)) > 0)
{
    fputs(name, fp);
    fputs("\n",fp);
    printf("Please enter a name: ");
}
```

The string input is performed within the `while` condition itself.

By using the filename "prn", you print each of the strings instead of saving them on a disk. Open the file with the command

```
if((fp = fopen("prn","w"))==NULL)
```

To create a typing program, you would declare the string with 81 characters so you can type a full line on the screen before pressing ↵. The program in Listing 12.2 shows how you can structure a simple word processor. Since the line isn't sent to the printer until you press ↵, you can use the backspace key to correct mistakes on the line as you are typing.

Listing 12.2: Program for Printing Line Output

```
/*wp.c*/
#include "stdio.h"
main()
{
FILE *fp;
char line[81];
if((fp = fopen("prn","w"))==NULL)
    {
    puts("Cannot access the printer");
    exit();
    }
puts("Type your lines of text, pressing Enter after each\n");
puts("Press Enter on a new line to stop\n");
gets(line);
while(strlen(line) > 0)
{
    fputs(line, fp);
    fputs("\n",fp);
    gets(line);
}
fclose(fp);
}
```

Reading Strings

You read a string from a file using the fgets() function with this syntax:

```
fgets(string_variable, length, file_pointer);
```

The function inputs an entire line up to the new-line code, but not more than length minus one character. The length is an integer, or an int variable or constant, that indicates the maximum number of characters that can be input.

Here is a program that will read back the names from the previous example:

```
/*fgets.c*/
```

```
#include "stdio.h"
main()
{
FILE *fp;
char name[12];
if((fp = fopen("MYFILE","r"))==NULL)
    {
    puts("Cannot open the file");
    exit();
    }
while(fgets(name,12,fp)!= NULL)
{
    printf(name);
}
fclose(fp);
}
```

The input is performed in the while parameter as long as the value read is not NULL. When reading strings, when the pointer reaches the end of the file, the NULL value is assigned to the string variable. So you should always use NULL to detect the end of the file when reading strings; use EOF when reading characters.

If you are writing a general program to read any text file, set the length argument at 80.

The printf() command, by the way, is being used here to output the contents of a string variable without a format specifier. Each string read from the file includes the new-line command that was written to the file by the fputs("\n",fp) instruction. No additional new-line command is needed within the printf() function.

Formatted Input and Output

Character and string file commands can only read and write text. If you want to create a file, or produce a printout, containing numeric values, you must use the fprintf() and fscanf() functions. The commands have the same syntax as printf() and scanf(), but they also include the file pointer to indicate where you want the data written to, or read from:

```
fprintf(file_pointer, control_string, data_list);
fscanf(file_pointer, control_string, data_list);
```

The program in Listing 12.3 inputs inventory information and writes it to a file. The first input is performed with a gets() command before the while loop starts. The loop continues as long as the length of each item name is at least one character. The loop ends if you press ⏎ instead of typing a name.

Listing 12.3: Recording Formatted Output

```
/*fprintf.c*/
#include "stdio.h"
main()
{
FILE *fp;
char name[20];
int  quantity;
float  cost;
if((fp = fopen("MYFILE","w"))==NULL)
     {
     puts("Cannot open the file");
     exit();
     }
printf("Please enter the item name: ");
gets(name);
while(strlen(name) > 0)
{
     printf("Please enter the cost: ");
     scanf("%f", &cost);
     printf("Please enter the quantity: ");
     scanf("%d", &quantity);
     fprintf(fp, "%s %f %d\n", name, cost, quantity);
     printf("Please enter a name: ");
     gets(name);


}
fclose(fp);
}
```

Notice that the next name is input as the last line of the loop. This lets you end the loop by just pressing ↲ once. Some beginning programmers might have written the loop like this:

```
do
{
    printf("Please enter a name: ");
    gets(name);
    printf("Please enter the cost: ");
    scanf("%f", &cost);
    printf("Please enter the quantity: ");
    scanf("%d", &quantity);
    fprintf(fp, "%s %f %d\n", name, cost, quantity);
}
while(strlen(name) > 0)
```

This would work as well, but to end the loop, you'd have to press ↲ three times: once for the name, then twice more to bypass the prompts for cost and quantity.

Within the while loop, the cost and quantity of each item are input using scanf() functions, and then the information is written to the disk file in one command:

```
fprintf(fp, "%s %f %d\n", name, cost, quantity);
```

Note that a new-line code is written to the file at the end of each line. If you looked at the file with the DOS command TYPE, each line of data would appear on a separate line:

```
disk 1.120000 100
ribbon 7.340000 150
toner 75.000000 3
```

If you did not include the new-line command, the text would run together in one stream, something like this:

```
disk 1.120000 100ribbon 7.340000 150toner 75.000000 3
```

Notice that there is no space between the quantity amount of one item and the name of the next item. You would still be able to read the file without problem because the compiler would detect the end of a numeric value and the beginning of a string.

However, suppose the first and last value of each item were strings, as in:

```
disk 1.120000 Memoryexribbon 7.340000 Okaydatatoner 75.000000 HP
```

When the program reads the string at the end of the first item, it would also read the string at the start of the next item. For example, the first item would be read as:

```
disk 1.120000 Memoryexribbon
```

All of the output data, even int and float values, is stored on the disk as text characters. You'll learn more about this later.

Reading Formatted Files

You input information from a formatted file using the fscanf() function. Fscanf() operates in the same way as scanf(), except that it obtains its input from the file rather than the keyboard. Unfortunately, fscanf() has the same drawbacks as scanf(). It cannot read strings that include spaces, and it will return incorrect results if the data in the stream does not match the expected data types specified in the control string.

Listing 12.4 shows a program that reads the formatted inventory file. Note that the while repetition continues as long as the input does not equal EOF (end-of-file).

Listing 12.4: Reading a Formatted Text File

```
/*fscanf.c*/
#include "stdio.h"
main()
{
FILE *fp;
char name[20];
int  quantity;
float  cost;
if((fp = fopen("MYFILE","r"))==NULL)
    {
    puts("Cannot open the file");
    exit();
    }
while(fscanf(fp,"%s %f %d", name, &cost, &quantity) != EOF)
    {
```

```
        printf("Item: %s\n", name);
        printf("Cost: %.2f\n", cost);
        printf("Cost: %d\n", quantity);
    }
    fclose(fp);
}
```

Working with Structures

One way to overcome the shortcomings of `fscanf()` is to combine data elements in a structure, and then output and input the entire structure at one time. You can write a structure to the disk using the `fwrite()` function, and read it using the `fread()` function.

The syntax of `fwrite()` is:

```
fwrite(&structure_variable, structure_size,
        number_of_structures, file_pointer);
```

This may look complicated, but it is really very easy to implement:

- `&structure_variable` is the structure variable with the address operator. This tells the compiler the starting address of the information that you want to write to the disk.

- `structure_size` is the number of characters in the structure. Rather than count the characters yourself, use the `sizeof()` library function like this:

  ```
  sizeof(structure_variable)
  ```

  This computes the size of the structure automatically.

- `number_of_structures` is an integer number indicating how many structures you want to write at one time. Always use 1 unless you are creating an array of structures and want to write the entire array as one large block.

- `file_pointer` is the pointer indicating the file.

For example, suppose you want to save information about your CD collection on the disk. Using the **CD** structure illustrated in Chapter 11, the command to write a structure would be:

```
fwrite(&disc, sizeof(disc), 1, fp);
```

The instruction is illustrated in Figure 12.5.

A program that inputs data into the CD structure and saves it on the disk is shown in Listing 12.5. The program uses the gets() function to input the name of the file you want to create. The variable storing the file name is then used in the fopen() command to open the file.

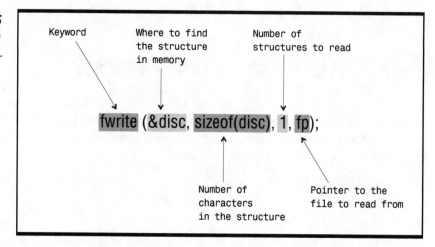

The information on each CD is input from the keyboard, and then the entire structure is written to the disk.

Listing 12.5: Recording the CD Structure

```c
/*fwrite.c*/
#include "stdio.h"
main()
{
    FILE *fp;
    struct CD
    {
    char   name[20];
    char   description[40];
    char   category[12];
    float  cost;
    int    number;
    } disc;
    char filename[25];
    printf("Enter the file you want to create:  ");
```

```
gets(filename);
if((fp = fopen(filename,"w")) == NULL)
{
      printf("Can't open the file %s\n",filename);
      exit();
}
puts("Enter disk information\n");
printf("Please enter the name of the CD: ");
gets(disc.name);
while(strlen(disc.name) > 0)
{
printf("Enter the description: ");
gets(disc.description);
printf("Enter the category: ");
gets(disc.category);
printf("Enter the cost: ");
scanf("%f", &disc.cost);
printf("Enter the slot number: ");
scanf("%d", &disc.number);
fwrite(&disc, sizeof(disc), 1, fp);
printf("Please enter the name: ");
gets(disc.name);
}
fclose(fp);
}
```

Reading Structures

To read an entire structure at one time, use the `fread()` function, which uses this syntax:

```
fread(&structure_variable, structure_size,
        number_of_structures, file_pointer);
```

It has the same syntax as `fwrite()` except for the function name. A program to read the CD file structure is shown in Listing 12.6. The data is read using this `while` loop:

```
while(fread(&disc, sizeof(disc), 1, fp)==1)
```

The `fread()` function returns the number of complete structures successfully read. Since the argument calls for reading only one structure at a time, the value returned should be 1. The `while` loop will continue as long as one complete structure can be read from the disk. If a structure cannot be read—because the end of the file has been reached—the function will return a zero and the loop will end.

Listing 12.6: Reading the CD Structure from the Disk

```c
/*fread.c*/
#include "stdio.h"
main()
{
    FILE *fp;
    struct CD
    {
    char  name[20];
    char  description[40];
    char  category[12];
    float cost;
    int   number;
    } disc;
    char filename[25];
    printf("Enter the filename to read: ");
    gets(filename);
    if((fp = fopen(filename,"r")) == NULL) {
        printf("Can't open the file %s\n",filename);
        exit();
    }
    while(fread(&disc, sizeof(disc), 1, fp)==1)
    {
    puts(disc.name);
    putchar('\n');
    puts(disc.description);
    putchar('\n');
    puts(disc.category);
    putchar('\n');
    printf("%f\n", disc.cost);
    printf("%d\n", disc.number);
    }
    fclose(fp);
}
```

Table 12.1 summarizes the input and output methods, and the test each function uses to stop reading data.

characters	putc(), fputc()	getc(), fgetc()	while != EOF
lines	fputs()	fgets()	while != NULL
formatted	fprintf()	fscanf()	while != EOF
structures	fwrite()	fread()	while != 1

Table 12.1
Summary of File Input and Output Functions

Reading into an Array

The programs used here to illustrate reading from a disk have merely displayed the input information on the screen. Once data is read into a variable, however, you can perform any operation on it, as well as use the data to load an array.

The program in Listing 12.7, for example, reads the information from the CD files into an array of the CD structure (assuming no more than 20 CDs). The subscript is used at each location of the structure name **disc**, so that each structure is input into another element of the array. After each structure is read and displayed, the total value of the collection is accumulated, and the subscript and count incremented, in these instructions:

```
total = total + disc[index].cost;
index++;
count++;
```

If you were only interested in the total and count information, you could have read each record into a non-array structure and kept a running total and count. However, once you read the data into an array, you can use the array to locate a specific CD, or to print any type of report.

Notice also that this program repeats asking for a filename until a file can be opened.

Listing 12.7: Reading the Structure into an Array

```
/*rarray.c*/
#include "stdio.h"
```

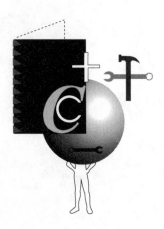

```
main()

{
FILE *fp;
struct CD
{
char   name[20];
char   description[40];
char   category[12];
float cost;
int  number;
} disc[20];
int index, count;
float total;
count = 0;
total = 0;
char filename[25];
printf("Enter the input filename? ");
gets(filename);
while((fp = fopen(filename,"r")) == NULL)
 {
printf("Can't open the file %s\n",filename);
printf("Enter the input filename? ");
gets(filename);
}
index = 0;
while(fread(&disc[index], sizeof(disc[index]), 1, fp)==1)
{
puts(disc[index].name);
putchar('\n');
puts(disc[index].description);
putchar('\n');
puts(disc[index].category);
putchar('\n');
printf("%f\n", disc[index].cost);
printf("%d\n", disc[index].number);
total = total + disc[index].cost;
index++;
count++;
```

```
        }
        fclose(fp);
        printf("The total worth of my collection is %.2f\n", total);
        printf("I have %d CDs in my collection\n", count);

}
```

C++ Notes

With C++ compilers, you can read and write files opened with the `ifstream` and `ofstream` functions using the << and >> operators. To read a file, use this syntax:

```
file_pointer >> variable;
```

To write a file, use this syntax:

```
file_pointer << variable;
```

Adding Data to a File

If you open an existing file using the w mode, any information in the file will be erased. To add new information to a file, open it in the **a** mode. In fact, with most compilers, you can use one program both to create a file and to add records to it. Using the **a** mode, the file will be created if it does not yet exist. If the file is already on the disk, the new information will be added to it.

When you append to a file, it is your responsibility to make sure that the data you add is in the same format as the existing data. For example, you can open a file created as a series of characters, then write to it a structure. You will get a runtime error, or some strange-looking data, when you try to read from the file.

Text and Binary Formats

The putc( ), fputc( ), and fputs( ) functions output text. If you look at the disk file using the TYPE command, you'll see the characters exactly as you entered them. You can create a file with any of these functions, then read it back using either getc( ), fgetc( ), or fgets( ). The character functions, for example, will simply read the file one character at a time, even if it were originally written as strings using fputs( ). Similarly, the string function will read the file back one line at a time, even if were written as individual characters.

The program in Listing 12.8, for example, copies one file to another, while displaying the file contents on the screen. The program would work with any file, no matter how it was created. Two file pointers are declared because you need to access two files at the same time.

Listing 12.8: A File-Copying Program

```
/*filecopy.c*/
#include "stdio.h"
main()
{
    FILE *fp1, *fp2;
    char infile[25], outfile[25];
    int letter;
    printf("Enter the filename to read: ");
    gets(infile);
    if((fp1 = fopen(infile,"r")) == NULL)
     {
        printf("Can't open the file %s\n",infile);
        exit();
     }
    printf("Enter the filename to write: ");
    gets(outfile);
    if((fp2 = fopen(outfile,"w")) == NULL)
     {
        printf("Can't open the file %s\n", outfile);
        fclose(fp1);
```

```
        exit();
    }
    while((letter= fgetc(fp1)) != EOF)
        {
        putchar(letter);
        fputc(letter, fp2);
        }
    fclose(fp1);
    fclose(fp2);


    }
```

The first file is opened in the r mode, so that its data can be input. If the file cannot be opened, the program ends. The second file is opened in the w mode so data can be output to it. If the output file cannot be opened, the input file is first closed, and then the program ends. This ensures that the input file, which was successfully opened, will not be damaged when the program ends.

The fprintf() function also writes all of its data as text. For example, if you use fprintf() to write the number 34.23 to the disk, five characters will actually be written, as shown in Figure 12.6. When you use fscanf() to read the file, the characters will be converted to a numeric value when inserted into the variable's address.

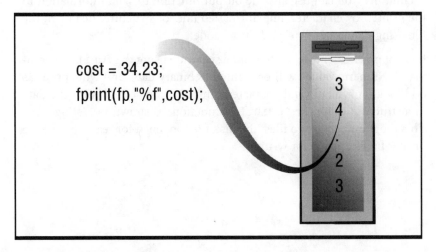

Figure 12.6
Fprintf() stores numeric values as text characters.

Since `fprintf()` stores all data as text, you can also read the file using `getc()`, `fgetc()`, or `fgets()`. However, these functions will treat the numeric data as text characters. Using `fgets()`, for example, the numbers will be read simply as characters that are part of the line. While you could display or print the file after reading it with `fgets()` or `fgetc()`, you could not perform any operations on the individual data items.

Binary Format

Use the `fwrite()` function to save numeric variables in binary format. The numbers will occupy the same amount of space on the disk as they do in memory. If you look at the disk file using the TYPE command, you'll see meaningless characters or symbols in the place of numeric data. These represent the ASCII characters equivalent to the stored values.

To read a file saved with `fwrite()`, you must use `fread()` and input the data into the same structure template. The structure can have a different name than the one used to write the file, and the member element names can be different, but the order, type, and size of the members must be the same.

Printing Data

Technically, you can use any file output function to send information to the printer: by character, line, formatted line, or structure. Just open the file using the name "prn" and the w mode.

It is not practical, however, to print a structure using the `fwrite()` command. Numeric values will be printed as binary data, and will appear as odd-looking symbols and characters. Instead, you should print the data in a structure using the `fprintf()` function, as shown in Listing 12.9. This program opens two files: the disk file is opened for reading, and the printer file is opened for writing.

Listing 12.9: Reading and Printing a Disk File

```c
/*fread1.c*/
#include "stdio.h"
main()
{
    FILE *fp, *ptr;
    struct CD
    {
    char  name[20];
    char  description[40];
    char  category[12];
    float cost;
    int   number;
    } disc;
    char filename[25];
    printf("Enter the filename to read: ");
    gets(filename);
    if((fp = fopen(filename,"r")) == NULL)
     {
         printf("Can't open the file %s\n",filename);
         exit();
     }
    if((ptr = fopen("PRN","w")) == NULL)
     {
         printf("Something is wrong with the printer\n");
         fclose(fp);
         exit();
     }
    while(fread(&disc, sizeof(disc), 1, fp)==1)
    {
    fprintf(ptr,"CD Name       %s\n",disc.name);
    fprintf(ptr,"Description:  %s\n",disc.description);
    fprintf(ptr,"Category:     %s\n",disc.category);
    fprintf(ptr,"Cost:         %6.2f\n",disc.cost);
    fprintf(ptr,"Location:     %d\n",disc.number);
    fprintf(ptr,"\n\n");
    }
    fclose(ptr);
```

```
    fclose(fp);
    }
```

Each structure is input with the `fread()` function, and then individual structure members are printed using `fprintf()` instructions. The `fread()` instruction can read strings that include spaces, so it is preferred over `fscanf()`.

The instruction

```
    fprintf(ptr,"\n\n");
```

puts two extra blank lines between each CD.

Program Design

Knowing how to write and read disk files gives you the ability to create sophisticated business and personal applications. In this chapter, the sample programs that input from the disk file read the entire file. There may be times, however, when you want to manipulate the data in other ways.

For example, you may want to search the disk file for a specific record. In this case, you open the file in the r mode, and then use a loop to input the data either structure-by-structure or line-by-line, depending on how the file was created. Each time through the loop, you test an input value against the data you are searching for. Use the `strcmp()` function, if your compiler has one, to test string values. Once you find a match, display the data and close the file.

The file functions described here perform *sequential* operations, meaning that they read the file in order starting at the beginning. You can use the a mode to add data to the end of the file, but you cannot go directly to a specific position in the file to change information stored there.

That's not to say that you cannot change information already in a file. You'll just have to use an algorithm that deals with the file sequentially. You'll learn this algorithm, and others, in the comprehensive programming example that follows this chapter.

Random-Access Functions

C++ and many ANSI C compilers provide functions for random access to files. *Random access* means that you can go directly to a specific location in the file to read or change the data stored there. The `fseek()` function, for example, moves the pointer to a location in the file. The next `fread()` function obtains its data from that location. The `ftell()` function reports the current location of the pointer, and the `rewind()` functions moves the pointer back to the beginning of the file.

Questions

1. What is a file buffer?

2. How is a file structure used?

3. Why is a file declared as a pointer?

4. Describe the difference between the r, w, and a modes.

5. Why do you close a file before the end of the program?

6. How do you output numeric data?

7. How do you print data on your printer?

8. What is the difference between `fprintf()` and `fwrite()`.

9. How do you print a structure?

10. What is the purpose of the `sizeof()` function?

Exercises

1. Write a program that uses `fputs()` to create a file of movie titles.

2. Write a program that reads the movie titles (Exercise 1) into a string array.

3. Write a program that uses `fprintf()` to create a product inventory file containing the product name, cost, and quantity.

4. Write a program that reads the product inventory file created in Exercise 3.

5. Edit the programs created for Exercises 3 and 4 to read and write the data as a structure.

6. Explain what is wrong in the following program:

```c
#include "stdio.c"
main()
{
    FILE fp;
    char letter;
    if((fp = fopen("MYFILE","w"))==NULL)
    {
        puts("Cannot open the file");
        exit();
    }
    do
    {
        letter=getchar();
        fputc(letter, fp);
    }
    while(letter!='\n');
    fclose(fp);
}
```

Thirteen

Putting It All Together

. . . .

Now that you know the basic elements of C and C++, you can write programs. The techniques that you've learned in this book are the building blocks. To develop an application, you apply these techniques in the correct order, building your program as a series of instructions, blocks of instructions, and functions.

In this final chapter, we will work though the development of a complete application. You'll see that the finished program contains the functions and commands you already know.

The Application

In previous chapters, you worked with a structure and disk file for cataloging a CD collection. You learned how to create a file and how to read a file containing information on compact discs. The sample programs in these chapters, however, just include the bare essentials of an application. There was no way to delete a CD from the collection, or to search the collection for information on a specific CD.

The program we will create here completes the application, enabling it to perform these seven tasks:

- Add a CD to the file.
- Delete a CD from the file.
- Change the CD's name or other data.
- Change the slot number where the CD is stored in your rack.
- Locate information on a specific CD.
- Sort the order of records in the file to match their order of location in the rack.
- Print a list of CDs in the collection.

We'll build the application as a series of functions. But before reading each section in this chapter, look at the section title, then write down the instructions that you think you'll need for the application. For example, start by writing down the global declarations that you'll need—any constants, file pointers, or structures. Then, read the section to see how the program is developed here. Remember, there are many ways to write this program. Your method isn't necessarily wrong just because your instructions are different than those given here.

You can find a listing of the complete application on the accompanying diskette. If you installed the sample files when you installed the PCC compiler, the program listing will be in the FIRSTC\SAMPLES subdirectory, under the name CDAPP.C. (Refer to the Appendix for more information on installing the PCC compiler and accessing the sample programs.) You should print this listing before studying the rest of this chapter. Then, after reading each section, refer to the program to see how the algorithms are applied.

Records and Structures

Even though we are cataloging CDs, you'll see the term "record" throughout this chapter. *Record* is a term used in database management, and this program is really a fundamental database management application. A database is a collection of information about a group of items. In this case, the group is a collection of CDs, but a database can be used to track business clients, a company's inventory, or a collection of any type.

Picture the database as an electronic version of an index card file. Each card is called a *record*, and it contains all of the data about one item. So, each record in a program about a CD collection contains the information on one CD.

When a program uses a structure, each record is one *instance* of the structure. Each time the program reads a structure from the disk, it is reading one record. Similarly, each time the program writes a structure to the disk, it is writing one record.

Global Declarations

The first task is to declare the necessary global variables. Since we'll be using disk files, we need to include the stdio.h header file:

```
#include "stdio.h"
```

As you will soon learn, we will be using three files: a printer file and two disk files. One disk file contains the data on your CD collection, and a second file serves as a temporary storage area. We define the disk file names as constants so that we can refer to them by using constant names:

```
#define FILENAME "CDfile"
#define TEMPFILE "Temp"
```

You can use any names for your own disk files, and the names can include the complete path, as in

```
#define FILENAME "C:\DATA\CD.DAT"
```

In addition, this application assumes the storage rack has spaces for 20 CDs, so we'll define a constant to be used to prevent entering rack numbers greater than 20:

```
#define MAX 20
```

Of course, you can increase this number as you see fit.

All three files are defined in one statement:

```
FILE *fp, *tp, *printer;
```

Next, you'll need to declare the CD structure, using the same definition illustrated in Chapter 11:

```
struct CD
   {
   char   name[20];
   char   description[40];
   char   category[12];
   float cost;
   int    number;
   } disc;
```

Finally, you will need some mechanism to prevent the user from assigning more than one CD to a slot. In this program, we'll use an integer array to store the assigned slot numbers and an integer variable to indicate the total number of CDs in the collection:

```
int slots[MAX];
int count;
```

The main() Function

Each of the program's major tasks will be performed in its own function. In main(), we need some way to select which task to perform and to call the appropriate function. The most efficient method of selecting a task is to display a menu of them. Thus, `main()` must perform these operations:

- Repeat the menu until you, the user, choose to stop the program.
- Display the list of tasks.
- Accept your keyboard entry to select a task.
- Call the function to perform the task.
- Stop the program when you make that selection.

To represent the menu selection, we need a variable local to `main()`. When you select a menu item (by typing a number), `main()` will read this value into a variable and use it to determine which function to call. So we start the `main()` function with this declaration:

```
char select;
```

Next, before we display the menu, we need to know which locations in the storage rack have already been assigned. We'll do that by calling the `getslots()` function. The function opens the file and reads all of the records, assigning each value of `disc.number` to an element in the `slots[]` array and counting the total number of records in the file:

```
getslots()
{
    int index;
    index=0;
    count=0;
    if((fp = fopen(FILENAME,"r")) != NULL)
    {

        while(fread(&disc, sizeof(disc), 1, fp)==1)
        {
            slots[index]=disc.number;
            index++;
            count++;
        }
        fclose(fp);
    }
}
```

Now, why repeat the menu? If we do not repeat the menu in a loop, the program would end after performing a single function. If you wanted to perform two tasks, such as adding new CDs and printing an updated list, you'd have to start the program twice. Since we don't know how many times you'll be repeating the menu, we use a do loop.

There will be eight menu options—one for each of the program's major tasks, and an eighth to end the program. Use puts() or printf() statements to display the menu, then getchar() to input the response. Using getchar() avoids the need to press ↵ after making your selection. If we use numbers for input, rather than letters, we don't have to worry about uppercase versus lowercase characters. So we can start main() like this:

```
main()
{
    char select;
    do
    {
    puts("    My CD Collections Program\n");
    puts("1  Add CD\n");
    puts("2  Delete CD\n");
    puts("3  Edit info CD\n");
    puts("4  Change location\n");
    puts("5  Sort CDs\n");
    puts("6  Locate CD\n");
    puts("7  Print List\n");
    puts("8  Exit Program\n");
    printf("Please enter selections: ");
    select = getchar();
    putchar('\n');
```

Once you select a menu item, main() needs to call the appropriate function. Eight menu options would require seven if statements. For more control, and an easier-to-read program, use a switch command that tests the value of the input variable. Remember to include a default section, in the event the user enters a number or letter not on the menu. We'll complete main() this way:

```
switch(select)
{
    case '1' :
        addcd();
        break;
    case '2':
        delcd();
```

```
                break;
        case '3':
                chcd();
                break;
        case '4':
                chloc();
                break;
        case '5':
                sort();
                break;
        case '6':
                locate();
                break;
        case '7':
                plist();
                break;
        case '8':
                break;
        default:
                puts("Invalid entry, try again\n\n");
        }
    }
        while(select!='8');
        return(0);
}
```

The do...while loop repeats the menu (that is, the switch statement) as long as you do not enter 8 to end the program. After you select an option, and the task is completed, the menu will reappear on screen so you can select another option.

Adding a Record: The addcd() Function

The function for adding the information about a CD follows the same pattern as the program for adding data in Chapter 12.

There are three differences between the addcd() function used in this application and the program shown in Chapter 12. In this application, the user cannot add a new CD to the collection if there is no location in the rack to place it. The `getslots()` function calculates the number of CDs already stored. When we've reached the maximum, a message appears on the screen, and the program returns to the menu:

```
int pause;
if(count>=MAX)
  {
     puts("Sorry. Your cabinet is full\n");
     pause=getchar();
     return;
  }
```

Also, in this application the file is opened in the **a** mode, so that it will be created if it does not exist:

```
if((fp = fopen(FILENAME,"a")) == NULL)
    {
        printf("Can't open the file %s\n",FILENAME);
        exit();
    }
```

If the file does exist, new data will be added to the end of it.

This function also requires you to input a slot number between 1 and 20. Because several of the program's tasks need this input, we can perform it in a separate function, called `getslot()`, and call that function when needed:

```
getslot()
{
int index, flag, pause;
    do
    {
    flag=0;
    printf("Enter the slot number:");
    scanf("%d", &disc.number);
    for(index=0;index<count;index++)
        {
            if(slots[index]==disc.number)
            {
                printf("Sorry that slot is used. Try again\n");
                flag=1;
            }
```

```
            }
        }
        while(disc.number < 1 || disc.number>MAX || flag==1);
        count++;
        slots[count]=disc.number;
    return;
    }
```

The `getslot()` function prevents the user from entering a location number that has already been assigned.

After the new CD is written to the file, the `getslots()` function is called to update the location array.

Deleting a Record: The delcd() Function

The function for deleting the information about a CD uses a standard algorithm for working with sequential files. With sequential access, we cannot go directly to a specific place in the file to change a record. When you open a file in w mode, its contents will be erased. If you open it in a mode, you can only add data to the end.

The solution is to use two files. The `delcd()` function opens the data file in the r mode and opens a temporary file in w mode:

```
if((fp = fopen(filename,"r")) == NULL)
{
    printf("Can't open the file %s\n",filename);
    exit();
}
if((tp = fopen(tempfile,"w")) == NULL)
{
    printf("Can't open the file %s\n",tempfile);
    fclose(fp);
    exit();
}
```

Then we input the name of the CD to be deleted:

```
printf("Please enter the name of the CD: ");
gets(delname);
```

A `while` loop reads each structure (record) in the original file:

```
while(fread(&disc, sizeof(disc), 1, fp)==1)
    {
```

If the record is not the one you want to delete, `delcd()` writes it to the temporary file:

```
if(strcmp(disc.name, delname) != 0)
fwrite(&disc, sizeof(disc), 1, tp);
```

This application uses the `strcmp()` function in several locations to determine whether the correct record has been read from the file. While `strcmp()` is not in K&R C, it is available in all ANSI C and C++ libraries.

When the correct record is found, `delcd()` does not write it to the temporary file, but instead sets a flag to later report whether a structure was deleted:

```
else
fflag='y';
}
```

We perform this process in a `while` loop to continue reading from one file and writing to another, until reaching the end of the file. At that time we close both files:

```
fclose(fp);
fclose(tp);
```

If `delcd()` did not find the record you wanted to delete, it tells you so on the screen, and then ends:

```
puts("\nDid not find the CD");
pause=getchar();
```

You now have duplicate files that contain the same data. The only drawback to this routine is that your disk must have enough free space to store two complete data files. You could consider the temporary file as a backup. If something goes wrong with the original file, the temporary will contain the data as of the last sequential operation. If you do not want to maintain the temporary file on disk, you could open it in write mode, and then immediately close it, as in

```
tp = fopen(tempfile,"w");
fclose(tp);
```

This leaves the file on your disk, but completely empty and taking up very little disk space.

If you did delete a record, you now have two different files. The original file contains all of the data, including the information you want to delete. Because delcd() did not write the structure you wanted to delete, the temporary file only contains the data you want to retain. But we can't leave the data this way. The program is set up to add data, and perform other functions, using the original file. So we have to get the updated data back to that file.

Some C++ compilers have a built-in command for changing a file's name, but many do not. For a generic approach, we can reopen the two files in reverse modes. That is, we open the original file in w mode, deleting its data, and open the temporary file in r mode. The openwr() function, called by delcd() and other functions, does this:

```
if((fp = fopen(filename,"w")) == NULL)
    {
    printf("Can't open the file %s\n",filename);
    exit();
    }
if((tp = fopen(tempfile,"r")) == NULL)
    {
    printf("Can't open the file %s\n",tempfile);
    fclose(fp);
    exit();
    }
```

the delcd() function then reads the records from the temporary file and writes them to the original file. When it closes the files, the original file will contain the updated information, without the deleted data:

```
while(fread(&disc, sizeof(disc), 1, tp)==1)
    fwrite(&disc, sizeof(disc), 1, fp);
fclose(fp);
fclose(tp);
```

Before the delcd() function ends, the program calls the getslots() function to update the array of assigned locations.

The application continues checking for a match even after a record is deleted. This way, you can delete more than one record with the same name—if you decide to throw away all of your Disco Duck CDs, for example.

You can enhance this routine by displaying the record and prompting for input to confirm the deletion. If you decide not to delete the record, your enhanced routine should write it to the file.

Changing CD Data: the chcd() Function

Changing the information about a CD requires the same basic algorithm as deleting a record: you write all the information to a temporary file and then read the unchanged records back to the data file again. Rather than just skipping over the record you want to change, however, you input new information for it, then write it to the temporary file.

The chcd() function first asks for the name of the CD you want to change, then starts a while loop to read each structure:

```c
openrw();
puts("Change Disc Function\n");
        printf("Please enter the name of the CD: ");
        gets(chname);

        while(fread(&disc, sizeof(disc), 1, fp)==1)
        {
```

Next, if the structure is not the one you want to change, the function writes it to the temporary file:

```
if(strcmp(disc.name,chname)!=0)
fwrite(&disc, sizeof(disc), 1, tp);
```

When the relevant record is found, `chcd()` displays its current data, and then prompts for input of the new information:

```
else
{
fflag='y';
puts("Old Data\n");
showdisc();
puts("New Data\n");
printf("Please enter the name of the CD: ");
gets(disc.name);
printf("Enter the description:");
gets(disc.description);
printf("Enter the category:");
gets(disc.category);
printf("Enter the cost:");
scanf("%f", &disc.cost);
if(count>=MAX)
    {
    puts("Sorry. You cannot change the location\n");
    pause=getchar();
    }
    else
    {
    getslot();
    }
```

The `if(count>=MAX)` instruction prevents the user from entering a new location number if the storage rack is full. When the rack is full, the `getslot()` function is not performed and the original slot number read from the disk will be rewritten with the rest of the edited record.

With the `cdch()` function, the user must retype all of the information for the CD, even to change only one item. You could customize the application so the user can just press Enter to accept an item's current contents.

For example, use these instructions to accept the new CD name:

```
printf("Please enter the name of the CD: ");
gets(name);
if(strlen(name)>0)
    strcpy(disc.name,name);
```

If the user enters a new name, it is assigned to disc.name and then written to the file with the rest of the record. If the user presses Enter without typing a name, the contents of disc.name remain unchanged, and the original name is written with the record.

Because we'll need to display a structure several times in the application, the routine has been created in a function called showdisc() and called when needed:

```
showdisc()
{
    printf("CD Name        %s\n",disc.name);
    printf("Description:   %s\n",disc.description);
    printf("Category:      %s\n",disc.category);
    printf("Cost:          %6.2f\n",disc.cost);
    printf("Location:      %d\n",disc.number);
    puts("\n\n");
    return;
}
```

After reading the new data, chcd() writes the structure to the temporary file:

```
fwrite(&disc, sizeof(disc), 1, tp);
```

After reading the entire fp file, chcd() closes both it and tp. If no record was changed (that is, the requested CD could not be found), the function reports this on the screen and stops:

```
fclose(fp);
fclose(tp);
if(fflag=='n')
nofind();
```

If a record was changed, chcd() reopens the files in opposite modes, then writes the data back to the original and updates the location array:

```
else
    {
    openwr();
    while(fread(&disc, sizeof(disc), 1, tp)==1)
```

```
        fwrite(&disc, sizeof(disc), 1, fp);
        fclose(fp);
        fclose(tp);
        }
        getslots();
    return;
    }
```

Changing Location: The chloc() Function

The function for changing a CD's location is essentially the same as for editing the entire record, except that only a new slot number is input:

```
puts("Old Data\n");
showdisc();
puts("\nNew Location\n");
getslot();
```

However, an if instruction at the start of the function prevents the user from changing the location if the storage rack is already full.

Displaying a Record: The locate() Function

To display a record, we input the name of the CD, open the file for reading, and then read each of the records until we find a match:

```
while(fread(&disc, sizeof(disc), 1, fp)==1)
    {
    if(strcmp(disc.name,name)==0)
        {
```

locate() calls the showdisc() function to display the information, then pauses to give you time to read the screen:

```
        fflag='y';
        showdisc();
        printf("Press Enter to continue");
```

Combining the Functions

The application in this book shows each task as a separate function. However, because the functions are almost identical, they could be combined into one. After finding and displaying the record, your revised program would use an `if` command to determine which parts of the structure are input:

```
if(select = '3')

    {
                puts("New Data\n");

                printf("Please enter the name of the
                CD: ");

                gets(disc.name);

                printf("Enter the description:");

                gets(disc.description);

                printf("Enter the category:");

                gets(disc.category);

                printf("Enter the cost:");

                scanf("%f", &disc.cost);

    }

        getslot();
```

If you selected 3 to edit the CD information, prompts would appear to input the name, description, category, and cost. Following the `if` command, the program would call the `getslot()` function to input the new slot number. If you selected 4, to change just the location, only a new location would be input.

```
        pause=getchar();
        putchar('\n');
        }
    }
```

`showdisc()` reads the entire file, so all CDs with the same name are displayed.

Printing a Report: The plist() Function

To print a listing of the CD collection, the program needs to open two files: the data file for reading, and a printer file using the standard DOS filename "prn" for writing:

```
if((fp = fopen(filename,"r")) == NULL)
  {
      printf("Can't open the file %s\n",filename);
      exit();
  }
if((printer = fopen("prn","w")) == NULL)
  {
      printf("Something is wrong with the printer\n");
      fclose(fp);
      exit();
  }
```

The `plist()` function reads each record and then prints the data using `fprintf()` functions:

```
while(fread(&disc, sizeof(disc), 1, fp)==1)
  {
fprintf(printer,"CD Name        %s\n",disc.name);
fprintf(printer,"Description:   %s\n",disc.description);
fprintf(printer,"Category:      %s\n",disc.category);
fprintf(printer,"Cost:          %6.2f\n",disc.cost);
fprintf(printer,"Location:      %d\n",disc.number);
fprintf(printer,"\n\n");
  }
```

Finally, the function closes both files and returns to `main()`:

```
      fclose(printer);
      fclose(fp);
      return;
  }
```

Sorting Records: The sort() Function

As you add CDs to your collection, you may not place them in consecutive slots in the storage rack. You may leave some slots empty, reserving them for a special title or type of CD. So when you add records to the file, you may not enter them in the same order as the corresponding CDs in the rack.

When you print a report, the CDs will be listed in the order you entered them. To find a CD by its slot number, you'd have to scan the entire listing.

Sorting the file, in this case, means rewriting it so that the CDs are stored in slot-number order. The CD in slot 1 is first, then the CD in slot 2, and so forth.

There are literally dozens of ways to sort a file. Some algorithms read all of the data into an array, sort the elements of the array in memory, and then write the array back to the disk. Other algorithms use two or more files, reading and writing in batches, then merging the files into one in the final sorted order.

The algorithm illustrated here, in the sort() function, needs only one file but uses an array of the structure. We need to declare the structure array and a number of variables:

```
sort()
{
struct CD temp[MAX];
int index, loop1, loop2, endloop;
loop1=0;
loop2=0;
endloop=0;
index = 0;
```

sort() opens the file for reading, then reads all of the data into the array, and closes the file:

```
while(fread(&disc, sizeof(disc), 1, fp)==1)
  {
    temp[index]=disc;
```

```
        index++;
    }
    fclose(fp);
```

The variable `index` is used as the subscript.

`sort()` reopens the file for writing, then sets up two `for` loops to write the data back to the file:

```
if((fp = fopen(filename,"w")) == NULL)
    {
        printf("Can't open the file %s\n",filename);
        exit();
    }
for(loop1=1;loop1<MAX+1;loop1++)
        {
                for(loop2=0;loop2<count;loop2++)
```

The outer `for` loop increments `loop1` from 1 to the maximum number of CDs. With the first repetition of the outer loop, the inner loop scans the entire array looking for discs in location 1. Whichever CD it finds with that location number is written to the file:

```
if(temp[loop2].number==loop1)
    {
    fwrite(&temp[loop2], sizeof(temp[loop2]), 1, fp);
    endloop++;
    }
```

The outer loop is then repeated, and the inner loop again scans the entire array, this time looking for a CD in location 2, writing the one it finds to the file. The process is repeated for all possible slot numbers.

However, once we've written all of the CDs back to the file, there is no need to continue looking for slot numbers. We use the variable `endloop` to keep track of the number of structures written to the file. After writing each structure, `sort()` increments `endloop`. When `endloop` equals the number of CDs, all of the structures have been written, and so the repetition can be ended:

```
if(endloop==count)
    break;
```

The file is then closed, and the `sort()` function ended.

Take your time and review the complete listing of the program again. Try on your own to add any improvements you'd like to see.

Appendix

Using the Sample Diskette

• •

ou're probably eager to begin writing C programs. The disk included with this book contains everything you'll need—an editor for writing programs, a compiler and linker, and sample programs to get your started. It also includes solutions for the exercises that appear at the end of each chapter.

Installing Your Compiler

To install the programs and other files on your hard disk, follow these steps:

1. Insert the disk into your disk drive.

2. Log onto the disk by typing A: or B:, depending on the drive you are using, then pressing ↵.

3. Type CINSTALL and press ↵. You'll need at least 750K of available disk space. If you do not have sufficient space, CINSTALL will report a warning and end. Delete some unnecessary files and start CINSTALL again.

A prompt will appear, listing the default directory where the programs will be installed—C:\FIRSTC.

4. Press ↵ to accept the default directory, or enter a new path and then press ↵.

5. The compiler, linker, and editor will be installed on your hard disk; then a prompt will ask whether to install the sample programs.

6. Select Yes to install the sample programs.

7. A message will appear, reporting that all of the files have been successfully installed. Then you will be asked if you want CINSTALL to check your CONFIG.SYS file. The compiler and linker require at least 25 files and 25 buffers set aside in CONFIG.SYS. If you select Yes, CINSTALL will check your configuration file and, if necessary, increase the settings. If CINSTALL changes your configuration file, it will save the original copy in the file CONFIG.OLD as a safeguard.

8. A message will appear asking if you want to reboot your computer. Rebooting will apply the changes made to your CONFIG.SYS file so that you can begin writing and compiling programs. Select Yes (or No if you decide to abandon the installation for any reason).

9. Press ↵ to end CINSTALL.

If you decide not to install the sample programs, you can manually install them later. Copy the file SAMPLES.EXE from the disk onto your hard disk, log into the directory where you copied the program, type SAM-PLES, and press ↵.

In the unlikely event that CINSTALL does not properly install the software, you can install it manually. Copy the following files to your hard disk:

PCC12C.EXE
EDITOR.EXE
SAMPLES.EXE

Log onto the disk where you copied the programs, then run each of them.

Using the CEDIT Program Editor

You can use any text editor or word processor to write the source code of your program. However, if you use a word processing program, you must save the file as ASCII text. This type of file will not contain any of the formatting codes or commands that most word processors record when you save a document. Your compiler would try to compile these codes and report a long series of error messages and warnings.

Included on the disk supplied with this book is a program called CEDIT.COM. This is a simple editor you can use to write and edit programs that are up to 1000 lines long.

To start CEDIT, log onto the directory where you installed your compiler, type *CEDIT*, and press ↵.

CEDIT does not have any text-formatting capabilities, and it does not wrap text when it reaches the end of the line. You have to press ↵ to move to the next line. But even though CEDIT is no-frills, it has all the capabilities you need to write programs.

On top of the CEDIT screen is a status line that shows the line and character position of the cursor, the name of the file being edited, and whether you are in insert (Ins) or overtype (Ovr) mode. In overtype mode, new characters you type take the place of existing characters on the line. In insert mode, characters will move over to make room for new ones.

Program lines can be no more than 78 characters long. You'll hear a warning beep when you are near the end of the line, and another beep when your line is full and won't accept any additional characters. If you are inserting text on a line, in insert mode, CEDIT automatically enters overtype mode when the line becomes full, preventing you from entering more than 78 characters on the line.

While you cannot select and copy text in CEDIT, you have these keys available:

Backspace	Deletes characters to the left of the cursor.
Del	Deletes characters to the right of the cursor.
PgUp	Moves the cursor up 20 lines.
PgDn	Moves the cursor down 20 lines.
Home	Moves the cursor to the start of the line.
End	Moves the cursor to the end of the line.
Ins	Toggles insert mode on and off.
F1	Inserts a blank line.
F2	Deletes an entire line.
F3	Displays help information.
F7	Displays options to save a program, clear the screen, and quit CEDIT.
F10	Loads a program.

Use the arrow keys to move the cursor around the document. Pressing the down arrow key at the end of the document will add new lines, just like pressing ↵.

Saving a Program

To save a document, press F7. A prompt will appear, asking if you want to save the program. Press Y. If the file already has a name, it will be saved immediately under the same name. If the program is new, and has not yet been named, a prompt will appear asking for a name. Type a program name, including the .C extension, and press ↵. You cannot save a program using the same name as a program already on your disk.

A prompt will appear, asking if you want to quit CEDIT. Press N to remain in CEDIT, and to start or load another program. Press Y to quit CEDIT.

Clearing the Screen

If you want to abandon a program you are typing and clear the screen, press F7 N N.

Quitting CEDIT

To quit CEDIT, press F7. Enter Y if you want to save the program on the screen, or N if you want to abandon the program. Then press Y to return to the DOS prompt.

Loading a Program

To load a program into CEDIT, press F10, type the name of the program, including its extension, and press ↵.

You can only load a file from a blank screen. You cannot load a file if any text is on the screen, or if you typed any text since last clearing the screen, even if you deleted it. To clear the screen so that you can load a program, press F7 N N.

Printing Program Listings

You cannot print a listing of your program from within CEDIT. When you installed the programs on the disk, however, a program called CPRINT.EXE was placed in the same directory as your editor and compiler. To print a program listing, you must log on to that directory, and then type *CPRINT* followed by the program name, as in

```
cprint myfirst.c
```

CPRINT will print the program, placing the filename before the listing.

You can use CPRINT to print a listing of the complete CDAPP.C program from Chapter 13.

Using The PCC Compiler

The PCC compiler provided with this book is not a scaled-down or demonstration version, but a full-featured compiler. It includes an extensive function library that contains string-handling and random-access file functions.

With PCC, you can both learn C and write complete applications. PCC even includes an assembler, if you want to learn assembly-language programming!

The compiler, and its associated programs, are copyrighted by C WARE Corporation, but are distributed as "shareware." This means that you can try out the program for 30 days to see if you like it. At the end of the trial period, you must either register your copy of PCC or discontinue using it.

Registration, which costs $30, entitles you to use the program on any and all computers available to you, as long as you use the program on only one computer at a time. You can also copy the program for the trial use of others. As a registered user, you can obtain updates as new versions are released by calling or writing C WARE Corporation. A handy form you can photocopy for registering your copy of PCC is included at the end of this appendix.

Educational institutions wishing to use PCC for courses involving C, as well as private or commercial institutions, should contact CWARE Corporation, or refer to the file PCC.DOC.

Installing PCC

When you ran the CINSTALL program as described earlier in this appendix, PCC and its associated support programs were installed on your hard disk.

If you are running low on disk space, you can delete some of the files installed with PCC. However, you need the following files to run the

PCC.DOC—Program Documentation

The file PCC.DOC contains the text of a 100-page manual on PCC and its library functions. The manual is not designed to take the place of a C textbook, but it thoroughly explains how to compile and link programs, the error and warning messages that may appear, and most of the library functions. You should print a copy of the file if you encounter problems or compilation errors that you cannot correct, or if you want to go beyond the fundamentals covered in this book.

programs shown in this book:

PCC.EXE	The first pass of the C compiler.
PC2.EXE	The second pass of the C compiler.
PCCA.EXE	The assembler and third pass of the C compiler.
PCCL.EXE	The object file linker.
PCCS.S	The standard C function library.
STDIO.H	Include file for the standard I/O package.

See PCC.DOC for a complete description of the PCC files.

Differences with ANSI C

PCC is completely compatible with the programs and techniques shown in this book, with two minor exceptions:

- PCC does not automatically insert a new-line code after a puts( ) command. If your lines of output run together, add the \n code when displaying literals, such as

```
puts("My CD Collection\n");
```

or insert the new-line character in `putchar()` commands, such as

```
putchar('\n');
```

The new-line codes have already been added to the sample files on your disk.

- PCC will report a warning when a program passes a structure between functions. You can ignore this warning, and it will not appear in later releases of the compiler.

Compiling a Program

To compile a program, type *PCC* followed by the name of the source-code file. For example, to compile a program named VIDEO.C, type

```
PCC video
```

and press ↵. PCC assumes your source-code files have the .C extension and that the program is in the same directory as the compiler. If the file has no extension, end the filename with a period, as in

```
PCC NOEXT.
```

If you used some other extension, include it in the filename:

```
PCC video.pgr
```

PCC will compile your program and create an object file, with the .O extension and the same name as the source-code file. The compiler actually uses three files to generate the object file: PCC.EXE, PC2.EXE, and PCCA.EXE. However, you only need to type PCC and your program name; the compiler calls the other programs itself when they are needed. If the compiler detects an error, it will display the line number where the error was detected, the line of code, and a brief explanation of the error. In some cases, the actual error may be in a previous line. For example, if you forget to end a line with a semicolon, the program logic may cause the error to be detected on another line.

In addition to errors, PCC may report warnings. These are less severe, and in some cases your program will still run properly. However, check each error and warning carefully. Correct the problems, then compile the program again.

Linking the Program

Once your program compiles without errors, you use the PCCL linker to create an executable program with the EXE extension. The linker adds the code for built-in functions from the PCCS.S library file and from any header files specified in your program. PCC includes two header files: STDIO.H is required for programs that use disk files or a printer; MATH.H for programs using complex mathematical functions.

To link the program, type *PCCL* followed by the name of the object code file. PCCL assumes the object file has the .O extension. For example, to link the file video.o (which was compiled from video.c), type

```
PCCL video
```

and press ↵.

The linking process will complete successfully as long as your program was compiled without errors, you have the necessary header files on your disk, and there is enough room on the disk to save the executable program.

Running Your Program

If the linking process does not report any errors, run your program by typing its name and pressing ↵.

Using the Sample Programs

When you install your compiler and editor, the sample programs discussed in the book are installed on your hard disk in the FIRSTC\SAMPLES subdirectory. Each program is listed by the name shown in the text.

For example, if you are reading Chapter 12, you'll see a program listing in a figure starting

```
/*fread.c*/
```

This means that you'll find the program under that name in the SAMPLES directory.

Also in the Samples directory is the source code of the CPRINT program, so you can study it on your own.

Exercise Solutions

At the end of each chapter you'll find exercises that require you to write programs. (There are also study questions; to find the answers to these, simply reread the relevant part of the chapter.) The solutions to the exercises are stored in the SAMPLES directory under the chapter and exercise number, starting with the letter E. For example, the solution to the second exercise in Chapter 11 is stored in the file E11-2.C.

You can review or customize the programs by loading them into your editor. You can compile and run the programs using PCC.

If you have another compiler, however, you may have to edit the programs that deal with files. Your compiler may require the stdio.h file to be included, with this syntax:

```
#include <stdio.h>
```

Carefully read any error messages that your compiler may list during the compilation process. Generally, however, you should be able to compile and run these programs with little or no editing.

In addition to these source-code files, the Samples directory also contains a text file containing all of the exercises and their solutions, as well as the answers to questions asking you to explain the errors in program listings. The file is called EXERCISE.TXT. You can use any word processing program to read or print the contents of the file.

Software Registration Form

Remit to:

C Ware Corporation

P.O. Box 428

Paso Robles, CA 94447

PCC version 1.2c

You can also order by phone using your P.O.#, Mastercard or VISA. (805) 239-4620,

9:00 A.M.-4:00 P.M., PST ONLY.

____ PCC Registration (Includes registration software OR latest version of PCC.)

@ $ 30.00 ea $_____

____ UPGRADE to the newest version (includes latest version of the program diskette, with

documentation on the disk.)

@ $ 5.00 ea $ _____

Orders are normally shipped by USPS at no additional charge.

For UPS shipment, please add $3.00

$ 3.00 ea $ _____

Subtotal _____

Total $ _____

Payment by: [ ] Check [ ] MC [ ] Visa [ ]

PO #   _____

Name: _____

Company: _____

Address: _____

_____

_____

Day Phone: _____ Eve: _____

Card #: _____ Exp. Date: _____

Signature of cardholder: _____

Index

In the following index, **boldface** page numbers indicate chapter sections in which the item is the main topic of discussion. *Italic* page numbers indicate illustrations.

fwrite.c sample program listing, 304–305

G

%g format specifiers, 75, 105
getc() function, 35, 293, 295, 310, 312
getch() function, 99, 186
getchar() function, 35
   buffers with, 186, 294
   for character input, **99–101**, *100*, 116
   for pausing, **101–102**, *102*
getchar.c sample program listing, 100–101
getche() function, 186, 294
gets() function
   simulating, **244–245**
   for string input, **97–99**, 116
getslot() function (CDAPP), 324–325
getslots() function (CDAPP), 321, 324–325
getstr.c sample program listing, 244–245
getw() function, 312
global variables, **158–159**, **174–175**, 319
graphic characters, **71–72**, *72*
greater-than signs (>)
   for comparisons, 179, 181
   in extraction operator (>>), 113–114, *114*, 291, 309
   for header files, 35
grouping instructions, braces for, 277–278, *279*

H

.H (header) files, 14–15, **34–35**, 286
hexadecimal numbers, 82, 105, 108
high-level languages, 7

I

IDE (integrated development environments), 23
if structures, **178–179**, *178*
   conditions in, **179–181**
   if...else, **182–184**, *183*
   multiple statements in, **181–182**, **190–191**
   nested, **189–191**, 195–197
ifstream operator, 291, 309
iftax.c sample program listing, **185–187**
#include directive, **34–36**
increment operator (++), **139–141**
incrementing values in for loops, 202–203, *202*
indenting, 28, *178*, 179, 181–182, 190
index variables in for loops, 202–203, *202*
information and data, 39, 121–122
initial values
   for array elements, **228–229**
   for structures, **262–264**, *263*
   for variables, 55, 115, 144
input, **95–96**, *96–97*. *See also* files
   address operator for, **102–104**, *103*
   in C++, **113–114**

P

parallel arrays, 240–243
parameters, **32–34**
  arrays as, **237–239**, *240*
  constants in, 51
  in macros, 172–173
  passing, 33, *33*, **161–166**, *162–163*
  pointers as, **276–280**, *278*
  structures as, **269–272**
parentheses ()
  for conditions, 268, *268*
  for functions, 26, *28*, 151
  for if, *178*, 179
  for precedence, 134–135, *134*
passing parameters, 33, *33*, **161–166**, *162–163*
  arrays, **237–239**, *240*
  pointers, **276–280**, *278*
  structures, **269–270**
patterns, **145–147**, *146*
pausing
  for loops for, **204–205**
  getchar() for, **101–102**, *102*
payroll1.c sample program listings, **135–136**
PC character set, 72
PC2.EXE file, 343–344
PCC compiler
  vs. ANSI C, 343–344
  installing, **338–339**, **342–343**
  using, **342–345**
PCC.DOC file, 35, **342–343**
PCC.EXE file, 343–344
PCC12C.EXE file, 339
PCCA.EXE file, 343–344
PCCL.EXE linker, 343, **345**
PCCS.S file, 343

percent signs (%)
  in assignment operators, 143
  for format specifiers, 75
  for remainder operation, 123, 125–126
periods (.), 264
planning, **19–20**, **61–62**
platforms, 13
plist() function (CDAPP), 333
plus signs (+)
  for addition, 123
  for assignment operators, 143, *144*
  for combining strings, 250
  for increment operator (++), 139–141
pointers, **272–275**, *273–275*
  declaring, 273, *273*
  file position, 289–290, *289*
  for files, 286–287
  with functions, **276–280**, *278*
portability, **13**, 16
precedence of operators, **131–136**, *132–135*
precision of numbers, 43
precompiled functions, 14
printf() function, **74–75**, 93
  converting data types with, **82–83**
  format specifiers with, **75–81**, *76–80*
  formatting with, **83–87**, *84–87*
  increment operator with, 140
  line feeds with, **81**
  for numbers, **75–81**
  for prompts, 98
  for string output, 299
  for troubleshooting, **147**

T

whitespace characters, 106, 108–109

width, display, **83–87**, *84–87*

word processing programs, 22

wp.c sample program listing, 298

write file mode, 288–290, 324

write file operations, 286

writing

    characters to files, **293–294**

    file structures, **303–305**

formatted file output, 300–302

X

%x format specifiers, 82, 105, 108

Z

\0 symbol, 56, *56*, 98, 243

zeros, leading, 86, *86*

A BOOK FULL OF SOUND AND FURY.

A New View Through Your Windows.

150pp. ISBN: 1119-X.

YOUR GUIDE TO DOS DOMINANCE.

1000 pp. ISBN:1442-3

DOS 6.2 can save you hundreds of dollars in hardware and software purchases. *Mastering DOS 6.2 (Special Edition)* shows you how.

Whether you're a beginner or expert, whether you use DOS or Windows, *Mastering DOS 6.2 (Special Edition)* will help you make the most of the new DOS utilities. Find out how to protect your computer work with ScanDisk, Backup, Undelete and Anti-Virus. Get a complete overview of disk caching and disk defragmenting. Discover the secret of expanding your memory by typing a single command.

You'll even find out about the new DOS utility DoubleSpace that will double the available space on your hard disk.

SYBEX. Help Yourself.

2021 Challenger Drive
Alameda, CA 94501
1-800-227-2346

SYBEX

POCKET-SIZED PC EXPERTISE.

550 pp. ISBN: 756-8.

The *PC User's es-sen'-tial, ac-ces'sible Pocket Dictionary* is the most complete, most readable computer dictionary available today. With over 2,000 plain-language entries, this inexpensive handbook offers exceptional coverage of computer industry terms at a remarkably affordable price.

In this handy reference you'll find plenty of explanatory tables and figures, practical tips, notes, and warnings, and in-depth entries on the most essential terms. You'll also appreciate the extensive cross-referencing, designed to make it easy for you to find the answers you need.

Presented in easy-to-use alphabetical order, *The PC User's es-sen'-tial, ac-ces'-si-ble Pocket Dictionary* covers every conceivable computer-related topic. Ideal for home, office, and school use, it's the only computer dictionary you need!

SYBEX. Help Yourself.

2021 Challenger Drive
Alameda, CA 94501
1-510-523-8233
1-800-227-2346

SYBEX

GET A FREE CATALOG JUST FOR EXPRESSING YOUR OPINION.

Help us improve our books and get a *FREE* full-color catalog in the bargain. Please complete this form, pull out this page and send it in today. The address is on the reverse side.

Name _____   **Company** _____

Address _____   **City** _____ **State** ___ **Zip** _____

Phone ( ) _____

1. How would you rate the overall quality of this book?

- ❏ Excellent
- ❏ Very Good
- ❏ Good
- ❏ Fair
- ❏ Below Average
- ❏ Poor

2. What were the things you liked most about the book? (Check all that apply)

- ❏ Pace
- ❏ Format
- ❏ Writing Style
- ❏ Examples
- ❏ Table of Contents
- ❏ Index
- ❏ Price
- ❏ Illustrations
- ❏ Type Style
- ❏ Cover
- ❏ Depth of Coverage
- ❏ Fast Track Notes

3. What were the things you liked *least* about the book? (Check all that apply)

- ❏ Pace
- ❏ Format
- ❏ Writing Style
- ❏ Examples
- ❏ Table of Contents
- ❏ Index
- ❏ Price
- ❏ Illustrations
- ❏ Type Style
- ❏ Cover
- ❏ Depth of Coverage
- ❏ Fast Track Notes

4. Where did you buy this book?

- ❏ Bookstore chain
- ❏ Small independent bookstore
- ❏ Computer store
- ❏ Wholesale club
- ❏ College bookstore
- ❏ Technical bookstore
- ❏ Other _____

5. How did you decide to buy this particular book?

- ❏ Recommended by friend
- ❏ Recommended by store personnel
- ❏ Author's reputation
- ❏ Sybex's reputation
- ❏ Read book review in _____
- ❏ Other _____

6. How did you pay for this book?

- ❏ Used own funds
- ❏ Reimbursed by company
- ❏ Received book as a gift

7. What is your level of experience with the subject covered in this book?

- ❏ Beginner
- ❏ Intermediate
- ❏ Advanced

8. How long have you been using a computer?

years _____

months _____

9. Where do you most often use your computer?

- ❏ Home
- ❏ Work

- ❏ Both
- ❏ Other _____

10. What kind of computer equipment do you have? (Check all that apply)

- ❏ PC Compatible Desktop Computer
- ❏ PC Compatible Laptop Computer
- ❏ Apple/Mac Computer
- ❏ Apple/Mac Laptop Computer
- ❏ CD ROM
- ❏ Fax Modem
- ❏ Data Modem
- ❏ Scanner
- ❏ Sound Card
- ❏ Other _____

11. What other kinds of software packages do you ordinarily use?

- ❏ Accounting
- ❏ Databases
- ❏ Networks
- ❏ Apple/Mac
- ❏ Desktop Publishing
- ❏ Spreadsheets
- ❏ CAD
- ❏ Games
- ❏ Word Processing
- ❏ Communications
- ❏ Money Management
- ❏ Other _____

12. What operating systems do you ordinarily use?

- ❏ DOS
- ❏ OS/2
- ❏ Windows
- ❏ Apple/Mac
- ❏ Windows NT
- ❏ Other _____

13. On what computer-related subject(s) would you like to see more books?

_____

_____

_____

_____

14. Do you have any other comments about this book? (Please feel free to use a separate piece of paper if you need more room)

_____

_____

_____

_____

- - - - - - - - - - PLEASE FOLD, SEAL, AND MAIL TO SYBEX - - - - - - - - - -

SYBEX INC.
Department M
2021 Challenger Drive
Alameda, CA
94501